Benin

Other Places Travel Guides

Benin

Michael Bolin | Erika Kraus | Felicie Reid

Published by
OTHER PLACES PUBLISHING

Second edition
Published November 2014

Benin
Other Places Travel Guide

Written by: Michael Bolin, Erika Kraus, and Felicie Reid

Cover designed by: Carla Zetina-Yglesias
Cover photograph copyright: Christoph Herby
Back cover photographs copyright: Christoph Herby

Published by:
Other Places Publishing
www.otherplacespublishing.com

All text, illustrations and artwork copyright
© 2014 Other Places Publishing

ISBN 978-1-935850-15-1

The Authors

Michael Bolin

Michael Bolin comes from northern California. He served two years in the Peace Corps as a teacher in a rural village in central Benin, where his strange customs amused the locals to no end. He plans to keep working with, and writing about, the people of this beautiful continent.

Erika Kraus

Originally from a small town in rural Kansas, Erika joined the United States Peace Corps after earning degrees in Biology and French. Erika was assigned to Benin where she immersed herself in the new surroundings and discovered everything her new home had to offer. This experience was an opportunity of a lifetime that formed Erika's professional direction. She is currently learning more about how people, especially the Beninese, create and interact with wooded sites. Erika is eagerly awaiting her first child with her husband and her dog.

Felicie Reid

Felicie Reid is a French-born aspiring writer with a degree in Environmental Science. Her passion for nature, travel, and adventure has taken her across much of Europe, the United States, South America, and West Africa. She served for two and a half years with the Peace Corps as an Environmental Action volunteer in Benin, where she had the opportunity to experience firsthand the culture and way of life of this amazing country. Felicie used the knowledge she had gained while living and traveling across Benin to write this book. She plans to continue her adventures around the globe with a second term with the Peace Corps in Morocco.

Acknowledgments

Many people contributed to this book, from Benin and around the globe. The following persons have all played a role in this project and deserve a great deal of thanks from the authors and publisher: Devon Abt, Dieudonné Adisso, Koudous Adoumbou, Jacob Affidji, Felix Agossa, Mathurin Akouete, Diane Albrecht, Darly Asse, Théodore Atrokpo, Guida Belco, Bill Biokou, Johnathan Bowler, Jessica Bruce, Tom Connelly, Andrea Cortez, David Cowell, Josh "Kora Kora" Cunningham, Kayla Curtiss, Hubert Dako, Kelly Daly, Drew Dilts, Abbe Eaton, Katherine Echeverria, Claire Eldred, Sarah Ellison, Jennifer Epstein, Edouard Ewodji, John Mark Feilmeyer, Jacy Gaige, Wesley Givan, Lissa Glasgo, Margaret Graham, Lisa Hembre, Christoph Herby, Leonore Hijazi, Adam Kendis, Novella Kirkland, Johanna Kretchel, Dismas Loko, Katie Lootens, William Lyle, Natalie McKennerney, Sara Miner, Elaina Murray, Ly Nguyen, Joseph Njie, Paul Oxborrow, Anastasia Pahules, Alicia Parrish, Sarah Pederson, Brigette Pohren, Caitlin Rackish, Daniel Ramirez, Stephanie Ranthum, Brian Readout, Clement Reid, Keith and Catherine Reid, Ryan Riley, Jim Rybarski, Heather Schultz, Jaren Tichy Schwartz, Samantha Speck, Andrew Spencer, Matt Terebessy, Jonny Thompson, Daniel W. Nara, Julie Wang, Cathy Wu, Tavor Yisrael, and Carla Zetina-Yglesias.

QUICK REFERENCE

Exchange rates at time of publication

Benin uses the West African Franc, known as the franc CFA or FCFA.

$1 US = FCFA 501

€1 = FCFA 656

£1 = FCFA 761

Electricity

Benin accommodates 220V.

Business Hours

Most businesses close for a three-hour break at midday. Common working hours are 8am–12pm and 3–6pm.

Time

GMT + 1

Telephone

Country dialing code +229. For calls from the US to Benin, you may need to dial 011 before the country code.

National Holidays

The following are civic holidays, when most businesses and offices will be closed. Businesses sometimes remain closed the day after the holiday to allow everyone to recover from the festivities.

Jan. 1: New Year's Day

Jan. 10: Celebration of Traditional Religions

May 1: Labor Day

Aug. 1: Independence Day

Aug. 15: Assumption

Nov. 1: All Saints' Day

Dec. 25: Christmas

Variable date (March/April): Easter Sunday and Easter Monday

Variable date (40 days after Easter): Ascension

Variable date (50 days after Easter): Pentecost

Variable date (January): Maoloud (birth of the prophet Mohammed)

Variable date (July/August): Ramadan feast

Variable date (October): Tabaski / Eid al-Adha (Muslim Feast of Sacrifice)

QUICK STATS

Official name: Republic of Benin / République du Bénin

Départements: Alibori, Atakora, Atlantique, Borgou, Collines, Couffo, Donga, Littoral, Mono, Ouémé, Plateau, Zou

Neighboring countries: Burkina Faso, Niger, Nigeria, and Togo

Population: 9.6 million (2012)

Official capital: Porto-Novo (population 276,000)

Political and economic capital: Cotonou (estimated population 700,000–1,000,000)

Type of government: Republic under multiparty democratic rule

Ethnic groups: Fon 39.2%, Adja 15.2%, Yoruba 12.3%, Bariba 9.2%, Peulh 7%, Ottamari 6.1%, Yoa-Lokpa 4%, Dendi 2.5%, other (including Europeans) 1.6%, unspecified 2.9% (2002 census)

Languages: French (official); Fon, Mina, Goun, Adja, Yoruba, Idaatcha, and others in the south; Nagot, Bariba, Ditammari, Fulani, Dendi, Tanguiéta, Tchabé, and others in the north

GDP (PPP): $15.51 billion (2012)

GDP per capita (PPP): $1,700 (2012)

U.N. Human Development Index Value: 0.427, ranked 167th of 196 nations (2011)

Life expectancy at birth: 60.2 years

Adult Literacy Rate: 42.4% (55.2% of men, 30.3% of women)

Percentage of population living on less than $2/day: 73.7%

Average temperature in Cotonou: 25–28°C, 77–82°F

USEFUL TRANSLATIONS

Anasara (anna-sah-ra): The northeastern translation for 'white person.' Heard mostly in Parakou, Kandi, Malanville, and Karimama.

Batouré (bah-too-ray): The northwestern translation for 'white person.' Common in Djougou and Natitingou.

Buvette (boo-vette): Typically an open-air bar that sells beer, soft drinks, and bottled water.

Doucement (doo-suh-mahn): Beninese-French word used for a variety of expressions, including 'watch out,' 'be careful,' and 'excuse me.'

Fétiche (fay-teesh): A site of Vodoun worship. Often with a small statue and the remains of previous sacrifices.

Féticheur (fay-tee-shure): The religious person responsible for a certain *fétiche* or sacred area.

Gendarme (jawn-darm): Local military stationed throughout the country at certain communal capitals and large cities. They are usually seen at *gendarmeries,* or local military posts, at check points along roads, and at border crossings.

Maison des Jeunes (may-zon day juhn): Youth Center, located in every major town and commonly used for any sort of public gathering, political meeting, concert, or cultural demonstration.

Maquis (mah-kee): Casual, open-air restaurant, often coupled with a *buvette* or bar, serving local cuisine by the plate from large cauldrons and coolers.

Marché (mar-shay): Market.

Oyibo (oh-yee-boh): The Yoruba and Idaatcha word for 'white person.' Mostly heard in the east-central regions.

Pagne (pah-nyah): A piece of fabric two meters long, typically used as a simple wrap or tailored into traditional outfits. A *pagne* is also used as a towel, a baby-strap, a head cushion for heavy loads, a blanket, and to provide shade from the sun.

Paillote (pah-y-ott): Thatch-roofed structure in the form of an awning, resembling a gazebo and used as a shaded place to rest, dine, or hold meetings.

Pirogue (peer-ohg): Dugout canoe commonly made from Samba, Iroko, or other local trees.

Yovo: The Fon word for 'white person.' This term can be extended to anyone who is not black, including Beninese people with lighter skin tones and albinos.

Zemidjan (zem-ee-djan): A motorcycle-taxi, the main mode of public transport in Beninese cities. See page 57 for more on *zems.*

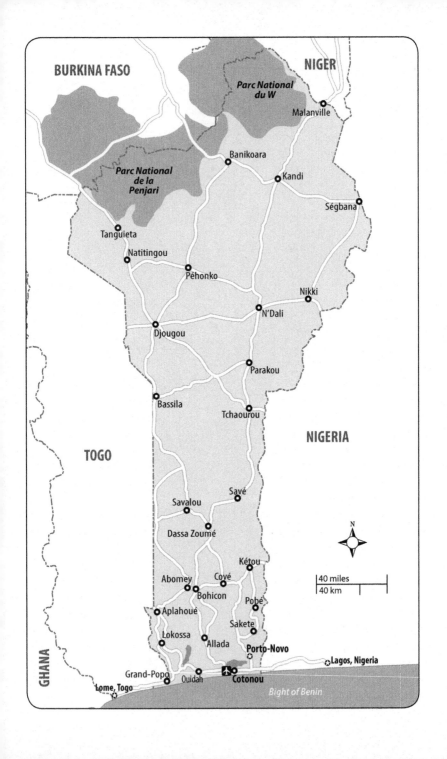

Contents

Introduction

An hour after I arrived in the Beninese village where I would spend the next two years, the villagers took over my house. Young men hoisted beds and tables and bookshelves onto their heads and summarily transported them outside, where children commenced to scrub the dirt off with wet rags. The few bags containing my possessions ended up under a mango tree. A legion of women brandishing palm-frond brooms attacked the naked floor and the cobwebs on the walls and ceiling, while in the backyard school-age boys uprooted the weeds with their short-handled hoes. The long-stagnant water in the cistern was judged to be unclean and dumped out, and a half-dozen girls were dispatched to the well to fetch some more.

When no more could be done, the entire scene rewound—furniture placed back on heads and put back in the house, water poured into the cistern, villagers streaming

Book Icons

INSIGHT Unique insight into the culture and people.

Author recommended accommodation or eatery.

Map Icons

- Accommodations
- Airport
- $ Bank/ATM
- Bar/Nightclub
- Bus/Taxi Station (Gare)
- Camping
- Capital
- Church
- City/Village
- Clinic
- Hospital
- Landmark
- Mosque
- Pharmacy
- Point of Interest
- Post Office
- Restaurant/Buvette/Eatery
- Train Station
- ———— Highway/road

Benin is divided into 12 departments and this book covers two departments in each chapter. The cultural nuances and unique characteristics found throughout Benin are insightfully explained, in a way only a local would know.

ALIBORI
ATAKORA
BORGOU
DONGA
COLLINES
ZOU
COUFFO
PLATEAU
MONO
OUEME
ATLANTIQUE
LITTORAL

back out my front door. The last one to leave, a middle-aged woman, stopped for a moment and turned to me. "If you need anything, let us know."

Benin offers beaches, safaris, markets, and museums, but for me its greatest attraction is its people. They have come through generations of poverty and oppression with a smile, always ready to share a good laugh with friends or open their doors to a stranger—even if that stranger is a 21-year-old kid with little knowledge of the country and a clumsy command of the language.

Too few foreigners ever truly experience Benin and its people. Many are intimidated by the mere idea of traveling to Africa. The ones who do visit can easily spend their whole trip in fancy hotels or on choreographed tours, shut off from the place they're trying to see.

This book attempts to fix that—to help visitors experience and appreciate everything Benin has to offer, from its traditional tourist attractions to its rich culture and amazing people. I and my co-authors each spent two years living and working in separate Beninese communities as Peace Corps Volunteers. As the only foreigners in our communities, we learned to live and thrive in places that few visitors ever see, and we've used that experience to write this book. Dozens of other Peace Corps Volunteers, Beninese friends, and local experts have also contributed inside knowledge from every corner of the country.

The result is this guidebook that gives travelers valuable practical advice on everything from lodging to transportation to bartering in the market, along with indepth descriptions of towns and villages across the country—all from a local perspective. We hope that it will help visitors get off the tourist track and experience the real Benin, a country that can constantly amaze those who know where to look.

- Michael Bolin

History

EARLY HISTORY

From the 17th century until French colonization, the most important state in present-day Benin was the Kingdom of Dahomey. The Dahomeyans traced their roots to the Adja people of Tado, a village on the banks of the Mono River in present-day Togo. Around the 12th or 13th century, the Adja migrated from Tado to present-day Benin. A war of succession split the Adja in the early 17th century as three brothers fought for the throne. The brothers eventually di-

> The country now known as the Republic of Benin was once called the French colony of Dahomey, the Republic of Dahomey, and the People's Republic of Benin.

vided the territory and founded their own kingdoms. Kokpon founded the Kingdom of Allada, Te-Agdanlin founded the Kingdom of Hogbonou—which the Portuguese later named Porto-Novo—and Do-Aklin founded the Kingdom of Abomey, which would soon be known as Dahomey.

An Oral History

Throughout Africa, history has traditionally passed from one generation to the next via oral traditions. Written records are rare, and traditional history varies according to the tribes involved and their religious beliefs. However, written accounts of West African oral tradition compiled by European explorers and anthropologists, as well as some African manuscripts dating as far back as the Middle Ages—such as those stored at Timbuktu—contribute to our understanding of the region's early history.

Over the next several generations, the Adja of Dahomey mixed with the local tribe to create a new people, the Fon. Legend has it that the first Fon came from the union of a Dahomeyan princess named Aligbonon and a spirit in the form of a panther. Today, the Fon are the largest ethnic group in southern Benin, while the Adja still live along the Mono River in southeastern Togo and southwestern Benin.

European observers called Dahomey the "Black Sparta" after the prowess of its soldiers and their ability to stand against the armies of more powerful neighboring nations. Dahomey's feared army included the Amazons, an elite corps of female warriors. (Europeans dubbed Dahomey's female warriors "Amazons" after the Amazons of Greek mythology.) The Amazons—known in Fon as *Mino*, "our mothers"—initially served as the king's personal guard, and many of them were among the king's hundreds of wives. By the mid-19th century they formed about a third of Dahomey's army. At the time, the Amazons were the only active-duty female military force in the world. "[They] fight with extreme valor," remembered one French Foreign Legionnaire who fought them, "always ahead of the other troops."

In 1718, King Agaja ascended to the throne of Dahomey and began an aggressive campaign of expansion. Agaja conquered Allada in 1724 and Ouidah, the region's main slave-trading port, in 1727. Dahomey's kings funded their constant wars by selling massive numbers of slaves to European traders. Some historians estimate that up to 20% of the slaves shipped to Europe and the Americas came through Dahomey. Slave-trading and constant warfare fostered each other: Dahomey needed a steady supply of slaves to trade for European weapons, and needed to fight wars in order to capture prisoners to sell as slaves.

In 1823, King Ghézo defeated Dahomey's main rival, the powerful Oyo Empire, based in present-day Nigeria. Dahomey would remain the preeminent power in the region until the French conquest in 1892.

EUROPEAN EXPANSION IN WEST AFRICA

> The first European settlement in present-day Benin was a Portuguese outpost established at Ouidah in the 16th century. The settlement's fort, built in 1721, still stands today.

Although Britain and France eventually colonized most of West Africa, it was the Portuguese who first explored the region and established its first European trading posts. Portugal began exploring West Africa in the early 15th century, and by the end of the 17th century, Portugal, Britain, France, and the Netherlands had established numerous settlements along the coast. Spain, Sweden, Denmark, and Prussia acquired less significant holdings in the region.

It's no coincidence that European expansion in West Africa coincided with colonization of the Americas. European prosperity in the New World was built on the backs of West African slaves.

The Slave Trade

Slavery had existed in West Africa long before Europeans arrived. Slaves were usually captured in battle or sold by their families to pay off debt. While West African slavery was far from pleasant, slaves could often work toward their freedom, and multi-generational slavery was uncommon.

Europeans introduced a new, more brutal kind of slavery to West Africa. They sold African slaves across the Atlantic, forever cut off from their homelands and families, where they and their descendants would be nothing but property.

The first known slave ship arrived in Lagos, Portugal, in 1441, and the last departed from Dahomey (now Benin) in 1885. During that time, between 11 and 13 million slaves were shipped from Africa. On the beach near Ouidah, the foremost slave-trading port in what is now Benin, a powerful monument called La Porte de Non Retour—the Gate of No Return—marks the spot where hundreds of thousands of people left their homeland forever.

While Europeans sometimes captured slaves themselves, more often they set up agreements in which African leaders sold slaves—often prisoners of war—to European slave traders in exchange for firearms or other European goods. European traders then shipped the slaves to the Americas, where they worked on European plantations and built European colonies, producing cheap raw materials that fueled the European powers' vertiginous growth in economic and military might.

But Europeans couldn't ignore the horrors of the slave trade forever. By the late 18th century, the Abolitionist movement had gained traction in Europe, especially in Britain. The British Parliament banned the slave trade in 1807. Within a decade, Britain had signed treaties with France, Portugal, the Netherlands, and other countries agreeing to shut down the trade. The American Congress also banned the international slave trade in 1807, though the domestic slave trade remained legal. Although the British and French navies monitored the Atlantic for slave ships, smugglers continued shipping slaves to Latin America and the Caribbean until the 1880s.

The slave trade ravaged West African societies. The most valuable slaves were men of working age: 56% of slaves shipped across the Atlantic were adult men. West Africa's adult male population fell about 20%, causing population growth to stagnate. Near-constant warfare and the threat of being captured destabilized much of the region. In present-day Benin, the Idaatcha and Mahi peoples fled the southern coastal region for the hills of what is now the *département* of the Collines, sparking conflict with the Tchabé and Nagot who already lived there. Their descendants still live in the Collines: the Idaatcha in Dassa, and the Mahi in Aklampa, Ouèssè, and other villages. Other refugees took shelter in the middle of lakes, building entire villages on stilts in the water. Many such villages, including the popular tourist destination of Ganvié, are still inhabited today.

> Organizations today study genealogy and link people of African descent to their genetic roots in Africa. For more information, visit www.africanancestry.com.

Cultural Implications Today

Most slaves from present-day Benin were sold in Brazil or the Caribbean. After emancipation, many of their descendants came home, bringing with them Afro-Brazilian and Caribbean culture. You can still see the influence on the architecture and cuisine of Ouidah and Porto-Novo. They also brought New World crops—corn, cassava, tomatoes, peanuts, and tobacco—that are now mainstays of Beninese cuisine and culture.

The Atlantic slave trade profoundly shaped not only Africa, but Europe and the Americas as well. Much of the European powers' eventual growth into world-spanning empires would not have been possible without the wealth and economic structures they gained from the trade and labor of West African slaves. And the slaves didn't just bring their labor to North America, Latin America, and the Caribbean—they also brought their cultures, religions, and languages. Haitian Voodoo comes from Vodoun, which originates in present-day Benin. Fon, the most widespread native language of southern Benin, is still spoken in parts of Brazil. Much of modern American music, from soul to blues to jazz, was developed by the descendants of slaves and draws on the structures of West African music.

Today, many Beninese still think of African-Americans as *"nos cousins vendus par-delà la mer"*—our cousins sold across the sea.

A Secret Code

Many West African manuscripts dating to the period of European expansion and colonization are written not in the Latin alphabet, but in a modified form of the Arabic alphabet called *Ajami*. While West African scholars had been using Ajami script to write in their native tongues for centuries, some historians today believe that, once Europeans began colonizing the region, Ajami became a way to keep out prying European eyes. Africans could criticize and mock the colonial administration without fear of colonial officials reading what they'd written.

CONQUEST AND COLONIZATION

In the mid-19th century, what is now southern Benin comprised the kingdoms of Porto-Novo and Dahomey. King Toffa I of Porto-Novo signed a trade and friendship agreement with the French in 1851; Dahomey's King Glélé followed in 1868 by allowing the French to occupy Cotonou. Both kings aimed to leverage French protection against potential aggression from the British in neighboring Nigeria.

France's interest in West Africa stemmed largely from the growing economic importance of products such as palm oil and peanuts. Importing agricultural products and raw materials to Europe under an economically-protected colonial regime promised huge gains for the French economy. While some recent historians have argued that colonization did less for French economic growth than previously thought, there's no doubt that, at the time, French political and business leaders intended to make a killing off their colonies. The French also aimed to limit the colonial growth of other European powers—notably Britain, which already had several footholds along the West African coast.

In 1890, Glélé's son, Béhanzin, succeeded him to the throne of Dahomey and immediately began to militarily resist French domination of the region. Dahomeyan warriors, including thousands of Amazons, fought bravely to defend their country, but they couldn't overcome French heavy arms and repeating rifles. France defeated Béhanzin's army in November 1890 and established a protectorate over Porto-Novo and Cotonou.

After another war broke out in 1892, a French army of 3,600 men—mostly West African troops—marched on Abomey, the capital of Dahomey. While the invading force included regular French troops and units of the French Foreign Legion, most of the troops were African soldiers fighting in the French army. The French called these troops *tirailleurs sénégalais*, or Senegalese skirmishers—a misnomer, since they hailed from throughout West Africa. After several fierce battles, they broke the Dahomeyan army and captured the town, effectively ending Dahomeyan resistance. The campaign, which cost the lives of 220 French soldiers and thousands of Dahomeyans, ranks among France's most costly African conquests—a testament to the Dahomeyans' stubborn resistance. In 1894, the French exiled Béhanzin and founded the French colony of Dahomey.

The following year, 1895, France grouped its colonies of Côte d'Ivoire, Dahomey, Guinea, the Haute-Volta (present-day Burkina Faso), Mauritania, Niger, Senegal, and the French Sudan (present-day Mali) into *L'Afrique occidentale française* (AOF)— French West Africa. By creating the AOF, France aimed to exploit the region's resources and to homogenize its hundreds of cultures and languages, all under the banner of progress and civilization. Officially, Paris administered the AOF via its regional capital in Dakar, Senegal. In practice, the colonial army exerted the most control over the colonized peoples. While white officers commanded the army, the bulk of its troops were African *tirailleurs sénégalais*.

The French colonial regime tried to have it both ways: to govern a vast territory with very few European troops and officials on the ground, while severely restricting opportunities for the African soldiers and administrators on whom the whole system relied. Only Europeans could become army officers or hold governmental positions. While France ostensibly aimed to assimilate the colonized peoples into French culture—to, in colonial parlance, "civilize" them—colonialism's driving motives were economic and political, and cultural assimilation progressed slowly. In 1937, out of an estimated 15 million people colonized, as few as 72,000 West Africans were French citizens. Only a few thousand of them had become French through cultural assimilation. Most simply lived in the earliest-formed colonies, where French citizenship was granted at birth. French law designated the rest of the AOF's population as *"sujets"*—subjects.

This all bred instability and resentment among the colonized peoples. Resistance to French rule swelled after the Second World War, ending with independence for all of French West Africa between 1958 and 1960.

INDEPENDENCE

Dahomey achieved independence from France on August 1, 1960. As with many African countries, Dahomey's early years witnessed a cycle of coups d'état and short-lived governments. Some stability came when Colonel Mathieu Kérékou took power in 1972. Kérékou established a Marxist-Leninist regime and, disdaining Dahomey's colonial name, renamed the country *La République Populaire du Bénin*, the People's Republic of Benin. "Benin," the name of a medieval kingdom in present-day Nigeria, was considered a neutral name that didn't favor any of Dahomey's many ethnic groups.

Kérékou's Marxist-Leninist ideology proved less than ideal for Benin. In 1990, under pressure from the population, international investors, and the Beninese diaspora, he agreed to the drafting of a new constitution. The constitution of 1990 established a democratic republic and renamed the country *La République du Bénin*. In 1991, after losing the country's first free presidential elections to former Prime Minister Nicéphore Soglo, Kérékou stepped down. It was the first time in sub-Saharan Africa's history that a dictator had peacefully ceded power to a democratically-elected government.

Benin's current president, Thomas Yayi Boni, took office in 2006 and won re-election in 2011. As an economist and former president of the West African Development Bank, Yayi has focused on the country's economic growth. He has also faced some controversies, including alleged involvement in a nationwide Ponzi scheme and a failed attempt to amend the constitution to allow himself to run for a third term in 2016.

Today, Benin is considered one of the most stable democracies in Africa, but it remains one of the world's poorest countries, with development and modernization often failing to reach the large rural population.

The Dawn of a New Day

Benin's national anthem, "*L'Aube Nouvelle*" (The Dawn of a New Day), elegizes Dahomey's past resistance to French rule and looks ahead to a brighter future free of colonial ties. A priest named Gilbert Jean Dagnon wrote and composed the song, which became the national anthem upon independence in 1960. Today, schoolchildren learn the anthem by heart, and it's one of few songs that nearly all Beninese—whatever their ethnicity, and whether or not they understand French—can recognize.

Politics

Since 1990, Benin has been a democratic republic. Its government comprises the Presidency, the National Assembly, and the judiciary. The President can be elected to a maximum of two five-year terms, while the 83 deputies of the National Assembly are elected every four years. The Supreme Court and the Constitutional Court hold final jurisdiction within the judiciary.

The country is divided into twelve provinces, called *départements*. *Départements* are divided into *communes*, and *communes* into *arrondissements*. While they no longer have any official power, village kings remain influential in local matters. The population, especially in rural villages, often trusts the king more than official law enforcement to fairly settle disputes.

During elections, every political party has an official symbol. You can see a seashell, the symbol of President Yayi Boni's coalition, on buildings and signs throughout Cotonou. During the electoral campaign, candidates work to associate their name with the representative political symbol, by which voters, many of whom are illiterate, will recognize the candidates on their ballots. As part of the campaigns, candidates and their associates visit local groups and hold animated rallies where they sometimes distribute "gifts"—anything from cash to t-shirts to free booze—to thank the population for their support. While this widespread practice rests on local traditions of leaders gaining support through personal gifts and favors, some Beninese are becoming more conscious of the harm it can do to a modern democracy.

On election day, official and circumstantially apolitical moderators supervise the voting, which takes place in a school building, in a thatched hut, or even at a table under a tree. Observers from the African Union found that, despite some problems, the 2011 presidential election was mostly free and fair.

Although Benin is a young democracy, its people know the value and fragility of democratic government. Shortly after winning re-election in 2011, President Yayi Boni proposed to change 40 of the 160 articles of Benin's constitution, including the provision limiting presidents to two terms. From government deputies to illiterate peasants, the population exploded in outrage. The recent civil war in Côte d'Ivoire, sparked when the incumbent president refused to leave office, remained fresh on people's minds. Even in regions that had heavily supported Yayi's re-election, billboards and graffiti demanded "Touche pas à ma Constitution!" (Hands off my Constitution!). Yayi renounced his proposals and promised to leave office at the end of his second term.

Voudoun and Politics

Vodoun divination is meant to be practiced on a purely familial or community level, yet Beninese politics have also gotten involved. During electoral campaigns, village diviners often receive visits from political candidates seeking support from spiritual forces.

Economy and Occupations

Most Beninese live on subsistence agriculture. Corn predominates in the south, while cassava and yams are more important in the north. Other significant crops include millet, beans, peanuts, oranges, bananas, and pineapples.

Cotton, mostly grown in the north, is Benin's most important cash crop. Other exports include palm oil (and its derivative products), cashews, shea butter, and coffee. The extraction of Benin's natural resources like phosphates, chromium, rutile (titanium dioxide), and iron ore are typically underdeveloped, though marble is sometimes mined.

Besides farming, many villagers have a second occupation. A man may fish, hunt, or work as a mechanic, tailor, blacksmith, or carpenter, while a woman may sell goods in the market or work as a hair stylist or seamstress. The wealthier members of Beninese society, who do not have to farm or do manual labor, are usually government functionaries such as bureaucrats, politicians, school administrators, law enforcement officers, and customs agents.

Widespread official corruption is an open secret in Benin. Many functionaries use their unofficial incomes to lead relatively lavish lifestyles, in stark contrast to the average family's hardscrabble poverty. In rural areas you'll often see, among the small mud houses and thatched market stalls, a gleaming mansion surrounded by high walls, or a late-model Mercedes speeding down the rough dirt road.

Tourism is a small but growing sector of the economy, particularly through the wildlife parks in the north and the cultural hot spots of Ouidah, Abomey, and Porto-Novo. Smaller communities are beginning to gain from tourism through the work of non-governmental organizations and tour guide businesses. Examples of community development initiatives are the Lake Doukon hippopotamus tours (p117) near Lokossa and the CPN eco-lodge (p151) in Camaté-Shakaloké.

EARLY ECONOMY

Before Europeans arrived, West Africans produced and traded salt, fish, soap, cloth, leather, and metals such as iron and copper. Coastal communities, such as present-day

Ouidah, harvested important quantities of sea salt. The salt was strained from blocks of mud collected between tides. Fishermen along the coast and rivers traded smoked fish throughout the region, and women made soap from ashes and boiled palm oil. Demand for this soap in Europe became so high that in the 17th century Portugal banned its importation to protect Portuguese soap-makers. West Africans also produced cloth and rope from animal skins and plant products. Even before 1000 CE, the Yoruba people of present-day Benin and Nigeria were adept at spinning, weaving, and dying wool and cotton. The Yoruba were also noted blacksmiths. They alloyed copper with zinc to form brass, and with tin to form bronze. In the north of present-day Benin and Nigeria, the Fulani and Hausa produced and traded leather goods such as harnesses, shields, bags, and sandals. West African commerce relied on barter and on a currency of cowrie shells. Today, the cowrie shell remains a symbol of prosperity: you'll often see it in jewelry and ceremonial clothing, and it's the symbol of President Yayi Boni's political coalition.

> The traditional system of inheritance excludes daughters from land bequests, but recent laws have banned this practice.

Media

Most Beninese get news and music via small battery-operated radios, which are cheap and can be used in areas without electricity. The government broadcasts the station ORTB (Office de Radiodiffusion et Télévision du Bénin) throughout the country, and many communes broadcast local radio stations, both in French and in local languages. You can pick up the BBC World Service and Radio France Internationale (RFI) on a shortwave radio.

Wealthier people have televisions at home. Satellite television is becoming increasingly popular, bringing international channels such as France 24 and the BBC into Beninese households. The Beninese particularly enjoy music videos and soap opera–type shows and movies, including some that are produced in West Africa. Many West African shows feed the people's love of drama and address topics that strike a nerve in West African society, such as polygamy, infidelity, official corruption, violence against women, and the pressure to have male children.

Benin has two daily newspapers, *La Nation* and *Le Matinal*, and several weekly or monthly papers. All newspapers are printed in Cotonou and Parakou. Delivery of printed news to outlying villages and towns is typically delayed or nonexistent. In Cotonou, local papers—which are usually in French—can be purchased at the Place de l'Étoile Rouge and behind the hospital, toward Cadjehoun. French newspapers and magazines are available at the Institut Français and at the bookshops near the Ganxi market and the Cathédrale Notre Dame des Apôtres. For neighborhood descriptions of Cotonou, see page 86.

Religion

You can't go long in Benin without passing a church procession in the street or getting woken up before dawn by a nearby mosque's call to prayer. The Beninese place religion and spirituality at the center of their lives and their culture.

> Special thanks to Johanna Krechel for her valuable insight into traditional religious beliefs and practices in Benin.

TRADITIONAL RELIGIONS

For centuries, the peoples of present-day Benin have practiced numerous traditional belief systems. The most well-known of these is Vodoun, whose complex cosmology links the spirits present in nature, ancestors, and human communities. Over time, Vodoun has mixed with traditional practices and beliefs from neighboring regions of West Africa, as well as with some aspects of Christianity and Islam: foreigners introduced Islam to the area beginning as early as the 9th century, and Christianity beginning in the 16th century. The result is a diverse, syncretic religious environment of today's Benin.

> In many towns, markets have a designated area where Vodoun talismans are sold. Wares can range from medicinal herbs to wooden figurines to dead animals. If you're respectful, vendors may be willing to explain the purpose of their merchandise.

Today the vast majority of Beninese are either Christian or Muslim, while also holding to some traditional religious beliefs and practices. They may not adhere to traditional beliefs as strictly as their ancestors did, but they believe that spirits and sorcerers exist and wield real power, which they may use for either good or evil. You may see someone crossing himself or invoking the name of Jesus or Allah as protection when evil spirits are perceived. When someone dies, the family may perform a traditional ritual as well as a Christian or Muslim funeral.

Oro 👣 INSIGHT

Oro is a guardian spirit still worshipped in the *départements* of Ouémé and Plateau, and in the villages of the Collines dominated by the Tchabé tribe. Since Oro originates from Yoruba traditions, it is not strictly considered part of Vodoun. The name "Oro" must never be uttered; villagers refer to it as *Le Fantôme*, the Phantom. The Phantom protects the community by chasing away evil spirits. It visits a village or town once a year, staying for a period ranging from a few weeks to a few months. Local sorcerers may summon the Phantom at another time if they believe that malicious spirits are active in the village. During that time, the spirit roams the village at night—and sometimes during the day. An eerie whooping sound accompanies the spirit's movement through the village.

While the Phantom is a benevolent spirit, its presence is so powerful that most people, especially women, are forbidden from seeing it. Everyone must stay inside their houses with doors and windows shut as it roams the village. Men caught outside by members of the Oro cult will be roughed up; women may be killed.

While the Oro cult isn't known to specifically target foreigners, foreign visitors should still take Oro seriously (for more, see *Safety and Security* on page 71).

> In some parts of the country you'll see temples of Vodoun and other traditional practices, while in other regions rituals and consultations mostly take place at a priest's or adept's house. In either case, it's best to visit in the company of a local.

The practice of Vodoun can involve worshiping specific gods and spirits, using talismans, or revering and calling upon ancestors. Since most Beninese now worship the Gods of Christianity and Islam, the worship of Vodoun's many divinities is often confined to the priests and initiated adepts of specific temples and cults. However, both ancestor-worship and the use of talismans remain widespread. You'll see talismans—which can take the form of a wide variety of objects—for sale in markets throughout the country. Many people, especially in rural areas, hang protective talismans above their doors.

Diviners are considered neutral spokespersons for spiritual forces. They act as mediums, interpreting physical signs to convey the meanings of past events or interpret messages from the gods and ancestors. A diviner usually works with some natural items, such as seeds, shells, bones, as well as some manufactured items, such as iron, that are important in daily life and associated with deities. He uses these items in a series of interactions with the subject in order to read messages from the spirits. More involved consultations may result in animal sacrifices, especially when a subject is advised that he must appease the gods to fulfill a wish or resolve a problem.

Today, Vodoun proper is found mostly in areas dominated by the Fon ethnicity. In other areas, Vodoun has often mixed with other traditional practices. In the Fon language, Vodoun is called *vaudou*, priests are *hounon* or *vaudounon*, and initiated adepts are *voudounsi* or *hounsi*. The French word *fétiche* (fetish) is commonly used to refer to talismans, rituals, cults, and traditional practices in general.

Foreigners often dismiss traditional belief systems like Vodoun as backwards superstition, or even black magic. In reality, these beliefs reflect the deep bond the Beninese feel between themselves, their ancestors, their communities, and their land.

Polygamy

Polygamy predates Islam in Benin. It is practiced by most ethnic groups, regardless of religion. A man's status traditionally relies on having many wives and children, which shows both his virility and his financial ability to support a large family. The practice of polygamy may have been encouraged by the slave trade, which skewed the ratio of young men to women.

Polygamy also reflects the relatively weak position of many women, who object to their husbands taking additional wives but, being economically dependent on them, usually can't do anything about it. Some co-wives live together in apparent harmony. Many do not. To defuse tension, husbands often have their wives live in different houses, or even in different towns.

While polygamy remains widespread, it is becoming less common, as attitudes slowly change and women gain more economic independence.

In many villages, a particular tree or hill is believed to house a spirit that guards the community. Most Beninese deplore Vodoun's darker side: attempting to use Vodoun to curse someone is a serious crime under Beninese law, punishable by steep fines and long prison sentences.

The Beninese discuss Vodoun and other traditional practices openly among themselves but can be reluctant to talk about them with a visitor. They know that foreigners often believe negative stereotypes about traditional African religions. But it's still possible for a respectful traveler to visit a Vodoun temple or talk with a priest— just ask a local where to find one and make it clear that you're curious, not hostile.

Vodoun Gods

Much of the following information is based on Marc Monsia's *Religions Indigènes et Savoir Endogène au Benin.*

> You can see representations of Vodoun gods and spirits at the Sacred Forest of Kpassè (p108) in Ouidah and the History Museum (p141) in Abomey.

Mahu-Lissa is comprised of both a male and female form, and is considered the Supreme Being, the Creator, in an expression of Positive and Negative. Mahu, the female form, represents the Negative and the "magnetic fluid." Lissa is the male form and represents the Positive and the "electric fluid." Lissa is also identified with the color white and the number one. Mahu is identified with the number two. Since one plus two equals three, three is believed to be the number that expresses life. The symbol of Mahu-Lissa is a calabash bowl.

The god **Hevioso** represents the element of Fire and its principles: Power, Will, Strength, and Justice. This deity is associated with thunder, lightning, and the color red, and is depicted holding a thunder axe.

Dan Ayidohwedo is symbolized by a rainbow uniting sun and water. This god represents the relationship between Fire and Water and acts as an intermediary between them. The name Dan represents the element of water, and *hwé* is the word for sun, representing Fire. The principles of this deity are Wisdom, Happiness, and Prosperity. It is said that Dan Ayidohwedo presides over all movement in the universe.

Dan and Ayidohwedo may also be represented as separate gods acting independently. Ayidohwedo is the god of Air, symbolizing the relationships between the material and immaterial, the sky and the earth, and the body and soul. Dan, who came from the ocean, is the god of Water and Love. In the Fon language, *dan* means snake: the movements of a snake and of water across the earth, are uninterrupted and leave a similar trace.

Sakpata, or Ayivoudou, is the most respected god because he represents the most important element: Earth. In Fon, *ayi* is pronounced two different ways: the level-tone pronunciation means earth, and the lowered-tone pronunciation means conscience. His symbol is a human with a sphere-tipped tail. The sphere represents the globe and the manifestation of all of the elements together. He can sense the electromagnetic forces in all actions. Sakpata is also worshipped as the God of Smallpox, the protector against diseases.

Legba, the messenger god, is a liaison between man and the spirits. Legba statuettes are found throughout the country. The most common and visible ones usually depict a creature with shapeless eyes, a hole with bits of bones representing the mouth, and a large phallus at its base. These Legbas are meant to serve as an altar where you can ask for a spirit's help in protecting a place or sending a message to another Vodoun deity. Many villages, homes, and markets have their own protective Legba statuette at the entrance. The less visible Legbas are those found in a secret place of worship or a spirit's physical home. These are usually managed by a vodoun priest and can only be seen by initiated cult members.

Ogoun is one of the principle deities in Orisha, the Yoruba traditional religious system. He is the god of war and iron. Representations of Ogoun can be found throughout the country, and as far as Brazil and the Caribbean. Ogoun altars usually consist of iron rods protruding from the ground.

Witch Hunts and Politics ✊INSIGHT

In the 1970s, President Mathieu Kérékou led a movement to replace local political leaders across the country with individuals loyal to him. Because many of the old leaders were Vodoun priests, Kérékou launched a campaign to uproot sorcerers and witches and punish evil-doers. Initially, this campaign only brought accusations against certain political leaders, but it ultimately shifted to a campaign that targeted mostly women and the elderly, who are commonly profiled as Vodoun sorcerers. This modern-day witch hunt used torture to extract confessions and caused severe family and community feuds. In the end, Kérékou succeeded and many local leaders were replaced with government loyalists.

CHRISTIANITY AND ISLAM IN BENIN

Origins

In a typical village that has significant Christian and Muslim populations, you'll probably find several small mosques alongside two or three large churches, which are sometimes the largest and grandest buildings in the village. This disparity reflects how each religion originally came to the region.

North African traders introduced Islam to present-day Benin beginning as early as the 9th century. (Benin's northern region, which had the most contact with traders coming across the Sahara, remains the country's most Muslim region to this day.) Traders came from Egypt and Libya, as well as from the medieval Songhaï Empire, a powerful and advanced Islamic state based in present-day Niger and Burkina Faso. During the 15th and 16th centuries, Songhaï's territory stretched from present-day Senegal to Timbuktu to present-day northeastern Benin and northwestern Nigeria. Islam initially took hold among the elite of northern Benin's major trading towns and acquired some prestige because of its association with stud-

The oldest Catholic church in Benin is the Cathedral in Ouidah, built directly across the street from the Vodoun Python Temple (p106).

ies of governance, poetry, natural sciences, and geography. Outside the towns, the spread of Islam was probably slow and informal, based more on personal connections than on an organized effort to win converts.

By contrast, Christianity came late and with more organization and resources behind it. Priests and ministers in the earliest European settlements generally focused on serving the European populations, not converting the locals. In the 19th century, when the slave trade gave way to colonial ambitions, some missionaries began attempting to win over Beninese rulers and to use them to spread their faith. By 1850, Catholic and Protestant missions had entered the territory and established churches, primary schools, and hospitals. Conversion to Christianity, however, was problematic at first. Local communities often ostracized a person who chose the European church, while missionaries asked that converts completely abandon their traditional belief system. However, the population's respect for literacy allowed churches to gain ground through schools. Colonial Dahomey's large number of schools earned it the nickname "the Latin Quarter of Africa."

Today

Christianity may not come from Benin, but the Beninese have given it their own flavor. Christians put on their most colorful traditional clothing to go to church, where they sing and dance to upbeat drumming. Even the choir dances while singing hymns. When offering donations, members of the congregation shimmy their way up to the altar. The practice of Islam is less flamboyant, but still fairly liberal. Muslim women rarely wear a veil, and some Muslim men drink beer, reasoning that only hard liquor really counts as alcohol.

Benin experiences little conflict between religions. Beninese Christians and Muslims alike shake their heads in disbelief when talking about the regular religious violence in neighboring Nigeria. They regard religious intolerance as an almost foreign concept and pride themselves on their country's relative religious harmony. You may even see Muslims celebrating Christmas with their neighbors, or Christians showing up at the Ramadan feast—religious differences are no reason not to party.

The Catholic, Methodist, and Evangelical churches have a strong presence in Benin. Places of worship range from massive structures of stone and stained glass to a few rough wooden benches under a thatched roof. As with Christians throughout the world, Beninese Christians' most important religious celebrations are Christmas and Easter. For both holidays, families spend the morning preparing large amounts of food and, if they can afford it, buying bottles of beer and soda from nearby *buvettes* (p66). Everyone then strolls around the village or neighborhood, visiting friends and neighbors, and families offer food and drink to anyone who comes to visit them.

Christian observance is most in evidence during Holy Week. On the morning of Palm Sunday, women dress in white robes and proceed through the village to the church, carrying palm fronds. Some Catholics commemorate Good Friday by simulating Jesus' tortuous journey to Golgotha: they follow their priest through the village in the afternoon heat, frequently stopping to kneel in the sun as the priest describes a stage of the Way of the Cross representations, which adorn the walls of Catholic churches around the world.

Benin has a homegrown Christian sect: **Celestial Christianity**, a mixture of traditional animistic and Christian practices. A carpenter from Porto-Novo named Samuel Oshoffa founded the Celestial Church of Christ in 1947 with the desire to create a form of worship free from foreign priests and greedy local Vodoun sorcerers. Every Sunday, Celestial Christians attend very long services wearing white robes and no shoes.

Eckankar 👣 INSIGHT

Another Christian denomination practiced in Benin is Eckankar, a religious movement founded in 1965 by American Paul Twitchell. This religion preaches spiritual practice that enables practitioners to experience what they call 'The Light and Sound of God.' The Eckankar church is based in Minnesota. Find more on the web: www.eckankar.org

---

In towns and villages that have a major mosque, the neighborhood surrounding the mosque is called *zongo*. In the *zongo* neighborhood, you can hear the call to prayer five times a day. Much of the neighborhood will pause for prayer. Before praying, Muslims must wash their face, hands, and feet, roll out a prayer mat, and face in the direction of Mecca. Many Muslim businesses keep plastic tea kettles full of water so that the faithful can wash before prayer.

Beninese Muslims place great importance on **Tabaski**, also known as Eid al-Adha—Arabic for "Feast of Sacrifice." According to Islamic tradition, God commanded Ibrahim (known to Jews and Christians as Abraham) to prove his faith by sacrificing Ishmael, his only son. Ibrahim told Ishmael about God's command and promised to obey it only if Ishmael were willing to be sacrificed. Ishmael agreed. But when Ibrahim tried to cut Ishmael's throat, a ram appeared in his place—God had rewarded their devotion by sparing Ishmael's life.

In remembrance of Ibrahim's and Ishmael's faith, Muslim families sacrifice a sheep—ideally a ram—on the morning of Tabaski. On the days leading to Tabaski, truckloads of sheep are brought from the north to a giant sheep market on the beach road between Cotonou and Porto-Novo. A sheep can cost up to FCFA 120,000, or US$240. Since many Muslim families can't afford a whole sheep, they often split the cost with several other families. On the eve of Tabaski, *zongo* neighborhoods are elaborately decorated while large white rams await the morning sacrifice.

The ram is divided into three parts: one part is eaten the day of the ceremony, one part is saved for the family, and one part is given to neighbors and friends. Muslims spend the rest of the day in prayer and celebration. As with other celebrations in Benin, friends and family don colorful matching outfits, and everyone wanders around the village, visiting friends and neighbors and giving gifts to children.

Culture

DIVERSITY

As with most African countries, Benin's borders were drawn by Europeans who had little knowledge of the peoples living here. Over 50 ethnic groups, each with its own culture, customs, and language, inhabit the area that is now Benin. Many Beninese, especially those living in rural areas and those who don't speak French, identify more strongly with their ethnicity than with their nationality. People who live in the territory of another ethnic group sometimes sardonically call themselves *"les étrangers du même pays"*—foreigners of the same country.

However, Benin witnesses relatively little ethnic tension. A villager may more readily identify with and trust someone of his own ethnicity, and may make the occasional sideways remark about another ethnic group, but serious conflict rarely, if ever, manifests itself.

Benin's multitude of ethnic groups gives the country an inexhaustible cultural and linguistic diversity. The peoples of southern and central Benin trace their roots to coastal populations originating in present-day Benin, Togo, and Nigeria, while those in the north are related to the savanna populations of Niger and Burkina Faso.

Primary ethnic groups settled certain regions of the country, then evolved and branched out over time. The Fon, southern Benin's dominant ethnic group, originally comes from present-day southeastern Togo, as do the Mina and Adja, who populate the *départements* of Mono and Couffo. The Yoruba migrated from present-day Nigeria beginning in the 12th century and eventually branched out into other ethnicities, including the Nagot, Tchabé and Idaatcha. Today, their descendants are found mainly in the *départements* of Ouémé, Plateau, and the Collines. The Gún, who mainly live in and around Porto-Novo, trace their roots to the division of the Adja in the early 17th century: the Adja who founded the Kingdom of Porto-Novo mixed with the nearby Yoruba, and today the Gún language is a blend of Fon and Yoruba influence. The Dendi, who live in north-central Benin, came from Mali in the 16th century. The Bariba, a mostly Muslim ethnic group from northern Nigeria, reside in the Borgou and Alibori departments. The Betammaribé, or Ottomari, and the Somba live in the Atakora and Donga regions.

In larger towns you find other African nationals. As in the major cities of many West Africa nations, merchants and shopkeepers from Asia and the Middle East, especially Lebanon and China, play an important role in Cotonou's economy.

With so many different ethnic groups, there are at least 50 languages and dialects spoken throughout the country. French is the official language of Benin and plays an important role in unifying the population for

> One ethnic group from Togo, the Kotokoli, reside only in and around the village of Alédjo, which is surrounded by Nagot villages. *Alédjo* is the Nagot word meaning "stranger" or "foreigner."

work, social exchanges, and formal education. Some local languages have recently been introduced into the public school system. See *Language Reference* (p197) for helpful phrases in some local languages.

ETIQUETTE

Greetings

While Westerners generally limit greetings to a brief "Hello, how are you?" the Beninese greet each other frequently and at great length. A Beninese may greet a friend or acquaintance by asking about how he slept the night before, as well as the condition of his work, household, wife, children, parents, health, and (if applicable) hangover, to name a few. Even casual acquaintances often exchange these pleasantries whenever they run into each other. People also wish each other luck in whatever they are currently doing: such greetings translate as good arriving, good working, good reading, good eating, good digestion, good sitting, good bathing, good partying, and so on. Other favorites include "Have you done a little?" and *"Tu es là?"*—"You there?"—to which you simply respond *"Oui."* This can all seem comical to a visitor, but it reflects the importance the Beninese place on personal relationships and on showing other people that they matter to you.

Handshakes also play an important role in Beninese etiquette. The basic handshake is the same as in Western countries. Two friends often end their handshake by snapping their middle fingers together, like when you snap your thumb against your middle finger. When shaking an important person's hand, it's tactful to place your left hand under your right forearm. It literally shows that you don't want them to have to support the weight of your arm during the handshake. When a child greets an adult,

---

Funerals in Benin

The Beninese place great importance on funerals. A large, well-attended funeral shows that the deceased touched the lives of many; a poorly-attended ceremony is a disgrace to the deceased and his or her family. To help avoid this disgrace, Beninese radio and television stations air death notices several times a day. People stop what they're doing and listen, in case they know one of the deceased. If he can afford the trip, a Beninese may take several days off work and travel across the country for the funeral of even a long-lost friend or distant relative.

Beninese funerals allow space for open and honest grieving, as well as for celebrating the life of the deceased and his or her impact on the lives of others. After the religious service and burial, everybody moves to the house of the family for a festive reception. Receptions often engulf the whole neighborhood and may last multiple days, with friends and strangers alike joining in. Food is always on hand and drink flows freely. Troupes of musicians and dancers wander around, instigating impromptu dance parties.

While guests contribute what they can, the cost of the ceremony and reception can swamp a working-class Beninese family. Groups of poor families sometimes form informal partnerships for this purpose: if there's a death in one family, all of the families will split the cost of the funeral.

he crosses his arms and bends his knees in a curtsy. In a large crowd, where shaking everyone's hands would take too long—even by Beninese standards—it's fine to clasp your hands above your head to acknowledge everybody. Alternately, some Beninese enjoy mimicking President Yayi Boni's habit of greeting crowds by nodding his head, extending both arms in front of him, and waving both hands simultaneously.

Names and Titles

In Benin, except between close friends, people generally don't call each other by their names. You refer to someone either by their professional title—*professeur* for a secondary-school teacher, *chauffeur* for a taxi driver, and so on—or, less formally, as if they were a member of your family. If you're a 25-year-old woman, you might call an 18-year-old woman *petite soeur* (little sister), a 35-year-old man *grand frère* (big brother), a 10-year-old boy *petit* (little one), and a 50-year-old woman *maman* or *tanti* (mom or auntie). A father or mother may be known by the name of his or her eldest child: a woman whose first child is a girl named Pépé becomes Maman Pépé, while Pépé's father is Papa Pépé.

A foreigner will usually be called either *yovo* or *monsieur*, *madame*, or *mademoiselle*. Since *mademoiselle*, the title for an unmarried woman, carries the connotation of a woman who's in search of a husband, many single women find it helpful to ask people to address them as *madame* (see *Potential Issues for Travelers* on p69).

> Turn an undesired marriage request into a good-natured joke, or simply respond with a white lie (you're already married).

Visiting a Beninese Home

Rather than knocking on the door, most Beninese announce their arrival by either clapping three times or shouting "Ko ko ko!," a practice left over from the days when entrances to homes were either open or covered with cloth, and there was no door to knock on. When the host asks "Who's there?" the visitor often simply replies "Me!" to see if the host recognizes his or her voice.

In Benin, it's highly important for a host to give his guest something to eat or drink. If you're visiting someone's home, you should accept any food or drink they offer you. Most commonly, you'll be offered either water or a shot of *sodabi* (p66). If you're not sure that the water's been boiled, put it to your lips without drinking. If it's mealtime, they'll offer to share the meal with you. If you don't find the food appetizing, it's fine to have a few bites and then say that it's good but *je viens de manger* (I've just eaten).

A shot of *sodabi* is a popular welcome gesture. If one prefers not to drink, a polite *non merci* will work—though sometimes the offer must be accepted to avoid offending the host. It is also perfectly normal to offer the drink to the ancestors by saying "*pour les ancêtres*," and pouring the *sodabi* on the ground. (Caution: do not pour the sodabi on the ground without saying "*pour les ancêtres!*" That would be considered impolite and rude.)

Traditional Kings

Beninese towns and villages usually have a traditional king. The king maintains the village's cultural heritage and mediates disputes within the community. Kings generally like receiving foreign visitors, as long as they are respectful.

If you're visiting a smaller village, going to see the king can provide both a memorable cultural experience and practical benefits: the king (or someone at his court) can tell you about the community, and maybe give advice on visiting any nearby attractions you're hoping to see. Visiting him also shows respect for local customs and demonstrates that your visit is well-intentioned.

If you visit a village king, there are a few points to remember. First, bow rather than shaking his hand. Touching the king is often forbidden. Remove your shoes before entering his courtyard or throne room. In the throne room, the person addressing the king kneels before him with both knees on the ground, while everyone else sits Indian-style. You will probably be asked to give the king money for the visit; about FCFA 1,000 should do it. If someone brought you to the king, he will probably expect a similar tip.

> Villagers often prefer to take a dispute to the king rather than to the local police station, where officers may be more interested in bribes than in justice.

Table Manners

In Benin, people traditionally eat with their right hand. Middle- and high-end restaurants will provide silverware. You may also find silverware at casual eateries, especially in cities. In casual eateries, cups of water are considered communal, but since the water probably hasn't been boiled, it's best to bring your own water anyway. Before and after eating, you can rinse your right hand in the provided bowl of water, which may or may not contain soap. (Bring hand sanitizer if you must have clean hands before eating.) The left hand is considered dirty—don't eat or hand people money with your left hand.

Many Beninese consider it rude to eat in front of someone without offering to share. They do not, however, always expect to be taken literally. If a stranger invites you to *"Viens manger"* (come eat), it's polite to simply say *"Bon appétit,"* *"Non, merci,"* or *"Je viens de manger."*

Taking Pictures

The Beninese generally love having their picture taken, provided you let them look at the pictures on your camera's screen when you're done. However, some people are opposed to it. To be safe, don't take picture of someone without asking their permission, and be discreet about taking pictures in public places where passers-by may end up in the photo. Be aware that even if someone gives you permission to take their picture, they may expect a small tip afterward—and this is especially true in areas frequented by tourists.

Dress

Dress is Benin is more conservative than in most Western countries. Visitors should follow suit, both out of respect for local customs and, for women, to avoid unwanted attention. Men should wear long pants, since shorts are worn only for outdoor work or by young boys. Women should keep their thighs, belly, and lower back covered.

> The weather is usually very hot and humid. Light, loose-fitting cotton or linen clothing is ideal.

Cleavage should be modest, and while it can be acceptable to show some upper arm and shoulder, tank-tops will attract unwanted attention. In the north, where dress is more conservative, women should cover their shoulders.

If you want to dress local, you can buy colorful local fabric at the market. It should cost FCFA 500–4,000 per square meter, depending on quality. Take the fabric to a *tailleur* (tailor) for men, or a *couturière* (seamstress) for women, to get it made into clothing. A shirt, skirt, or pair of pants takes two meters, while a complete outfit takes 4–8 meters.

Music, Literature and Art

MUSIC

Beninese of all ages love music, especially when it's upbeat and highly rhythmic. Channeling the beat through your body is central to the Beninese view of music: they rarely listen to music that you can't easily dance to. When music is playing, impromptu dancing is prone to break out—anywhere, anytime, by anyone of any age.

Traditional Beninese Music

Beninese music traditionally consists of drumming and singing—and, of course, dancing. Village drummers still make their own drums from local materials and perform at funerals, weddings, religious holidays, and other occasions. Their traditional drums come in two varieties. One type of drum has a single drumhead and rests on the ground between the legs of the drummer, who beats the drumhead with his hands.

The other type of drum can function as a talking drum. It has two drumheads, one at each end, and hangs from the drummer's shoulder by a leather strap. The drummer beats the horizontal drum with a curved stick while, with his other hand, pulling on the thin leather cords connecting the two drumheads. By pulling and relaxing the cords, he controls the tension of the drumhead and thus the pitch of the sound. A skilled drummer can manipulate the pitch so precisely that he can send messages through his drumming. In the days before phones and motorized transport, villagers could make announcements throughout the village—and even talk with neighboring villages—using these drums. Today, drummers in some villages still pass this knowledge down to their children, and some Beninese can still understand messages sent by drum.

You'll mostly see traditional drummers at ceremonies and celebrations. They often roam the crowd, accompanied by a troupe of dancing women in matching traditional outfits, collecting donations from everyone. Part of the money goes to the drummers and dancers, while the rest goes to the family or families who sponsored the party.

Contemporary Beninese Music

Benin is home to a vibrant and inventive music scene, combining native folk music with rhythms from Ghana, the Congo, Latin America, France, and the United States. Some of Benin's most influential post-colonial musicians and groups include Ignacio Blazio Osho, Gnonas Pedro, G.G.Vickey, Les Volcans de la Capitale, and Picoby Band d'Abomey.

Gnonas Pedro (1943-2005) performed in the famous salsa band Africando All Stars. Orginally formed in 1990 under the name Africando, the group fused New York–based musicians and West African vocalists. Because salsa-style music has been popular in Central and West Africa since the 1940s, the group formed to blend African rhythms with New World influences. They sang in Wolof (a native language of Senegal), Spanish, or a mix of both. Gnonas Pedro's last recording is the posthumously-released title track *Ketukuba* (2006).

Angélique Kidjo is a world-renowned Beninese artist, especially popular in Europe. She sings in Fon, Yoruba, French, and English. Mesmerized as a child by a Jimi Hendrix album cover, Kidjo followed African music to the United States, Brazil, and the Caribbean. As a teenager she began recording and toured West Africa. Shifting politics prevented her from becoming an independent artist in Benin, so in 1983 she moved to Paris to study music. Kidjo started out in Paris as a backup singer for local bands, but by 1985 she had become the lead singer for Three Pili Pili, a Euro-African jazz/rock band. By the end of the decade, she was one of the most popular live performers in Paris. She has won four Grammy awards for her albums *Oremi*, *Black Ivory Soul*, *Oyaya*, and her most recent work, *Djin Djin*, whose title references the sound of a bell ringing in a new day for Africa. The percussionists in *Djin Djin*, Crespin Kplitiki and Benoît Avihoue, are members of the Gangbe Brass Band (see below). Their Beninese roots, along with Kidjo's, give the music a Beninese flavor. To learn more and get a taste of her music, visit kidjo.com.

The **Gangbe Brass Band** was formed in 1994 by eight Beninese musicians who aimed to blend Western jazz and big-band music with native rhythms. *Gangbe* means "the sound of metal" in Fon. They draw on instruments and rhythms native to Benin, as well as those imported by French colonists, who introduced European-style military and dancehall music to the region. The unique combination of instruments and rhythms bridge the past and present. The group sings in Fon—its members' native tongue—about societal problems, political injustice, and women's suffering. They have released three albums: *Gangbe* (1998), *Togbe* (2001), and *Whendo* (2004).

In addition to music from their own country, the Beninese enjoy the music of other West African nations—mainly Nigeria and Côte d'Ivoire—as well as some American pop.

> Orchestre Polyrythmo' was a popular group in Benin in the 1970s. Though they haven't produced new material in a while and the members are in their 60s, the music still sounds good.

LITERATURE

Literature in Benin, as in many African countries, has historically suffered several disadvantages. Most of the population is illiterate, restricting the numbers of readers and potential writers. Writers must choose between writing in their native tongue, which likely has a very small readership in Benin and no readership abroad, and writing in French, which can feel like a concession to European hegemony. Writers also face a tough publishing market: African publishers are few and generally ill-funded, while European publishers may be wary of taking on an African writer whose work is not guaranteed to appeal to European readers.

All of this belies the fact that Benin enjoys a long, rich tradition of oral story-telling. Beninese love telling and listening to stories, and are prone to recount a myth or proverb to make a point in any situation, from a barroom argument to a business meeting. Several acclaimed writers who call Benin home have channeled this tradition into written literature.

Perhaps Benin's most important writer is **Jean Pliya**. His short story collection *L'Arbre Fétiche* (*The Spirit Tree*) and play *La Secrétaire Particulière* (*The Private Secretary*) are popular among Benin's literate population for their sharp critique of Beninese society. Pliya was born in 1931 and has studied and taught in Benin, Togo, Niger, Senegal, and France, as well as having served as Vice Chancellor of the University of Benin and Minister of Education. He has recorded Fon oral traditions and histories in French, and in 1967 he won the Grand prix littéraire d'Afrique noire, an annual award for francophone writers from Sub-Saharan Africa, for his work *Kondo le Requin* (*Kondo the Shark*), which depicts King Béhanzin's resistance to French rule.

Félix Couchoro's work *L'Esclave* (*The Slave*), written in 1929, is considered the first African novel. Couchoro was born in Ouidah in 1900 and moved to Togo in 1939. He worked as a teacher, businessman, journalist, and newspaper editor, gaining local and international acclaim by publishing his works in serial form in Togolese newspapers. In *L'Esclave*, set in a village in southwestern Dahomey, he satirizes the Dahomeyan elite of the colonial period. He later shifted his writing style, adapting his French grammar to the local vernacular and incorporating Ewe and Fon expressions and proverbs. His later works include *Amour de féticheuse* (*Sorceress' Love*, 1941), *Drame d'amour à Anecho* (*Love Story at Anecho*, 1950), and *L'héritage cette peste* (*Heritage Is a Plague*, 1963). He died in Lomé, Togo, in 1968.

Ken Bugul, whose real name is Mariètou Mbaye Biléoma, was born in Senegal and now lives and writes in Benin. Her name means "one who is unwanted" in Wolof. She studied in Belgium and, for a time, was one of 28 wives in the harem of a village marabout in Senegal. In 1991, her work *Le Baobab Fou* was published in English as *The Abandoned Baobab: The Autobiography of a Senegalese Woman*. She won the Grand prix littéraire d'Afrique noire in 2000 for *Riwan ou le Chemin de Sable* (*Riwan; or, the Sandy Path*). She lives in Porto-Novo.

Florent Couao-Zotti was born in Pobé in 1964 and published his first work, *Ce* *soleil où j'ai toujours soif* (*This Sun-Scorched Place Makes Me Thirsty*) in 1996. In his wide-ranging work, which includes novels, plays, short stories, and comic books, he skewers Benin's political and economic elite. In 2010 he won the Prix Ahmadou-Kourouma for his detective novel *Si la cour du mouton est sale, ce n'est pas au cochon de le dire* (*If the Sheep's Pen Is Dirty, the Pig Shouldn't Point It Out*).

Djimon Hounsou

Beninese-American actor Djimon Hounsou was born in Cotonou in 1964. He immigrated to France as a teenager, where he dropped out of school and was homeless for a time. He eventually moved out of poverty by modeling. In 1990 he immigrated to the United States and began acting, and in 2005 he became a dual American/Beninese citizen. He has appeared in numerous American films and TV shows, starring in *Amistad* (1997), *Gladiator* (2000), and *Blood Diamond* (2006). He has been nominated twice for an Academy Award.

ART

Art flourished in present-day Benin prior to colonization. The royal family of Dahomey patronized artists who produced carvings in wood and ivory; pieces worked in silver, brass, and iron; and bas-reliefs. Dahomeyan artists also practiced *toiles appliquées* (applied canvas), a method of layering different pieces of cloth to create a kind of patchwork tapestry.

As in much of Africa, Dahomeyan art focused on sculpture, abstraction, and representing the human body. Statues and figurines of people are usually elongated or otherwise distorted; ceremonial masks have exaggerated features. One unique feature of Dahomeyan art is that statues and masks sometimes use zoomorphic representation, depicting specific people—often kings—as half-human and half-animal. (Each Dahomeyan king was traditionally linked to a different animal.) Another unique practice is the production of small bronze figurines that were purely decorative, whereas figurines in other African art traditions usually served a religious purpose.

West African art heavily influenced European artists in the early 20th century and played a crucial role in the birth of the Cubist movement. Pablo Picasso and Henri Matisse, among others, studied African art and applied African artists' distortion of perspective and ratio to their revolutionary work.

Beninese Art Today

Museums in Abomey, Ouidah, and Porto-Novo display some original artwork from what is now Benin. However, much of Benin's original art is now housed in European museums, including the Louvre and the Musée de l'Homme in Paris. Most artworks in Beninese museums are replicas.

You can still see original Dahomeyan bas-reliefs at the Royal Palaces in Abomey. They mostly focus on warfare and on the martial exploits of Dahomeyan kings, reflecting the importance of war in this kingdom that was constantly fighting with its neighbors. You'll also see more recent statues in town centers, especially in the center of major roundabouts. These statues usually date to the time of Mathieu Kérékou's Marxist-Leninist regime and employ motifs common in Communist art. One statue in Bohicon shows several peasants collectively holding up a large pot, while another in the Place des Martyrs in Cotonou depicts three men wielding a machete, a sword, and a Kalashnikov striding forward together.

You can find artwork for sale in artisans' markets in most of Benin's larger towns. While most of these artworks are simply imitations of art from previous generations, you can also buy original contemporary art from artists in some towns. Communities of artists in Cotonou, Porto-Novo, and Dassa promote the development of Beninese art and the collaboration of contemporary artists by hosting international symposiums and festivals.

Contemporary Beninese Artists

Joseph Njie is a Gambian-born painter who lives and works in Natitingou. He paints original pieces and makes all of his own paint pigments from stones that he mines from the Atakora Mountains surrounding Natitingou. He enjoys visiting with foreigners and has been a good friend to many Peace Corps Volunteers over the years. If you're in Natitingou, you can go to his home, which doubles as his studio, to look at (and maybe purchase) his work, as well as to chat about art, African politics, and food—he speaks impeccable English. Call 98.62.40.42 or 96.08.46.90 and say that Jonny sent you.

Born in Parakou, **Félix Agossa** began his artistic career while still in high school. In 1987 he created his first cement sculpture, *L'Élève Inconnu* (The Unknown Pupil), in a dusty Parakou schoolyard as a tribute to Benin's students. It still stands today, braving the elements and inspiring younger generations.

Immediately recognized as a promising artist, Agossa was invited to Liège, Belgium, for a nine-month study in an animation studio. By 1993, the young artist had become well-known in the West African art scene. Jovial and easy going, Agossa became a highly solicited sculptor and author-illustrator throughout West and Central Africa, from Senegal to the Congo. In 2000, he set off once again for more exhibits and artist residencies in Marseilles, Bordeaux, Brussels, and Berlin.

Shortly after his return from Europe, the Beninese clergy took notice of Agossa's work and hired him to decorate many of Benin's churches and cathedrals. Agossa thus began a new stage of his career: spiritual art. Today he continues to explore this realm of art, combining Vodoun, Christianity, and Islam. His paintings contain indigenous and personal emblems and symbols that can be applied to all forms of personal and spiritual journeys.

Agossa's work depicts the everyday expressions and shapes of the people he observes. Like many African artists, Agossa makes use of local materials in order to create an authenticity in his work, true to his African origins.

Richard Korblah was born in Côte d'Ivoire in 1978 and raised in southern Benin. He has been showing his work in Cotonou since 1998, and has traveled to Europe for numerous artist residencies. He often works shirtless, a bandana tied around his neck and a Neem stick—used by the Beninese as a kind of toothbrush—in his mouth. He likes to sleep among his unfinished canvases, and says he doesn't grasp their full significance until he has completed them and can take a step back. His art often veers toward the spiritual, and his paintings regularly contain a representation of the cross. Korblah sometimes becomes so consumed with his work that he falls ill after completing a piece.

In one series of paintings, Korblah uses a combination of photographs, paint, and fabric to create distorted images of the suffering and jubilation expressed in the traditional scourging ceremonies practiced by the Fulani people of West Africa. These mixed-media compositions embody the ceremonies' brutality and power through bold streaks of paint. A medley of earth tones and blood-red and blue hues represent the harsh yet vibrant Fulani lifestyle.

Sports

Soccer is by far the most popular sport in Benin. Since it requires relatively little equipment and has fairly simple rules, it's well-suited to areas with little funding or organization for team sports. You'll often see children of all ages playing impromptu soccer matches in a schoolyard, in a field, or on any other open patch of ground. Many villages field a local team that plays against other village teams, and some schools organize annual soccer tournaments, both intramural and against schools in neighboring villages. These village-level tournaments can be very informal: teams often lack uniforms, and even shoes. In larger towns, teams are more organized and well-funded—some even have team buses.

In much of the country, people tend to believe that sports aren't for girls. Schools and villages often field only boys' and men's soccer teams. However, with the spread of physical education programs to rural public schools, girls are beginning to receive more opportunities to play.

The inhabitants of cities and large towns enjoy a greater variety of sports, including basketball, handball, volleyball, and tennis. Running is also popular, and some towns host annual marathons.

The Squirrels

Les Écureuils—the Squirrels—is Benin's national soccer team. There have been a few debates regarding the ferocity of squirrels, yet the name remains. In 2008, the team made history by advancing to the final round of the Africa Cup of Nations (CAN). The main stadium in Cotonou, Le Stade de l'Amitié (Friendship Stadium), hosts the team and also contains track and field facilities.

The Environment: Geography, Flora and Fauna

Benin is a relatively flat country characterized by plateaus and valleys in the south, rolling hills toward central Benin and the northeast, and a modest mountain range in the northwestern Atakora region. The highest point is Mount Sokbaro (658 meters) in the Atakora Range, just west of the village of Alédjo.

Benin is part of the **Dahomey Gap**, also known as the Intertropical Convergence Zone (ITCZ). The Dahomey Gap is an oscillating low pressure zone created by cold sea currents flowing close to the coastline. High pressure winds blow toward the Dahomey Gap from two directions: the tropical winds from the Atlantic blow northeast from April to October, and the dry winds from the Sahara, also known as the **Harmattan**, descend southeast from November to March. The Gap runs along the coast of Benin, Togo, and part of Ghana. In this region the wooded savanna reaches farther south, nearly touching the coast. The land to the east and west of the Gap is part of the Guinea Forest zone. It was once densely wooded, but deforestation has created a "derived savanna" consisting of cultivated fields, farm-bush, secondary-growth forests, and savanna grasses.

> Even though sacred forests are venerated and protected by traditional beliefs, they are not immune to deforestation and have begun to give way to the quest for more farmland.

Benin is mainly covered by open and wooded savanna, though there are patches of the Guinea Forest the south. Some sacred forests, such as the Lama Forest in central Benin and the forest of Niaouli, just north of Cotonou, have been partially protected from deforestation.

During the dry season, the Harmattan spreads a veil of dust over the country. The vegetation becomes dry and brown, and water becomes scarce. In this period, many farmers burn their fields in an effort to rejuvenate the soil and to clear the weeds in preparation for the next planting season. Hunters take advantage of the reduced undergrowth during the dry months to hunt wildlife.

Floods are a serious concern throughout the country. Cotonou, which sits on a narrow strip of land between the ocean and a large lagoon, is especially vulnerable.

Environmental Concerns

Management of trash and wastewater is a problem in Benin. In the past, all of the household waste was organic and decomposed naturally; the scrap and debris could simply be thrown into piles outside the home and be used later to fill low spots. However, stagnant water provides a habitat for breeding mosquitoes, and thus the malarial parasite. Today, the introduction of modernized items into daily life has resulted in non-biodegradable waste, such as tin cans, plastic bags, and batteries. The cities are too crowded and poorly planned to compensate with a more efficient and environmentally sound waste management system. In these dense populations, household waste is discarded in nearby fields, burned, or buried within the household courtyard. Refuse collection services exist in larger towns, but do not reach all the neighborhoods, nor is there priority for keeping the city clean. There are no public trash cans; piles develop along the sidewalks, transforming gutters and open-air canalizations into veritable public dumps. Trash located near concessions, schools, wells, and community clinics emit stinking odors, attracting many insects and rodents that cause health issues for the population. More than 80% of industrial and household waste in Cotonou does not reach the municipal dumps.

The Mono River typically floods about every five years. It floods in increments: the first couple waves empty back into the riverbed, but the third wave often creates eddies and ponds throughout the vast flood plain, destroying fields and homes. Roads are completely blocked for up to a week before the water recedes to its banks and the land begins to slowly dry. Due to poor drainage systems, heavy rainstorms can also flood towns and cut roads.

Clash of Livelihoods INSIGHT

In the north, where cattle herding is more common, the seasonal migration of herders (mostly of the Fulani people) with their livestock causes serious friction with local farmers. Farmers accuse herders of letting their animals eat and trample their crops, while herders allege that farmers have over-cultivated the region, leaving little grazing ground.

FAUNA

Pests

Beware: do not bother the ants! In the countryside you'll often see thick columns of ants filing across paths and roads. They definitely bite. They will even invade homes in search of food and moisture. Villagers employ fire, boiling water, gasoline, and other extreme measures to fight them off.

Also watch out for scorpions, especially during the dry season and in the north. Some are about the size of an average person's hand, while others are much smaller and harder to spot. A sting is extremely painful and causes significant swelling, and should be treated as soon as possible at a hospital or health center. Carry a flashlight at night to avoid stepping on one, and sleep under a tucked-in mosquito net—after checking that you don't have any bedmates first.

Golden Orb Spiders

In the north, you may see Golden Orb Spiders high up in trees or power lines. You will probably be hoping that they stay up there. These massive black-and-gold spiders spin golden webs whose color attracts unfortunate bees. Their webs are among the strongest spiderwebs in the world.

Reptiles

Many snake species call Benin home, including the black cobra, spitting cobra, boomslang, and green and black mambas. All of these snakes are venomous and greatly feared by villagers, who enthusiastically kill them on sight. Pythons aren't venomous and, being venerated in Vodoun, enjoy limited protection from humans. Avoid walking off the path in tall grass, and if using a latrine, shine a flashlight around before sitting down. If you're bitten, take note of the snake's appearance and get to a hospital in a larger town as quickly as possible—village health centers may not have the appropriate antidote.

Lizards in Benin are quite harmless and even help deplete the cockroach population. Large agama lizards, popularly called *margouillat* in French, are gregarious. The males come in an array of flashy green, blue, red, and yellow hues and can be seen perched on rocks and walls, bobbing up and down as they survey their surroundings. Female agama lizards are smaller and more slender, with bright green dots on their heads.

Geckos tend to hang around in houses, providing natural pest control as they dart across walls and ceilings, catching and eating moths and insects. Chameleons aren't common, but can be found in the bush and for sale in local markets. Chameleons have a mean bite, so be aware before handling one.

Crocodiles can be found in rivers distant from human populations. Sea turtles come seasonally to the beaches, especially around Grand Popo (p113).

Mammals

Most of the original mammal species of Benin have been hunted out of the countryside, though they still live in very remote, unpopulated areas. Small mammals, like the bush rat (agouti), small deer, and monkeys are heavily hunted. In the protected territories of the wildlife parks, species such as the elephant, hippopotamus, warthog, harnessed bushbuck, Western kob, Western hartebeast, oribi and Western bush duiker attain populations of several thousand. The most numerous species are the African water buffalo and the Western roan, with numbers exceeding ten thousand. The territory also supports smaller populations of the sing-sing waterbush, nagor reedbuck, and the korrigum, a West African species of topi.

In the feline family, there are an estimated 750 lions and a number of leopards, servals, caracals, African wild cats, and possibly even one to two dozen cheetahs, one

---

Endangered and Vulnerable Species in Benin

Wildlife populations in the parks have declined over the past 25 years, resulting in the giraffe and the African wild dog now reportedly extinct in the region. On the other hand, the roan, elephant, hippo, and buffalo numbers seem to have increased.

Endangered
  Red-bellied Monkey (Cercopithecus erythrogaster)
  Wild Dog (Lycaon pictus)

Vulnerable
  African Elephant (Loxodonta africana)
  African Golden Cat (Profelis aurata)
  Cheetah (Acinonyx jubatus)
  Fox's Shrew (Crocidura foxi)
  Ja Slit-faced Bat (Nycteris major)
  Lion (Panthera leo)
  Red-fronted Gazelle (Gazella rufifrons)
  Spotted-necked Otter (Lutra maculicollis)
  West African Manatee (Trichechus senegalensis)
  White-thighed Black-and-white Colobus (Colobus vellerosus)

of the last surviving populations in West Africa. Other predators include jackals, hyenas, the African civet, genets, otters, badgers, and several species of mongoose.

Hippopotamuses are somewhat common in the parks of the north, the Ouémé River near Dassa and Idadjo, and around the Mono River near Lokossa. There are an estimated 2,000 hippopotamuses throughout the combined West African nations of Côte d'Ivoire, Ghana, Togo, Benin, and Burkina Faso.

The West African Manatee

The West African Manatee is an elusive creature in both myth and reality. Though previously thought extinct in the region, some evidence shows that the species is still present in several West African nations. In 2000, for example, Côte d'Ivoi reclaimed a population of up to 800 manatees. These mammals are herbivores that inhabit estuaries with mangroves or freshwater with overhanging vegetation. Of all manatee species, the West African Manatee is the most threatened. Though legally protected worldwide, manatee populations continue to decline due to hunting and incidental trapping in fish nets, turbines, and control gates in dams.

Mistaken Identity ✊INSIGHT

In West African coastal communities, the goddess Mami Wata is a mermaid deity who represents irresistible beauty and wealth. There are legends of people following Mami Wata to a deep and watery death. It is possible that the female manatee, which has a somewhat scaly body with lungs and mammaries to nurse her young, could easily resemble a woman on the surface of the water and thus be at the source of these spiritual beliefs.

BIRDS

Small Birds

The **common garden bulbul** lives up to its name in that it is very common, much like the American robin. This species of bulbul has a dark head and drab brown body. It measures roughly the length of a hand and is most often seen on the ground, or in low bushes and trees.

Village weavers are colloquially called *oiseaux gendarmes*, or "army birds." They are oriole-sized with a black head and a yellow-orange body. They measure about seven to eight inches tall and live in colonies. A colony of village weavers will invade a tree, where they weave nests and make incessant, obnoxious noise. The weavers will inhabit this tree until it either falls down or, if in a village, the villagers cut the tree down or smoke the birds out.

Pin-tailed whydahs, when in breeding season, make wonderful cat toys: the males grow long tail feathers, perhaps two feet long at most. Out of breeding season, one can identify a pin-tailed whydah by its distinct orange beak, black and white spotted coloring, and its small size, about three to four inches tall. These birds are most often seen while feeding on the ground.

Red bishops, also known as black-winged bishops, are fairly common birds and easily spotted in the tall grass on which they float. They have a red mane, a black body, and measure about five inches tall.

The Senegal firefinch, or red-billed firefinch, is so named from the male's bright red coloring. This bird is four to five inches tall, and is most commonly seen feeding on the ground.

Medium-sized Birds

Senegal kingfishers are often perched high, not necessarily near water. About eight inches tall, their bright blue color, orange beak, and terrific screech make these birds easy to identify.

The **white-throated bee-eaters** are beautiful green birds often seen perched on electrical wires, usually in groups. Their white throat is quite visible in contrast to the black stripes on their face and throat. Their flight is graceful, with the couple of pin-tail feathers trailing neatly.

The **common fiscal shrike** is also seen on electrical wires, though not in groups. The shrike has black and white coloring, and a helmet shaped head with a stout black beak. This bird is about seven inches tall.

African black crakes and **African jacanas** are sure to be seen in freshwater ponds and marshes. The crake is about ten inches tall, and has an amusing clown colored body with long, bright orange legs, a yellow beak, and red ringed eyes. Jacanas are also known as lily trotters, as they use their large feet and long legs to walk on lilies. The jacanas have longer legs and more graceful coloring than the crake, with a soft blue colored forehead, a white throat, and a brown body. Both of these water birds are trapped by locals for consumption.

The **helmeted guinea fowl** roams wild throughout the north of Benin and is commonly raised for consumption. The **double-spurred francolin** and the **stone partridge** are also part of the local diet and have a pleasant, sweet meat.

Large Birds

Western grey plantain eaters are found in the crown of mid-sized trees, thrashing about for plantains or other fruit. They are large and grey with a yellow beak, and almost two feet tall including the tail feathers.

The **Senegal coucal** has a noticeably clumsy gait, aerial or terrestrial. The call sounds like big, fat drops of water: *blop blop blop blop blop*. It measures about a foot long, and is very dark colored with a black head, brown body, and red eyes. It is most often low to the ground in brush.

Black kites are notorious pullet-killers; Beninese paint their baby chickens in neon colors to fool these constantly-circling predators. Black kites have a telltale screech, yellow beak, forked tail, and dark brown body.

The **piping hornbill** is a forest-dwelling bird, usually seen flying between stands of trees, calling nasally. Their undulating flight is an identifiable characteristic, along with their black and white coloring and horned bill.

FLORA

The vegetation in Benin varies greatly from the north to the south due to the diversity in soil, climate, and human activities. Coastal communities—notably Cotonou, Ouidah, Grand Popo, and around Lake Ahémé—have many lagoons and mangroves. Farther north, the vegetation visibly reflects the low average rainfall as it becomes less dense and more scrub-like.

Southern and Central Regions

Indigenous vegetation in this region has practically disappeared, replaced by a mosaic of cultivated fields and fallow farmland. Plantations of coconut palms, mangroves, teak trees, and oil or raffia palms dot the flood zones of the south. The Beninese use the oil palm in many ways. The leaves are used to construct huts and cabins, or are stripped to the central vein and used as poles for maneuvering *pirogues*. The sap is harvested as palm wine and distilled into the infamous *sodabi*. Red oil is extracted from the palm nuts and used for cooking. As you move away from the coast, you find not only oil palm plantations, but also orchards of mango and cashew trees. The lovely red flowers of the **flamboyant tree**, common in the south, make it one of the most beautiful trees in West Africa.

Northern Region

The most common trees in the north are the néré, shea tree, boabab, ronier palm and kapok tree. The **kapok** can grow very tall, with white flowers and spines all over its trunk. It is often regarded as sacred. **Ronier palms** are mostly seen throughout the far North, especially in Park Pendjari. Its leaves are used to make hats and bracelets worn by Bariba tribes and nomadic Fulanis. Ronier shoots are a tasty, earthy snack, often eaten with chunks of coconut. The **kola tree** produces the kola nut, which contains alkaloids and is widely chewed across the Sahel due to its stimulating virtues, similar to those of caffeine. The kola nut also serves as a traditional gift in ceremonies and rituals. The **cailcedrat** is used for making furniture.

The Basics

When to Visit

Most of Benin experiences three distinct seasons. For a visitor, each season has its pros and cons.

> Benin's annual rainfall is about 1,100 mm (43 inches), and the average temperature is 27° Celsius (82° Fahrenheit).

The rainy season, from May to October, is humid and moderately warm. Rain typically falls a few days a week, often at night. Afternoon highs can reach around 30° Celsius (86° Fahrenheit), though rainstorms help cool things off. Intense thunderstorms can interfere with travel plans. Some dirt roads wash out and become nearly impassable. The national parks in the north remain open, but wildlife is more dispersed and harder to see in the undergrowth. Despite these disadvantages, frequent rains turn the landscape green and lush, making this the most scenic time to visit the country.

A cool dry season sets in from November to January. The Harmattan wind blows down from the Sahara, chasing off the heat but also blowing dust everywhere. Temperatures fall, especially in the north, ranging between around 15° Celsius (59° Fahrenheit) at night and 25° Celsius (78° Fahrenheit) in the

> The drier months cause dirt roads to become dusty; those traveling on *zemidjans* will quickly be covered in red dirt.

afternoon. The landscape dries up and turns brown. Villagers often burn the foliage around their villages, creating a moonscape in some areas. Since the weather is cooler and undergrowth is cleared away, this is the best time to go hiking.

The Beninese call the period from February to late April *La Chaleur*, or The Heat. The weather remains dry, but cool wind gives way to searing heat, which becomes nearly unbearable in the north. Afternoon highs can reach 40–45° Celsius (104–113° Fahrenheit) in the southern and central regions, and up to 50° Celsius (122° Fahrenheit) in the north. However, this is the best time to go on safari: animals gather at the few remaining watering holes and are easier to see through the withered or burned foliage.

Where to Visit

Your trip itinerary will depend on how long you plan to spend in Benin and what kinds of sights and experiences you're looking for. Listed below are a few places you shouldn't miss. However, as many visitors and foreign residents in Benin can testify, it's often in the little-known corners of the country where you'll find your most profound and memorable experiences. A simple meal with a Beninese family or afternoon at a *tchoukoutou* market (p67) can teach you more about Benin's people and culture than a trip to any museum. Try to set aside part of your trip to check out some of the less well-known towns and villages that we've highlighted in this book.

THE SOUTH

To discover the history of the Kingdom of Dahomey, the slave trade, and Vodoun, spend some time in the south. If you're spending less than a week in Benin, the south is probably the only region you'll have time to see. Here are the main attractions:

Ouidah (p104), pronounced "wee-dah," was once this region's main slave-trading port. It owes its diverse culture to heavy Portuguese influence, as well as to the descendants of slaves who returned here after the end of the slave trade, bringing Brazilian and Caribbean culture with them. It is also the capital of Vodoun for Benin, if not for the world.

Abomey (p139) was the capital of the Kingdom of Dahomey. You can visit the haunting palaces of the kings of Dahomey and learn about Dahomey's enthusiastic participation in the slave trade and stubborn resistance to French colonization.

Porto-Novo (p125) is Benin's capital, though Cotonou is its main city. As with Ouidah, Portuguese influence over the centuries shows itself in the architecture and culture of the town, as does French colonization.

Grand Popo (p110) is Benin's premier beach town. This otherwise sleepy village houses several hotels and restaurants along the beach, ranging from backpacker hostels to high-end resorts.

THE NORTH

If you're spending over a week in Benin, take a trip up north as well. The climate and cultures of the north markedly differ from the south—you may find yourself wondering if you're still in the same country. Since the north is less developed and has historically had less European influence than the south, traditional customs and ways of life are better preserved here. The locals also tend to be friendlier toward foreigners. However, Western-style cuisine and amenities are harder to find. Here are the north's main attractions:

Pendjari National Park (p192) is the more popular of Benin's two wildlife parks. On a two– or three–day safari in the park, you're likely to see elephants, lions, warthogs, water buffalo, hippopotami, baboons, and various species of antelope, monkeys, and birds.

Boukoumbé (p189) is a village set in the scenic Atakora Range. The surrounding landscape makes it one of the most beautiful places you'll visit in Benin. It's also home to the *tata sombas*, traditional fortified houses built as protection against enemy tribes. You can visit a *tata somba*, and even spend the night on the roof.

Natitingou (p183), also set in the Atakora Range, is Benin's most scenic major town. It combines decent lodging and excellent African and European cuisine with the hospitality and laid-back feel that's typical of rural northern Benin. It's also one of the best places to find quality Beninese artwork and handicrafts at reasonable prices.

Getting There

VISA REQUIREMENTS, COSTS, AND PROCEDURES

You must obtain a Beninese visa from your local Beninese embassy or consulate before leaving your country. You will not be allowed to board the plane in Europe without a visa. There is no official body that issues tourist visas within Benin. Transit visas, valid for 48 hours and meant for people who are briefly traveling through Benin en route to another country, are available at the main border post between Benin and Togo (east of Lomé) for FCFA 10,000. Transit visas are not available at other border posts.

United States

Embassy of the Republic of Benin, Consulate Office *Tel: (202) 232.6656; Website: beninembassy.us; Email: info@beninembassy.us; 2124 Kalorama Road NW, Washington, DC 20008*

Visa requirements:

▷ One passport-size photo

▷ International certificate of vaccination (yellow fever)

▷ Passport valid for at least six months

▷ Completed application form, available on embassy website

Plus one of the following:

▷ Copy of a flight itinerary

▷ Supporting document from an employer or travel agency

▷ Letter from a bank indicating sufficient funds for the trip

Visa fee:

▷ $140 for a multiple-entry visa valid for 36 months. This is currently the only option available.

Visa procedures:

▷ When you submit your visa application, include a self-addressed prepaid certified envelope or express mail envelope. Allow 72 hours for the embassy to process your application.

Canada

Ambassade de la République du Benin, Consulate Office *Tel: (613) 233.4429; Website: benin.ca; Email: amba.benin@yahoo.ca; 58 Glebe Avenue, Ottawa, ON K1S 2C3*

Visa requirements:

▷ Two recent passport-size photos with the date they were taken stamped on the back

▷ International certificate of vaccination (yellow fever)

▷ Passport with at least two blank visa pages

▷ A photocopy of your passport's identification pages

▷ Itinerary for a round-trip ticket

▷ Completed application form, available on embassy website

Visa fees:

▷ 90-day single-entry visa: $100

▷ 90-day multiple-entry visa: $120

Visa procedures:

▷ If you come to the embassy when it opens in the morning, they can return your passport the same day. Otherwise, your passport will be returned by post and processing will take up to 72 hours.

France

Consulat Général du Bénin à Paris *Tel: 01.42.22.13.14; Website: consulat-benin. fr; Email: paris@consulat-benin.fr; 89, rue du Cherche Midi, 75006 Paris (Note: Don't confuse the Consulate General with the Embassy of Benin in Paris, a separate entity which does not issue visas.)*

Visa requirements:

▷ One passport-size photo

▷ International certificate of vaccination (yellow fever)

▷ Passport

▷ Completed application form, available on the consulate's website

Visa fees:

- ▷ 30-day tourist visa: €50

- ▷ 90-day tourist visa: €80

Visa procedures:

- ▷ The consulate is open Monday through Friday. They accept applications from 9am to 1pm, and allow applicants to pick up their passports from 4pm to 5pm. Allow 48 hours for the consulate to process your visa. Plan on picking your passport up in person. If you live outside the Île-de-France, the consulate can return your passport on the same day.

United Kingdom

Republic of Benin UK Consulate *Tel: (020) 8830.8612; Website: beninconsulate.co.uk; Email: beninconsulate@hotmail.co.uk; Millennium Business Centre, Humber Road, London NW2 6DW*

Visa requirements:

- ▷ One passport-size photo

- ▷ International certificate of vaccination (yellow fever)

- ▷ Passport

- ▷ Completed application form, available on the consulate's website

Visa fees:

- ▷ 15-day single-entry visa: £60

- ▷ 30-day single-entry visa: £70

- ▷ 30-day double-entry visa: £80

- ▷ 90-day single-entry visa: £100

- ▷ 90-day double- or triple-entry visa: £110

Note: If you live in the Republic of Ireland, add £8 for return postage.

Visa procedures:

- ▷ The consulate is open Monday, Wednesday, and Friday, 10:30am to 4:00pm. Include a self-addressed Prepaid Registered or Recorded Delivery envelope.

TRAVELING BY AIR

From North America

All flights from North America to Benin involve a layover in Europe. Air France and its partner Delta operate regular flights from the US to Paris and from Paris to Cotonou. However, it can be cheaper to fly to Brussels, Paris, or London on an American airline and then transfer to Air Brussels or Royal Air Maroc for the rest of the journey. The same is true if you're traveling from Canada.

From Europe

Air France has direct flights from Paris to Cotonou, and Air Brussels has direct flights from Brussels. Royal Air Maroc flies from London and Paris to Cotonou via Casablanca.

Regional

Direct flights are available between Cotonou and the following cities: Abidjan, Accra, Addis Ababa, Brussels, Casablanca, Douala, Johannesburg, Lagos, Nairobi, Ouagadougou, and Paris.

Airline Offices in Cotonou

Air Burkina *Tel: 21.31.68.28; Website: air-burkina.com; Email: cotonou@airburkina. bf or cotonou2j@intnet.bf; Cotonou office: Immeuble Govinda, Avenue Steinmetz, Quartier Guinkomé*

Air Côte d'Ivoire *Tel: 21.30.98.65; Website: aircotedivoire.com; Email: reservation@ aircotedivoire.com; Cotonou office: Immeuble 40 logements, Place des Martyrs, across the street from the ORTB*

Air France *Website: airfrance.com; Cotonou office: Lot Q 23, Quartier des Cocotiers, Route de l'Aéroport*

Brussels Airlines *Tel: 21.30.16.82; Website: brusselsairlines.com; Email: salesbenin@ brusselsairlines.com; Cotonou office: Lot G24, Les Cocotiers, Avenue Jean-Paul II, Cadjehoun 1*

Camair-Co (Cameroon) *Tel: 21.31.80.30 / 97.97.09.38 / 67.03.30.38; Website: camair-co.cm; Cotonou office: Avenue Steinmetz, across the street from the MTN building*

Ethiopian Airlines *Website: ethiopianairlines.com. Represented in Cotonou by Vitesse Voyages. Tel: 21.31.07.18; Email: marcel.allide@gmail.com*

Kenya Airways *Tel: 21.31.63.32; Website: kenya-airways.com; Cotonou office: Avenue Steinmetz, across the street from the MOOV headquarters*

Royal Air Maroc *Tel: 21.30.86.04; Website: royalairmaroc.com; Email: anazih@yahoo. fr; Cotonou office: Lot Q 13, Quartier des Cocotiers, Route de l'Aéroport*

South African Airways *Tel: 21.31.84.08 / 21.31.46.45; Website: flysaa.com; Cotonou office: Immeuble Kougblenou, intersection of Avenue Steinmetz and Rue Chagas*

Travel Agencies

See the next section, *Tours and Travel Agencies,* for more travel agencies in Benin that can book hotels, transportation, and guided tours.

Satguru Travel & Tours Service can help you find and book flights to and from Benin. They are based in Dubai and have offices all over the world, including in Benin and several neighboring countries. They work with all the airlines in Africa and are efficient at obtaining the cheapest flights in a timely manner. *Tel: 21.31.35.43 / 21.31.61.85; Website: satgurutravel.com; Email: sales.coo1@satgurutravel.com / satgurutravelscotonou@yahoo.com; Cotonou office: Next to Continental Bank in Dantokpa*

TRAVELING BY LAND

Togo

Taxis to Lomé, Togo leave from the Godomé intersection in Cotonou and should cost FCFA 3,500–4,000. Intercity Lines (www.intercity-lines.com) operates a bus line between Cotonou and Abidjan via Lomé and Accra. It runs three times a week.

There are other border crossings farther north, such as by the Beninese towns of Athiémé, Aplahoué, Bassila, and near Boukoumbé. For these crossings, you'll need to take a bush taxi or a zemidjan. You may need to switch taxis or zems at the border.

> **Visas for Togo** Tourist visas for Togo can be obtained at the **Embassy of Togo** in Cotonou. Bring your passport, two passport-size photos, and FCFA 15,000. With luck, the consular officer will be in his office and can sign off on your visa while you wait. *Location: Across the street from the Cathédrale St. Michel.*

Ghana and Côte d'Ivoire

Intercity Lines (www.intercity-lines.com) operates a line between Cotonou and Abidjan via Lomé and Accra. It runs three times a week. You can also take a bush taxi to Lomé (see previous section), then get another taxi from Lomé to Accra.

> **Visas for Ghana** Currently, the Embassy of Ghana in Cotonou does not issue tourist visas to non-Beninese nationals. If you are planning to visit Ghana during your trip, get a visa from the Ghanaian consulate in your country before leaving home.

Burkina Faso

Intercity Lines (www.intercity-lines.com) operates a line between Cotonou and Ouagadougou. It runs three times a week and costs FCFA 18,000. Bush taxis leave Natitin-

---

Travel to Niger and Nigeria

Since January 2011, when two French citizens were kidnapped and later killed in Niger's capital city, Niamey, Western governments have strongly advised their citizens against traveling to Niger. As of 2013, the U.S. Department of State advises Americans to avoid all non-essential travel to the country. The 2012–13 civil war and French intervention in neighboring Mali have further destabilized the region and made Western hostages a prime commodity for allies of northern Mali's Islamist rebels. Al Qaeda in the Islamic Maghreb (AQIM) is active throughout Niger and openly seeks to kidnap Westerners.

Travelers, especially light-skinned Westerners, should also avoid Nigeria. Numerous terrorist groups are active throughout the country, especially in the north, and bombings and kidnappings occur regularly. The Nigerian government's years-long war with Boko Haram, a militant Islamist organization based in the north, has destabilized much of the country. Militants may target foreigners for kidnapping.

In recent years, some Western governments have issued travel warnings for Benin's northeastern region as a result of its proximity to Niger and northern Nigeria. However, there have been no recent targeted attacks against foreigners in this area. If you're planning to travel northeast of Parakou and Kandi, check your country's travel recommendations before your trip, and remain vigilant while traveling.

gou at least once a day for the Benin–Burkina Faso border crossing at Porga. It should cost about FCFA 2,000. Taxis are most frequent on Monday, Porga's market day.

Visas for Burkina Faso Single-entry tourist visas for Burkina Faso valid for 90 days are available at the **Consulate of Burkina Faso** in Cotonou. Bring your passport, two passport-size photos, and FCFA 22,000. Processing your visa should take about 48 hours. *Tel: 21.31.25.73. Location: Haie Vive.*

Tours and Travel Agencies

Depending on your language skills, your budget, and how adventurous you're feeling, you may want to hire a tour guide for all or part of your stay in Benin. (Note that traveling in Benin can be very difficult unless someone in your group speaks some French.) Some Benin–based travel agencies can coordinate your flights, lodging, and transportation as well.

Bill Biokou, a Porto-Novo–based interpreter and guide, runs a network of professional English-speaking guides who can accompany you throughout the country. Their services are flexible, depending on how much you want them to take care of. They can arrange lodging and transportation, and even provide you with a full itinerary. A guide costs FCFA 30,000 per day, or FCFA 25,000 per day for three or more days. If you hire a guide for multiple days, you either directly pay for his lodging or pay him FCFA 10,000 per night, and he'll find his own lodging. If you want to reserve a tour, contact Bill at least two weeks in advance. *Tel: 97.18.08.45; Email: bipro.services@gmail.com*

Théodore Atrokpo, better known as **Théo**, is a highly recommended local guide who conducts tours throughout Benin. His mission is to get visitors off the regular tourist track by showing them the more authentic aspects of Benin's people and culture that most foreigners never see. His tours are mostly cultural, though he's knowledgeable about Benin's natural environment as well. He places particular emphasis on helping visitors experience and understand Vodoun. His base rate (not including transportation or lodging) is FCFA 6,000 per person per day for 3–5 people, with lower prices for larger groups. He can also organize custom all-inclusive tours based on your interests, your budget, and how much time you have. While his English isn't fluent enough to conduct a tour (though his French is excellent), he can find an English-speaking translator if you need one. *Tel: 93.84.91.09 / 97.44.81.96 / 95.69.67.96; Email: letourdetheo@yahoo.com*

TransAfrica conducts tours and visits to special events throughout Benin, Burkina Faso, Côte d'Ivoire, Ghana, Niger, and Togo. They can provide English-speaking guides. Their office in Lomé, Togo, handles tours to Benin. *Tel: +228 22.21.68.23; Website: transafrica.biz; Email: transafrica@transafrica.biz; Lomé office: Rue Moyama, 666*

Agence Africaine de Tourisme (ATT) is based in Cotonou and organizes tours in Benin and neighboring countries. They can also book flights, cars, and hotel rooms. *Tel: 21.31.54.14 / 21.31.54.96 / 21.31.44.69; Website: aatvoyages.com; Email: info@aatbenin.com*

Concorde Voyages & Tourisme organizes tours in Benin and neighboring countries. They can book flights, car or bus rentals, and hotel rooms. You can also purchase travel insurance or receive money transfers at their Cotonou office. *Tel: 21.31.34.13 / 21.31.51.01; Website: concordevoyage.com; Email: cvt@concordevoyage. com; Cotonou office: Concorde building (Immeuble Concorde), behind the Librairie Notre Dame, Ganxi*

What to Pack

Backpack It's helpful to be able to carry all your stuff on your back, especially when riding zemidjans. A solid pack with a hip belt will help you balance as your zem careens through traffic.

Lightweight clothing Benin's weather is hot and, in the south, humid. Cotton and linen are best. Women should dress modestly. See *Dress* (p35).

Malarial prophylaxis Get it from your doctor before you leave home. See *Malaria* (p75).

Mosquito net Budget and midrange hotels may not provide one. You can buy one in Cotonou and carry it with you.

Motorcycle helmet It's difficult to get around Beninese towns without taking the zemidjans, or motorcycle taxis. You can buy helmets in Cotonou.

Poncho Dramatic thunderstorms can strike with little warning, especially during the rainy season.

Sandals Closed shoes can get uncomfortable in the West African heat. Solid sandals with good support, such as Chacos or Tevas, are best.

Soap and towel Budget and midrange hotels will probably not provide them. Soap is easy to find throughout Benin. You can buy a cotton towel in any town's market, or buy a quick-drying microfiber towel before leaving home.

Toilet paper You can buy it throughout Benin. Be sure to have some on you at all times: unless you're at a high-end hotel, you probably won't find any in the bathroom.

WHO (World Health Organization) Card or other proof of vaccination. Without proof of vaccination against Yellow Fever, you will not be allowed to enter the country. See *Mandatory Vaccinations* (p76).

Visa You must have a current Beninese visa to enter the country. Get your visa in your country; you won't be able to purchase one when you get to Benin. See *Visa Requirements* (p49).

Transportation

Bush Taxi

Bush taxis are the most common mode of long-distance transport. The vehicles are usually old Peugot sedans that have been deemed unfit to be driven in Europe. They usually have poor suspension and no air conditioning, and they frequently break down. A bush taxi trip can be uncomfortable, unpredictable, and frustrating—but, from the bumpy roads to the eight adults crammed in the cab to the goats in the trunk, it's a quintessentially African experience.

Each town has a taxi station, called an *autogare* or *gare routière*. Larger towns have multiple *autogares*, usually located according to destination—northbound taxis at the station on the north side of town, southbound taxis at the station on the south side of town. When you arrive at an *autogare* you'll be swarmed by porters, who will try to grab your luggage and put it in their taxi. Hold on to your bags until you verify that a taxi is going to your destination—some porters will lie about their taxi's destination in order to fill it up with passengers as quickly as possible. Negotiate the price with the driver before getting in. If the station has a list of prices, insist on paying the posted price.

Then you wait. Drivers usually don't leave until their taxis are full. "Full" is defined as 2–3 passengers in the front and 4–5 in the back, plus children. (The legal limit is six passengers, but it's seldom enforced.) While waiting, you can chat with your fellow passengers, purchase snacks from roving vendors, and reflect on the mercurial nature of life. If you want, you can offer to pay double price to get the front seat to yourself. Luggage goes in the trunk or on the roof. Before the taxi leaves, make sure your bags are securely fastened in or on the vehicle.

You should pay no more than half the price up-front; insist on paying the rest when you get to your destination. Sometimes, your driver will only take you partway to your destination, and you'll have to move into another taxi for the rest of the trip. In this case, it's the driver's responsibility to find you another taxi. Re-negotiate the price with the new driver before your old driver takes off, and make sure your bags get transferred.

Bus

Intercity buses are a more comfortable and reliable alternative to bush taxis, but they only run between major towns and depart only once or twice a day. From Cotonou, you can get a bus to Tanguiéta, Natitingou, Djougou, Dassa, Bohicon, Parakou, and Malanville. If you want to get off in a smaller town that's on the way—for example, if you take the Parakou bus but want to get off in Savé—talk with the porter when you get on the bus.

Most buses leave Cotonou from La Place de l'Étoile Rouge. The safest and most reliable bus companies are Ayina Transport et Tourisme (known simply as ATT) and La Poste, both of which operate bright yellow buses. Their buses are relatively new, in good condition, and have functional air conditioning—assets not to be taken for granted in Benin. Several bus companies have offices at Étoile Rouge, where you can buy tickets in advance. (If the company you're looking for doesn't have its office at Étoile Rouge, a zemidjan should know where it is.) It's only imperative to buy tickets in advance around major holidays, such as Christmas and Easter, when a lot of people will be traveling. Otherwise, you can just show up at the bus about half an hour before it leaves and buy a ticket from the porter.

Buses for most destinations leave Étoile Rouge at 7am, with a few leaving at 6:30am. For more common destinations, such as Parakou, more buses leave in the late morning or early afternoon. There are a few overnight lines that leave Cotonou late in the evening.

Many buses now have an onboard TV screen or two. You'll probably be watching either West African music videos or West African soap operas. While this can be intriguing for a while, after six hours you'll probably be ready for a break. Bring your iPod.

Cheaper bus lines have no TV. Instead they have salesmen who will often ride the bus for a while, exhorting their captive audience to buy their wares. They're usually selling lotions or powders purported to have healing powers, or some such thing.

> *Train service*: While there is a railroad running from Cotonou to Parakou, it has been out of service for several years.

Buses usually stop in Bohicon or Dassa so passengers can take a bathroom break and have lunch. Vendors swarm each bus as it stops, offering fried snacks, street meat, fruit, and cold drinks. Women nearby sell avocado sandwiches and Beninese dishes such as *pâte*. Be careful not to wander too far from the bus—the driver won't wait for stragglers when it's time to leave.

Zemidjan

To get around town, take a motorcycle taxi, known as *zemidjans* or *zems*. In a city or larger town, you can stand on the side of the street and wait for one to pass by. You'll recognize them by their distinctive shirts, a different color in each city, with their registration numbers painted on the back. They wear yellow shirts in Cotonou, blue

> Be careful to mount from the left side of the motorcycle to avoid a nasty burn from the hot muffler on the right side.

Navigating Beninese cities

Cities and towns in Benin are loosely planned and haphazardly laid out. Except for a few major boulevards, streets do not have names—or if they do, no one knows them—and businesses do not have street addresses. People give directions on the basis of landmarks: traffic circles (which do have names), pharmacies, hotels, schools, large restaurants and *buvettes*, and major government offices or business headquarters.

Unless you have a hired car, you'll probably be getting around cities by *zemidjan*. If your *zemidjan* doesn't know your destination by name, you'll need to give him the name of a well-known nearby landmark. In the regional sections of this guide, the locations of venues will, if necessary, be accompanied by the directions you should give a *zem*.

shirts in Porto-Novo, and green and yellow shirts in Parakou and Natitingou. To flag one down, wave your arm prolifically and shout "kékéno!" if you're in the south or "zé!" if you're in the north.

When a zem pulls over, make sure he knows your destination and negotiate the price before you get on his motorcycle. If he seems unsure of exactly where you're going—even if he says he knows how to get there—send him away and find another zem. Some zems will take a passenger without understanding the destination, drive around in circles, wait for you to get fed up, and then demand to be paid anyway when you get off. Most of them, however, are honest and reliable. Prices are very reasonable: getting around Cotonou should cost about FCFA 100–400, depending on how far you're going.

If you're not familiar with the city, you probably won't know the "real" price for your trip—the price you should be aiming for when negotiating with your driver. To avoid this, ask a local how much the trip should be before you go look for a zem.

Once you get on the *zem*, you'll be alternately thrilled and terrified. They're called *zemidjans*—Fon for "get me there fast"—for a reason. They ignore speed limits and bend traffic rules—running red lights, cutting off other drivers, driving on sidewalks and down the wrong side of the street. On rural dirt roads, they drive through streams and over bumps that can send you flying out of your seat. Wear a helmet, strap your backpack on tight, and hold on to the rack behind you—not the driver.

Car Rental and Hire

To rent or hire a car, you have a few options. The cheapest option is to hire a bush taxi. It should cost around FCFA 20,000 per day plus gas. However, bush taxis are generally older sedans in poor condition: they aren't built for Benin's rough roads, rarely have air conditioning, and break down frequently.

You can hire a jeep or SUV through a tour company (see *Tours and Travel Agencies* on page 54) for about FCFA 60,000 per day plus gas. These vehicles are generally comfortable and in good condition.

Finally, you can rent a car and drive yourself around. This can be an adventurous proposition if you're not used to West Africa's rough roads and chaotic cities. The following international car rental agencies have offices in Cotonou:

Avis *Tel: 21.38.33.40 / 97.97.70.80; Website: avis.com; Located at the Cotonou airport; Open Mon–Fri 8am-12:30pm and 3pm-6:30pm*

Europcar Benin *Tel: 21.31.44.44; Website: europcar.com; Located at the Cotonou airport and at Hôtel du Port, off Avenue Clozel, near the Ancien Pont*

You'll find **gas stations** in large towns and at infrequent intervals along the paved highway. However, most of Benin's gas is smuggled from Nigeria and sold in glass bottles on the side of the road. Due to the inherent volatility of the pirating-siphoned-gas-from-Nigeria business, gas prices can widely and frequently fluctuate. If you're hiring a car, check out the day's prevailing gas prices first—the driver may try to overcharge you by saying that gas is more expensive than it really is.

Money

Like the rest of French-speaking West Africa, Benin uses the West African CFA franc (franc CFA or FCFA). Since very few establishments beyond high-end hotels accept credit cards or travelers' cheques, plan on paying for everything in cash. The condition of your bills and coins is more important than you'd think. Vendors may not accept torn or dirty bills, or coins that are so worn that the date is no longer visible. If a vendor tries to give you such bills or coins as change, you should refuse—you might not be able to spend them later. The same applies to the 250–franc coin: in some parts of the country, vendors don't believe it's real money and won't accept it.

> All travelers' cheques should be exchanged in Cotonou, as the banks in other large cities such as Bohicon and Parakou are not consistent with their exchange procedures.

Another issue is getting change. Many street vendors, especially in rural areas, won't break bills for small purchases. Zemidjans are also unlikely to have change for a bill. Plan ahead: break your large bills at places that are likely to have change, such as boutiques, supermarkets, and restaurants, and save your coins for smaller transactions.

In Cotonou there are several **banks** and foreign exchange offices around the Ganxi market. The larger banks include Bank of Africa (BOA), Société Générale Bancaire Béninoise (SGBB), and Ecobank, each of which offers Western Union services and has branches in all of Benin's major towns. Each bank has an ATM where you can withdraw money in FCFA. You can also go into the bank and exchange bills at the counter. The teller may refuse your money if you have bills smaller than $50 or €50, or if your bills appear even slightly dirty or wrinkled. If you insist, they may give in, but it's easier to plan ahead and come to Benin with large bills in mint condition. A quicker bill exchange can be done on the black market: Nigerian money vendors in Jonquet or Zongo sit on their wooden benches under parasols and beckon any foreigner walking by with promises of cheap rates. However, it's best to avoid them. They're notorious for peddling in counterfeit bills, and a foreigner exchanging large amounts of cash in the street is a ripe target for a mugging. If you do use their services, check the latest exchange rate before negotiating and be sure to count the money before leaving. Only exchange from U.S. dollars or Euros to FCFA, and not the other way around—false bills can cause issues once back home. Also note that British pounds are generally not accepted, so it's best to travel with Euros or U.S. dollars.

NEGOTIATING

In open-air and artisans' markets, prices are rarely posted, and negotiating is normal and expected. Vendors will demand the highest prices in areas frequented by tourists, and you'll need to haggle if you don't want to get ripped off. Casually ask the vendor how much an item costs, without acting too interested. Your first counteroffer should be about one-third of the vendor's opening price, though feel free to go lower if his price seems ridiculous. The vendor may get dramatic, and you should feel free to do so as well: act shocked or offended if he insists on a high price. It's all part of the game.

However, not all prices are negotiable. Brick-and-mortar stores (except stalls in artisans' markets) have fixed prices, as do restaurants, *buvettes*, and vendors selling food by the roadside. Intercity bus companies also have fixed prices. You can negotiate with taxi drivers, except in taxi stations where the drivers' union has posted a list of prices. Zemidjan etiquette varies by region: while zemidjans in the south will usually ask for a high price and expect you to make a counteroffer, zemidjans in the north will often begin with the standard price and not expect to negotiate. When in doubt, remember that zemidjans are among the lowest-paid workers in Benin and could use a few extra francs.

The Art of the Deal

Your most intensive bargaining experiences in Benin will probably come when you're shopping for souvenirs in artisans' markets and boutiques. In Cotonou and in touristy areas, vendors know that foreigners aren't used to negotiating prices and may feel uncomfortable doing so. They attempt to charge foreigners up to ten times the normal price—and some tourists fall for it. Don't be one of them. Even if bargaining seems like a chore at first, it's part of the experience, and you may even enjoy it. Here are a few tricks:

Know the price beforehand. Vendors will give in more easily if you show that you know the real price. Before you go shopping, ask a local, such as your guide or the receptionist at your hotel, what a reasonable price would be for each item you're planning to buy. Or see our list of *Real Prices of Popular Handicrafts* (p92).

Bring a limited amount of money with you. While bargaining, you can open your wallet and show the vendor that you don't have the cash to pay the astronomical price he's demanding.

Don't act too interested. Give the impression that you don't really care whether you end up getting what you're bargaining for. You can even point out a minor flaw in the item and dramatically act like it's a huge deal.

Walk away, and look like you mean it. If the vendor doesn't offer a lower price as you're leaving, come back a few minutes later to see if he's had a change of heart.

And here are some of the strategies that vendors often use:

Having you choose an item. For example, if he has several similar paintings, he'll ask you which one you like best. There's no difference in value. He just wants to make you feel attached to one of them.

Having you hold an item. He may try to physically hand it to you. Again, this makes you feel attached to it. You feel like it's already yours, and become more willing to pay a higher price to keep it.

Throwing in other items you don't want. Instead of lowering the price, he'll offer to throw in a free Benin-shaped keychain or something.

The poverty card. He will remind you that Benin is a poor country, and why are you trying to rip off poor people? He has a point. Take the money you saved by negotiating well and donate it to one of the organizations listed in *Helping And Experiencing Local Communities* on page 78.

BUDGET

The amount you should budget when visiting Benin depends on your itinerary and preferred level of comfort. Daily expenses in Cotonou and other cities will be higher if you choose to stay in high-end hotels and eat at Western restaurants. In rural areas, the choices are more limited and less expensive. In small villages, apart from lodging, it is difficult to spend more than FCFA 2,000 a day. Budget travelers should calculate an average of FCFA 7,000 per night for lodging, plus FCFA 3,000–5,000 for food. Getting around in cities by zemidjan can cost an additional couple thousand FCFA per day. Remaining costs would be for long-distance travel, museum fees, and souvenir shopping. Also consider the cost of safaris in the national parks, which can quickly increase the budget.

TIPPING

Tipping is generally not expected in hotels, *buvettes*, or restaurants. However, feel free to round up a tab at a *buvette* to give the server a couple hundred extra francs.

In general, the Beninese are very welcoming and eager to help strangers, but they will assume that a foreigner has some money to spare. If someone helps you out—such as by translating for you or directing you to a restaurant you're looking for—he may expect a tip. This is especially true if someone approaches you and offers his assistance, rather than you approaching him, or if (as often happens) he physically accompanies you to your destination rather than giving verbal directions. On the other hand, some people who help you may refuse payment, while others won't ask for payment but will politely accept it. Basically, don't be afraid to ask locals for directions or advice, but be ready to pay a couple hundred francs if needed.

Food and Drink

BENINESE CUISINE

Beninese cuisine includes traditional West African flavors, as well as Brazilian flavors brought from descendants of slaves returning to their ancestral land. In general, meals are based on a starch staple, with far less protein and fresh vegetables than Westerners are used to. Food varies from region to region, largely dependent on the climate and soil composition. Southern staples include corn, cassava, and rice, usually served with fish. Farther north, yams or sorghum are more frequently the starch staple, with protein coming from game meat, goat meat, beef, pork, or a spongey cheese called *wagasi*. Sauces commonly include tomatoes, onions, chili peppers, various vegetable oils, leafy greens, and spices such as garlic, ginger, and black pepper. Okra sauce, called *sauce gombo*, is characteristically slimy and usually quite spicy. Some leaves are used to make slimy sauce, while others, such as the gboma leaf, are used to make a sauce that resembles spinach. The Maggi cube, a chicken or shrimp flavored bouillon, is commonly used to add flavor. Starches are sometimes served with a small side of raw or fried ground hot peppers, referred to as *piment*.

LOCAL DISHES

Staples

The main staple throughout Benin is *pâte*, a paste similar to mashed potatoes. You make the most common variety, called *pâte blanche* (white pâte), by stirring corn flour or ground cassava into boiling water. *Pâte* made with corn flour is considered to be of higher quality. *Pâte rouge*, the variety that most often appeals to foreigners, is made by stirring spices, ground tomatoes, and chicken grease into corn-based *pâte* while it is still boiling. In poorer areas, people sometimes eat *pâte noire*, which is made from yams that have dried out and can no longer be used to make *igname pilée* or *ignames frites*. All varieties of *pâte* are traditionally dipped in sauce and eaten by hand, and accompanied by fish, meat, or *wagasi* cheese.

Igname pilée, or pounded yam, is popular in central and northern Benin. West African yams—a white tuber that can grow up to half a meter long—are peeled, chopped, boiled, and then pounded with mortar and pestle into a paste that's thicker and more filling than *pâte*. As with *pâte*, you eat it by scooping up a mouthful with your right hand and dipping it in sauce. Served with the right sauce, quality *igname pilée* can satisfy even a foreigner who's unfamiliar with Beninese cuisine.

Akassa is fermented *pâte blanche*. It's basically slightly sour Jello. Unlike *pâte* and *igname pilée*, however, it doesn't quickly spoil and can be eaten several hours after it was prepared. You can see chunks of *akassa* for sale in the market, wrapped in large teak leaves. It's often eaten with a strong pepper sauce to mask the taste.

Rice and **beans** are common throughout the country, served separately or together. Beans are often mixed with **gari**, a coarse flour made with cassava which—like *pâte* and *akassa*—has little nutritional value but gives the sensation of being full. In the north, you'll find two local rice dishes: **riz au gras**, a greasy and sometimes spicy rendition of brown rice, and **waché**, brown rice mixed with a small portion of beans. Foreign visitors usually like both *riz au gras* and *waché*.

In towns and larger villages, you can find **pork** and **piron**. Chunks of pork are slow-cooked in a rudimentary oven and served with *piron*, a paste made of *gari* and pork fat, as well as ground fresh peppers. If you like pork, this isn't a meal you'll want to miss.

Yams

The West African yam, the sole domesticated crop that is native to the region, is central to cuisine and culture in much of West Africa. The first people to domesticate yams ran into a problem: wild yams are poisonous. Some historians believe that the practice of pulverizing boiled yam in a mortar and pestle—still seen today in the preparation of *igname pilée*—was originally an attempt to make the yam safe to eat. The Festival of the First Yam, still observed in August or September in parts of central Benin, may have had a similar purpose. The festival marks the formal beginning of the yam harvest. It is forbidden to eat from the new yam crop before the festival—perhaps in recognition that prematurely-harvested yams are likely to be poisonous.

> The sap from the yam tuber is a skin irritant.

Meat, Fish, and Cheese

In the south, any meal is usually accompanied by fish. Farther north, meat and cheese become more common. In towns and larger villages, the most common meats are easily recognizable to a foreigner: beef, chicken, and pork, as well as goat and guinea fowl. More unusual meats crop up in rural areas. Antelope, wild rabbit, and bush rat are common. You may even find elephant, hippopotamus, lizard, or snake.

In Benin, "cheese" means *wagasi*, a spongy wheel that is usually served in sauce. (The kinds of cheese that Westerners are familiar with can be found only in some supermarkets in major towns.) While *wagasi* may not look appetizing, you'll probably like it, especially if it's been cooked in a good sauce. The Fulani people, who generally make their living by herding cows, produce *wagasi* and sell it to everyone else. Since

---

Pâte Recipe

Ingredients:

- 1.5 cups corn meal homogenized with 1.5 cups water
- 1.5 cups additional corn meal
- 2 cups water

After thoroughly mixing the corn meal and water, heat the two cups of water until just before boiling. Add the homogenized corn meal/water to the heated water, without decreasing heat. Stir. When boiling, add additional corn meal and beat with wooden spoon over heat. Reduce heat slightly and let the mixture thicken for 3-5 minutes. Remove from heat and pour into serving dish.

Sauce:

- 4 tbs oil
- 2 large onions
- 3 cloves garlic
- black pepper to taste
- 14 oz. crushed tomatoes (or, in Benin, 'many' crushed tomatoes)
- 2-3 chili peppers, or to taste
- 1 tbs chicken or beef bouillon, or vegetable or meat stock.

Sauté all ingredients, except the bouillon, in hot oil for about five minutes or until the onions are soft. Add the liquid and let simmer for about 20 minutes, or until the ingredients are well mixed. Add other spices, green leaves, and/or meat and fish as desired.

the Fulani live mostly in northern and central Benin, that's where you find *wagasi* most often. If you buy a wheel of *wagasi*, boil it for ten minutes before eating it. *Wagasi* served at an eatery has generally already been cooked and is fine to eat.

Cassava

Also known as *manioc* in English and French, cassava is a dry, starchy tuber native to South America. The descendants of West African slaves brought it over with them when they returned from Brazil after the abolition of the Atlantic slave trade. It is now ubiquitous throughout West Africa and is the third largest source of carbohydrates for humans in the world. It's easy to see why cassava has flourished: it can grow in poor soil and withstand drought, and the harvested tuber can be easily stored in a hot climate for long periods of time. But while it can make you feel full, cassava contains few nutrients. Over-reliance on cassava contributes to malnutrition in Benin, especially among children.

SNACK FOODS

Snack foods are prevalent in Beninese cuisine. **Beignets**, fried balls made from a dough of beans, bananas, or wheat flour, are sold throughout the day in almost any location. In the afternoons and evenings bean *beignets* are served with ground chili pepper sauce. There is a fried, spicy, corn flour *beignet* called

> Ignames frites, or fried yams, are a popular substitute for French fried potatoes.

avoomi, which means 'dog poop' in Fon. These are made by rolling corn flour dough into teaspoon-sized balls, pressing five of them together in a line (tapering the ends) and then deep frying them. It's a delicious, crunchy snack, and fun to talk about!

Dokons, also known as *paté*, are sweet, fried balls of wheat flour. They're most often eaten in the morning or around sunset with a bowl of **bouille**, a sweetened corn flour porridge. **Gateaux** are a crunchy form of dokon, like fried cookies. **Klouie-klouie** are crispy and crunchy snacks made with corn or peanut butter that vary in shape and form according to region. In the Couffo they resemble dry rings of fried peanut butter. In Djougou and much of the north, they are stick-shaped and sometimes made with the added ingredients of ginger or hot pepper and sugar.

Other filling snacks, ideal for lunch or before dinner time, are deep fried breadfruit slices, plantains, sweet potatoes, cassava, or yams. All of these snacks taste best and are safest to eat when hot. Little bags of roasted peanuts, boiled corn and peanuts, and sweet cookie-like snacks such as soy biscuits and coconut milk cookies are sold at taxi stops and market stalls. There are endless varieties of fried staples to be discovered: sweet, salty, or spicy.

Bread is popular in Benin, and most larger towns have a bakery that produces fresh baguettes daily. Vendors bike or drive through the town and countryside to sell fresh bread, yelling "*Pain chaud!*" ("Warm bread!"). *Brioche*, a sweet bread baked in rectangular loaves, is sold at street stands and in the market. Because it's only found in cities and large towns, *brioche* is a traditional Beninese gift—when a villager travels to a town or city, he brings some back for his friends and neighbors.

Basics

Cafeterias in Benin typically consist of an outdoor bar with a bench or stools where you can buy instant coffee or tea saturated with sweetened condensed milk. Some cafeterias also serve fresh baguettes, onion-and-tomato omelettes, spaghetti, and yogurt or curdled milk. They generally do not sell alcohol, and are often open early in the morning and late at night.

WESTERN FOOD

Western cuisine is not widely available in Benin. You can find Western dishes—such as fries, chicken, pasta, and salad—in some *buvettes* and mid-scale eateries in large towns. (Be careful with fresh salad: the vegetables may not have been properly washed and may make you sick.) More extensive and expensive Western offerings, such as pizza, steak, hamburgers, and French cuisine are found in upscale restaurants and hotels, mostly in Cotonou but also in Parakou, Natitingou, and Porto-Novo. Middle Eastern and Asian cuisine are generally confined to Cotonou, though, oddly enough, you can find places selling Lebanese *schwarma* (a kind of Mediterranean burrito, also spelled *chwarma*) in several towns throughout the country.

FRUITS AND VEGGIES

There are many fruits available according to the season and climate. Fresh tomatoes, chili peppers, onions, and other typical vegetable ingredients are mainly available during the rainy season. You can find a wide, though not exhaustive, variety of vegetables for sale in major cities throughout the year. **Mango** and **avocado** season is from mid-March to June. Wild mangos are small and the flesh is stringy, though the flavor is wonderful. Grafted mangos, which are larger and have a smoother texture, are much more popular. **Papaya** season is usually from November to January. The south has an abundance of **bananas**, **plantains**, **pineapples**, and **oranges**, which you can buy in markets and by the roadside throughout the year. Less common fruits include **guavas**, **watermelons**, and **breadfruit**. Guava and breadfruit availability depends on the trees, while watermelons depend on water availability in the region.

Inside a Beninese Kitchen 🐾INSIGHT

A typical Beninese family cooks its meals over a fire, which they build outdoors or in an outbuilding to keep the heat and smoke out of the house. If firewood isn't available for scavenging, the fire burns on locally-made charcoal. (Camp stoves using propane gas are available in cities but unheard of in most of the country.) A stove is either a short cylinder of clay or dried mud, with the fire inside and the cast-iron cooking pot resting on top, or simply three rocks arranged in a triangle to support the pot. Another kitchen necessity is a flat stone slab on which tomatoes, garlic, onions, peppers, and spices are ground before being added to the sauce on the fire. Since the Beninese insist on eating their meals extremely hot, food is kept warm in plastic coolers until the whole meal is ready. Men often eat separately from women and children. Men customarily receive the most food, including the best pieces of meat, fish, or cheese; sometimes the entire meal is served to the men first, and the women and children get what's left over. If eating with a guest, the host often shares a plate with the guest as a sign of hospitality.

DRINKS

In Benin, drinking **water** from a well, a pump, and even a faucet will probably make a visitor sick. Fortunately, you can find bottled water in most restaurants and *buvettes*. A large 1.5 liter bottle should cost FCFA 500. Before buying, make sure that the cap's seal is still intact; otherwise it may be a recycled bottle filled with tap water. You can also find clear plastic sachets of water, called PurWater, on nearly any street corner. PurWater is tap water with chlorine added. At FCFA 25 for a half-liter sachet, it's the cheapest option, but quality isn't guaranteed. For water treatment options, see *Other Health Concerns* on page 76.

Buvettes

Easy to find in both towns and villages, *buvettes* are establishments that sell beer, soda, bottled water, and sometimes food. A *buvette* can be a building, a thatched shade struc- ture, or simply a few tables under a tree. The atmosphere is generally laid-back and the fare is cheap. If you see an establishment whose sign reads "Restaurant," "Bar," "Club," or "Café," it's probably just a *buvette*: Western-style restaurants, bars, and clubs are found only in larger towns.

The Beninese love their **beer**. While the price of beer—FCFA 600–1,200 for a large 66mL bottle—may seem cheap to foreigners, it's quite expensive for the average Beninese villager, and only wealthier Beninese can afford to drink it on a regular basis. *La Beninoise*, brewed in Cotonou, is the most common brand. You can also find Cas- tel, Flag, "33" (pronounced "tree-tree") and more expensive brews such as Heineken, Tuborg, Star, and Guiness.

Palm wine is harvested directly from a felled palm tree. This milky white liq- uid is sweet and tangy and best when refrigerated. A liter should cost about FCFA 300–500. It is available for sale roadside or served cold by the glass at some *buvettes*.

Sodabi, Benin's moonshine, is highly important in Beninese culture. It is served to guests at home and often used in Vodoun ceremonies. Various roots and leaves are often soaked in *sodabi*, changing its color and, according to some Beninese, giving it a wide range of medicinal powers. Being open to trying *sodabi* can help show people that you're not just a snobbish foreigner. However, you should be careful.

There are two types of *sodabi*. The first is traditional *sodabi*: a clear, harsh liquor distilled from palm wine. The second is basically a chemical cocktail that's cheaper to make than the traditional version. Both varieties pose health risks. Production is not regulated and alcohol volume can vary widely. Analyses have found that sodabi some- times contains a large percentage of methanol, or wood alcohol, the consumption of which can cause blindness.

However, if you still want to try sodabi, insist on the higher-quality tradition- al variety. (Say that you want "*sodabi de bonne qualité*" or "*sodabi à base du vin de palme*.") You can distinguish the two varieties by smell and taste. While traditional sodabi has a strong smell and a harsh taste, the chemical cocktail is positively rank. When in doubt, err on the side of caution.

Tchoukoutou, or *tchouk*, is locally-brewed millet beer. It is brown or red and has a bitter, slightly acidic taste, somewhat similar to cider. On market day, village women sell their *tchouk* in thatched stalls in the market. You can also find permanent *tchouk* stands open every day in larger towns, especially in the north. When you sit down at a stall, the vendor will ladle a bit of *tchouk* into a calabash bowl for you to taste. If you like it, she'll fill the bowl for you.

Tchoukoutou can be an acquired taste, but while enjoying it you'll see a side of Benin that foreigners rarely get to see. Since tchouk is cheap—FCFA 50–100 per bowl—the market is a gathering place for farmers, laborers, and other villagers who have little money and who may never have talked with a foreigner before. If you're up to the linguistic and cross-cultural challenge, chatting with them can be a fascinating and enlightening experience for both of you.

Non-alcoholic drinks are served at all restaurants and *buvettes* and include Coca-Cola, Sprite, Fanta, and various flavors of Fizzi or Youki drinks. In the south and along the Togo border, another popular sweet drink is Lion Killer, which resembles Sprite but with a slight orange flavor.

FanMilk is a brand of ice cream, yogurt, and fruit juice snack packaged in Ghana and sold in larger towns throughout Benin. Teenage boys sell it by pushing insulated handcarts or riding specially-designed bicycles through commercial areas, sounding a small horn to signal their presence. Flavors include chocolate, vanilla, fruit, and tapioca. Prices range from FCFA 100–200.

Women and children at the market often sell **local iced drinks**, either from coolers or from baskets they carry on their heads. Frozen hibiscus juice, lemon water, sweet Lipton tea, and tap water are sold for FCFA 25–100 in clear plastic bags. They're refreshing, but are usually prepared with tap water and may make you sick.

> Bottles are recycled and must be returned intact if you take drinks from a *buvette*. The barman may ask you to put down a deposit of FCFA 50–100 per bottle.

Accommodations

Cotonou offers a broad range of accommodations, from backpacker hostels to multi-national luxury hotels. The majority of hotels across the country fall into three categories: Budget (FCFA 4,000–10,000), midrange (FCFA 10,000–30,000), and upscale (FCFA 30,000 and up). Budget hotels offer both a private shower and toilet in the room, or have a shared toilet. In rural locations, modern plumbing is often replaced with communal pit latrines and bucket showers. Midrange hotels usually have private bathrooms with running water, a fan or air conditioner, and in-room television. Due to frequent water cuts throughout the country, most hotels provide a bucket of water in the bathroom, which you can use to take a bucket bath or to flush the toilet by pouring water into the toilet bowl. Some upscale hotels in Cotonou have their own water reserves, so they usually remain immune to water cuts.

> It's a good idea to carry a mosquito net if planning to stay in more budget accommodations.

Only upper-end hotels in Cotonou such as Novotel, Hôtel Marina, and Hôtel du Port accept major credit cards and Euros. The rest accept only FCFA. The hotel will usually ask you to leave your room key at the front desk when you leave the building. If you prefer to keep the key on you, you should discuss it with the receptionist.

Camping isn't common in Benin, but there are facilities in tourist hotspots such as Grand Popo and the wildlife parks in the north. Camping typically costs FCFA 2,000–5,000 per person. You need permission to camp on hotel properties in other towns for a similar rate. (See hotel descriptions by region.)

Comforts

Toilets are not available in much of Benin, especially in rural areas. To urinate, men can simply find a corner or a patch of tall grass. Women can go to a shower stall, with the owner's permission. For other needs, there are pit latrines, which vary widely in cleanliness and presence of spiders and insects. The Beninese generally don't use toilet paper, so you should carry your own. It's called *papier hygiénique* in Beninese French and can be found in boutiques in towns and larger villages.

If you're using a toilet, be aware that plumbing is often not up to Western standards and toilets are easily clogged. In some cases, there may be a toilet but no running water, in which case you'll need to dump a bucket of water into the bowl when you're finished.

Feminine hygiene can be complicated in more remote areas. It's best to use O.B. brand tampons to reduce waste. Do not attempt to flush tampons, since they may clog the toilet. Tampons should be dropped down a latrine, burned with the trash, or disposed of in one of the abundant black plastic bags. Feminine napkins should be similarly disposed of. Simply ask for soap and water when you're done.

You can buy feminine napkins and tampons at some supermarkets in Cotonou, such as Erevan, LeaderPrice, and Mayfair. This is the only city where these items are certain to be sold, though you may find them elsewhere.

Laundry is done by hand. You can easily find someone willing to wash your clothes. You should pay about FCFA 500–1,000 per sack of clothes. Undergarments are considered intimate and should be washed privately in a sink or washbasin and hung to dry in a place hidden from public view.

Communication

Most larger towns have a few internet cafés, called *cybers* (pronounced *see-bear*). Credit should cost about FCFA 200–500 per hour, depending on how many hours you buy at once. In most *cybers*, you can either use one of their computers or bring your own. Power outages and internet service cuts are common, especially outside of Cotonou, Porto-Novo, and Parakou. Some upper-end hotels also provide wifi, at least in the lobby.

Cell phones are quite cheap and worth purchasing for longer stays. A basic Nokia phone costs about FCFA 11,000 and a SIM card costs FCFA 1,000–2,000. All phone credit is sold on a pay-as-you-go basis from boutiques or bright yellow or green kiosks. Coverage is good in cities and larger towns, but can get spotty in rural areas. The phone companies MTN and MOOV have the best coverage.

Potential Issues for Travelers

SKIN COLOR

The Beninese generally like foreigners, and malicious harassment of light-skinned visitors is rare. However, Western notions of political correctness do not apply, and a foreigner will often be treated differently and judged by stereotypes. A visitor of East Asian descent, for example, may be assumed to be Chinese, greeted with *"Ni hao,"* and asked if he knows karate. These stereotypes aren't always meant to be rude. Since Benin isn't a racially diverse country, its people often don't realize that talking openly about race and invoking racial stereotypes can be annoying and hurtful.

Foreigners, especially those with light skin, will be called by the local word meaning "white person." Throughout the south, this word is *yovo*, while further north it becomes *oyibo*, *anisara*, or *batouré*, to name a few. Children will shout this word, or sing it in a song, as the foreigner passes by. Attempting to stop it will probably just encourage them. If an adult addresses you as *yovo*, he probably doesn't mean to offend you, but considers it similar to the Beninese custom of addressing a teacher as "teacher" or a carpenter as "carpenter": people call you what you are.

MONEY

The Beninese often assume that foreigners, especially those of European descent, have vast amounts of money and connections. Random people may ask you for favors such as paying for a relative's surgery, helping their kid go to university in Europe, or a simple gift of cash.

While much of Benin's population lives in dire poverty, it's best not to give money to people you don't know. As a visitor, you'll probably have no way of knowing where that money is really going. If you want to give back to the people of Benin, see *Experiencing And Helping Local Communities* on page 78 for a list of organizations that will use your contributions well.

Beyond getting hit up for money, you'll also be charged the tourist price for anything from a souvenir to a taxi ride. Beninese vendors often base their prices on how much they believe the customer can afford to pay. It's not just foreigners who get overcharged: an apparently wealthy Beninese person, or one who doesn't speak the area's local language, will often be charged more as well. In general, overcharging is most egregious in the south and in areas that see a lot of tourists, such as Grand Popo and the areas around the national parks in the north. To avoid getting ripped off, see our tips for bargaining in *Money* on page 59.

LANGUAGE

Traveling in Benin can be difficult if you don't speak French, even in cities. It's best if someone in your group speaks at least some French. You can also hire an English-speaking guide (see *Tours and Travel Agencies* on page 54).

French is widely spoken, but not by everyone, especially in rural areas. Over 50 local languages are spoken in Benin. Learning some phrases in local languages can help you communicate with non-French speakers (see *Language* on page 197). It can also help you ingratiate yourself with the locals, who don't often hear foreigners making an effort to speak their language.

ISSUES FOR FEMALE TRAVELERS

In Beninese courtship, men are often expected to be more forward, while a woman is expected to resist a man's advances at first, even if she feels favorably toward him. This means that a female visitor, especially a young woman, may receive unwanted advances ranging from compliments to marriage proposals, and that her admirer may not understand "no" to really mean "no." There's no perfect approach to dealing with unwanted advances. You can firmly insist that he leave you alone, turn it into a joke, or tell a white lie. If he persists, you can ask a nearby middle-aged or older Beninese woman to intervene: they have a lifetime of experience in yelling at men.

Beninese women dress more conservatively than many Western women. Men may assume that a woman who dresses less conservatively is looking for attention, or is even a prostitute. This is especially true in rural areas and in the north. For female travelers, dressing modestly shows respect for local customs and helps avoid unwanted attention. See *Dress* on page 35 for details on the kind of clothing you should bring to Benin.

ISSUES FOR LGBT TRAVELERS

If you ask about homosexuality, the average Beninese person will tell you that it either doesn't exist or isn't "recognized" in Benin. Despite a small gay rights movement in the country, understanding and acceptance of homosexuality remains distant.

Under Beninese law, homosexuality is a crime punishable by one to three years in prison. No one has ever been convicted of this crime, but in recent years several Westerners have been arrested on charges such as "moral indecency." However, homophobia doesn't thrive in Beninese culture as it does in some other African countries. When asked about homosexuality, the Beninese tend to react with confusion or vague disapproval, not anger or hatred.

Basically, unless you're talking with a friend you trust, it's probably best to remain discreet about sexual preferences that aren't strictly heterosexual.

Safety and Security

Traveling in Benin is relatively safe if you observe a few precautions:

▷ Do not travel after dark unless it is an emergency, especially off the paved highway. Bandits sometimes attack travelers on rural roads at night.

▷ As in other countries, avoid walking alone at night, especially in Cotonou.

▷ Muggings are common at the beach in Cotonou, even in daylight. Don't go to the beach alone, and choose a part of the beach where there are people nearby.

▷ Only take *zemidjans* who are wearing the colored shirt with a registration number painted on the back, and take note of this number when you get on. Fake *zemidjans* have been known to take foreigners to locations where bandits are waiting to mug them. If you have a problem with your *zemidjan*, you can report his registration number to the local authorities.

▷ Don't share a *zemidjan* with another passenger. Not only does it make the motorcycle more difficult to control, but the law limits *zemidjans* to one passenger. If a police officer sees you breaking this law, he may hold both you and your driver accountable.

▷ Avoid crowds and political rallies.

▷ The authorities periodically set up roadblocks to check vehicles traveling along the highway. If your taxi or bus is stopped, they may ask to see your passport or other identification.

BENINESE LAW ENFORCEMENT

Law enforcement forces are found throughout the country, even in remote areas. While officers are usually helpful toward foreigners, they generally don't patrol and won't immediately respond to emergency calls, as the police do in Europe and North America. If you need help, you should go in person to the nearest *gendarmerie* or police station. Be aware that while all law enforcement officers speak French, few speak English.

Law enforcement officers are poorly paid, and many use bribes to augment their official income. A gendarme or police officer may request, with a variable degree of subtlety, a modest bribe if you ask for his help. However, while it's common practice, attempting to bribe an official is technically against the law. Don't initiate the transaction, and don't try to bribe someone to do something illegal. Benin has a few organizations responsible for law enforcement:

▷ Officers of the **Police Nationale** handle routine police work. They wear dark blue uniforms. They're mostly found in larger towns, but their presence in villages is expanding. An officer is called a *policier* and their police stations are called *commissariats*.

▷ The **Forces Armées Béninoises (FAB)** is the army. They wear khaki or camouflage uniforms. While law enforcement is not their primary job, they sometimes man checkpoints on the road.

▷ The **Gendarmerie Nationale** is a unit of the FAB charged with local law enforcement both in towns and in rural areas. They wear khaki or camouflage uniforms. Its members are called *gendarmes*, and a local station is referred to as *la brigade* or *la gendarmerie*.

▷ You may see members of **local militias** in some rural areas. They don't wear uniforms and often carry hunting rifles or shotguns. They're generally on guard against highway bandits and don't bother foreigners.

If you are the victim of a crime while in Benin, it is important to contact both the local police and your country's nearest embassy or consulate, where the staff can assist you with the legal process. Your country's representation can also help you find medical care and contact family or friends. Except under special circumstances, the investigation and prosecution of the crime is solely the responsibility of local authorities, but embassy officers can explain the local criminal justice process and find an attorney if needed. The loss or theft of a passport should also be reported immediately to the local police and the nearest embassy or consulate.

Foreigners traveling in Benin are subject to Beninese law and may be arrested and tried for committing a crime, even if the offense is not a crime in their home country. This includes possession and use of illegal drugs, including marijuana.

FOREIGN EMBASSIES

If your country has diplomatic representation in Benin, they can provide assistance if you are the victim of a crime or if you need to find medical care.

Embassy of the United States of America *Tel: 21.30.06.50; Website: cotonou. usembassy.gov; Location: Rue Caporal Bernard Anani (between Camp Guézo and the French embassy); Hours: M–Th 8am–12:30pm and 1:30–5pm, F 8am–1:30pm. Note: For after-hours emergencies, call the number listed above and ask to be directed to the duty officer.*

United Kingdom *The UK has no diplomatic representation in Benin. There is a Community Liaison Officer at the British School of Cotonou who can help British citizens in emergencies only. His name is Simon Collins. Tel: 21.30.32.65 / 95.30.19.51 / 21.30.32.65 / 95.85.38.73; Email: simonmcollins@gmail.com; Location: The British School of Cotonou, Haie Vive.*

Ambassade de France (Embassy of France) *Tel: 21.36.55.33; Website: amba-france-bj.org; Email: ambafrance.cotonou@diplomatie.gouv.fr; Location: Avenue Jean Paul II; Hours: M–F 8am–12:30pm and 3–6pm.*

Embassy of Germany *Tel: 21.31.29.67 / 21.31.29.68 / 21.31.54.51 / 21.31.56.93; Website: cotonou.diplo.de; Email: info@cotonou.diplo.de; PO Box: 01 B.P. 504, Cotonou. Location: 7 Avenue Jean Paul II; Hours: M–F 8am–12pm.*

Canada Canada has no diplomatic representation in Benin. Services are offered through the Embassy of Canada in Abidjan, Côte d'Ivoire.

EMERGENCY CALL NUMBERS

Cotonou

Centres de Secours (Emergency Centers) with phone numbers:

Cotonou–St. Jean: 21.30.22.22

Cotonou–Dantokpa: 21.32.10.29

Cotonou–Sodjatimey (Akpa): 21.33.46.26

Police d'État (State Police): 21.31.58.99

Sûreté urbaine de Cotonou (Cotonou Urban Safety): 21.31.20.11

The all-purpose **emergency number** in Cotonou is 118. Calls to 118 are free, but it can be difficult to get through to someone.

Cotonou's main public **hospital** is the Hubert K. Maga National University Hospital (Centre National Hospitalier et Universitaire Hubert K. Maga), generally known as the CNHU. *21.30.01.55 / 21.30.06.56; Location: Avenue Jean-Paul II, east of the Place des Martyrs and west of the French embassy.*

For medical emergencies requiring air transportation or medical evacuation, call Benin International Medical Assistance (97.88.90.03), a private company that, for a price, can provide evacuation from anywhere in Benin to Cotonou or to another country.

Alternate medical evacuation is available through Benin's public Medical Emergency Service (Service d'Aide Médicale d'Urgence / SAMU), which is based at the National University Hospital (CNHU) in Cotonou. *94.86.07.07 / 97.67.37.36; Dr Martin Chobli, head of the Medical Emergency Service 95.36.11.01*

Parakou

Centre de Secours (Emergency Center): 23.61.10.81

Parakou's main **hospital** is the Hospital of the Borgou (Centre Hospitalier Départemental du Borgou), known as the CHD or simply "l'hôpital." *23.61.07.13 / 23.61.07.17; Location: On the paved road leading east from the Carrefour de la Colombe, the second traffic circle you come to if you're heading north from the main Arzéké Market.*

Natitingou

Centre de Secours (Emergency Center): 23.82.15.81

Natitingou's main **hospital** is the Regional Hospital (Hôpital de la Zone).

Basics

Other Cities

Emergency center telephone numbers for the following cities:

Calavi: 21.14.15.28

Allada: 21.37.14.68

Ouidah: 21.34.19.18

Porto-Novo: 20.21.51.67

Lokossa: 22.41.16.09

Bohicon: 22.51.01.83

ORO

One traditional practice that can pose a security risk to travelers is Oro. In the *départements* of Ouémé and Plateau, and in some villages of the *département* of the Collines, a spirit called Oro roams each village or town for an annual period ranging from a few weeks to a few months. This area includes Porto-Novo.

Since uttering the name "Oro" is forbidden, it is known as *"la fétiche,"* the fetish, or *"le Fantôme,"* the Phantom. The Phantom usually roams a village or town at night, beginning between 9pm and midnight. It may also go out during the day, especially on Saturdays. When the Phantom is nearby, you'll hear an eerie whooping sound. Most people, especially women, must stay inside with doors and windows shut while the Phantom is out. Men caught outside by members of the Oro cult will be roughed up; women may be killed.

While this can sound terrifying, you'll be fine as long as you take it seriously. If you are in one of the areas listed above, do the following:

Discreetly ask the locals whether the Phantom will be coming out at night.

If the answer is yes, it's best to simply leave the area—assuming the Phantom isn't currently roaming the village.

If you end up somewhere while the Phantom is out, stay inside with all windows closed and doors locked. Do not attempt to go out or to look outside.

If anyone offers to show you the Phantom, it's best to decline unless you're a man and the person is someone you trust.

Swimming Off the Coast

Swimming in Benin's coastal waters is dangerous due to violent currents and rip tides. There are no lifeguards or established emergency services on the beaches, and local fishermen frequently drown close to shore. Swimming should be kept to the safety of hotel swimming pools.

Health

MALARIA

Malaria, a noncontagious parasite spread by mosquitoes, is the most deadly disease in Benin and poses a serious threat to travelers. While mosquitoes are most prevalent during the rainy season, from April to November, they are present year-round.

Before coming to Benin, you should see your doctor to obtain antimalarial prophylaxis. Common prophylaxes include Lariam (Mefloquine), Doxycycline, and Malarone. When taken as prescribed, they can greatly reduce the danger posed by malaria. Talk with your doctor about which prophylaxis is suitable for you.

Since mosquitoes are most active at night, you should take precautions to protect yourself against getting bitten while sleeping. Here are a few options:

▷ Sleep under a mosquito net. If you're planning to stay in budget accommodations, buy a net in Cotonou for about FCFA 2,000 and bring it with you—not all low-end hotels provide them. If your hotel provides a mosquito net, check it for holes.

▷ If your budget permits, stay in hotels with A/C. A functioning in-room air conditioner will usually keep mosquitoes away.

▷ Burn an anti-mosquito coil, which you can find in most boutiques, near your bed. A coil lasts about 6–8 hours. Its smoke doesn't kill mosquitoes, but it keeps them away.

▷ There's a device called Vape that, when plugged into an electrical outlet, is a convenient way to keep mosquitoes away. You can find it in some pharmacies and supermarkets in Cotonou, such as Championne and Supermarché du Pont.

▷ Buy anti-mosquito spray at a boutique and fumigate your room before going to bed. This is a less desirable option—the spray often irritates people as well as mosquitoes.

▷ Spray yourself with anti-mosquito spray *that is intended to be sprayed on skin.* Check the label before buying to make sure it's safe to spray on yourself. This kind of spray can be difficult to find, even in Cotonou.

▷ In the evening and after dark, wear thick long pants, long sleeves, and socks. Mosquitoes can bite through thin clothing.

Symptoms

Symptoms of malaria include fever, headache, back and joint pain, nausea, vomiting, shivering, and, in some cases, episodes of severe convulsions. Since many of these symptoms can also indicate other illnesses, such as the flu, a blood test is needed before making a definite diagnosis.

Basics

If you believe you've contracted malaria, get to the nearest hospital or health center (*Centre de Santé*). The standard treatment for malaria is a pill called Coartem and is widely available at hospitals, health centers, and pharmacies throughout Benin. You should insist on being treated with Coartem rather than with quinine, which some hospitals still use.

OTHER HEALTH CONCERNS

Waterborne diseases and parasites such as giardia, amoebas, and cholera are endemic in Benin. If you drink unfiltered water, you will likely get sick. Here are a few ways to get clean water:

▷ Buy bottled water, which is available at *buvettes*, boutiques, and supermarkets throughout the country. A 1.5 liter bottle should cost about FCFA 500. Check that the cap's seal is unbroken before buying; vendors are known to fill recycled bottles with tap water.

▷ Boil water from a faucet or a pump. Keep the water at a boil for three minutes to make sure it's safe to drink.

▷ Bring iodine tablets from home. When dissolved in water, they will kill many of the microbes that can make you sick.

▷ Buy PurWater sachets—clear half-liter plastic bags of chlorinated tap water—which street vendors sell for FCFA 25. Quality can vary, so use this as a backup option only.

▷ Be careful of ice cubes and of local beverages and frozen refreshments that may have been prepared with tap water.

Benin also experiences high rates of food-borne intestinal illnesses, such as E. coli and typhoid fever. Avoid consuming raw foods, including vegetables, lettuce, and fruits that cannot be peeled. When you're buying food on the street or from a low-end eatery, look at how sanitary the vendor's setup appears to be; avoid places that are very dirty or have a lot of flies.

Before traveling to Benin, ask your doctor about any other health concerns you should keep in mind.

Mandatory Vaccinations

You must be vaccinated against **yellow fever** before entering Benin. As soon as you step off the plane, a doctor will check your proof of vaccination. If you don't have it, you won't be allowed to enter the country.

Your proof of vaccination will most likely be a **WHO Card**, an internationally-recognized vaccination record issued by the World Health Organization and signed by the doctor who administers your vaccination. Before your trip, talk to your doctor about obtaining the proper proof of vaccination.

Travelers to Benin are recommended, but not required, to have current vaccinations against Tetanus, Polio, Meningitis, Typhoid Fever, Hepatitis A, Hepatitis B, Rabies, and Diphtheria.

MEDICAL FACILITIES IN COTONOU

Medical facilities in Benin are limited and not all medicines are available. Travelers should bring their own supplies of prescription drugs and preventive medicines. Not all medicines and prescription drugs available in Benin are USFDA–approved. However, pharmacies, hospitals, and private clinics are located in most major towns. Consultations and lab tests aren't expensive and commonly required medication and antibiotics are widely accessible. You may, however, have a hard time finding an English-speaking doctor, especially in smaller towns.

Below are some recommended private medical facilities, doctors, and pharmacies in Cotonou.

Private Clinics

Polyclinique Les Cocotiers *Dr. Assani: 21.30.14.31 / 21.30.14.20; Location: Carrefour Cadjehoun, across from the Cadjehoun post office.*

Clinique Mahouna *Tel: 21.30.14.35; Location: near Carrefour Cadjehoun, off the paved road.*

Polyclinique POSAM *Tel: 21.31.83.83; Director Dr. Athanase Sodjiedo: 90.90.08.33 / 95.49.43.43.*

Polyclinique Hôtel Dieu Cotonou *Dr. Justin Lewis Denakpo: 95.42.67.19; Dr. Fassassi Alimatou, cardiologist: 97.46.08.98.*

Clinique d'Akpakpa *Tel: 21.33.14.37 / 21.33.06.40; Location: PK 2 on the road to Porto-Novo, on the right.*

Doctors

The following doctors can be consulted in their offices. Some will make house calls.

Dr. Dominique Atchade *Tel: 21.30.10.70; Speaks English; Office location: the National University Hospital (CNHU) (see page 73).*

Dr. Anne Brunet Apithy *Tel: 21.31.35.26; Speaks English; Office location: in the "La Residence" neighborhood.*

Dr. A.M. Caudron-Tidjani *Tel: 21.31.56.34; Office location: in the SCOA-Gbeto neighborhood.*

Major Pharmacies

Pharmacies are major landmarks, and zemidjans usually know them by name.

Pharmacie Cocotiers *Near Haie Vive*

Pharmacie Jonquet *In the center of Jonquet*

Pharmacie Camp Guézo *Near the Camp Guézo and the U.S. embassy*

Pharmacie Notre Dame *on Avenue Clozel in Ganxi*

For more information on medical facilities in Cotonou and elsewhere in Benin, see *Emergency Call Numbers* on page 73.

Helping and Experiencing Local Communities

Visitors can contribute to Beninese communities in several ways. Many Benin-based nongovernmental organizations (NGOs), including orphanages and environmental and health education groups, welcome volunteers and donations. Below is a list of NGOs in Benin where you can volunteer for a few days or weeks.

Another way to contribute is to help children attend school. While most Beninese children attend primary school, very few finish high school, partly because of the cost. When you add up the cost of tuition, uniforms, school supplies, and housing (since many students have to leave their villages to attend school), a year at a public secondary school can run upwards of 300 U.S. dollars—a huge sum for the average Beninese family. The high cost of schooling disproportionately hurts girls: when parents can't afford to send all their children to school, they usually prioritize their sons' education, reasoning that a girl will probably end up being a stay-at-home mother anyway. If you want to support a student, you can donate to the **Benin Education Fund** (see the following page).

If you have connections with a school in your country, you can set up a correspondence program between that school and a Beninese school. Talk with the school administration or an English teacher if you're interested. You may also be able to observe a class at a local school.

Finally, there are a number of international organizations that are active in Benin. Several of them are listed below.

Be aware that some Benin-based NGOs are run by corrupt leadership and don't properly spend donations. If you're considering donating to an NGO that isn't listed below, be sure to verify that it actually does the work it claims to do.

DEVELOPMENT ORGANIZATIONS ACTIVE IN BENIN

Local

Local NGOs in Benin are not likely to have English-speaking staff on hand. If you don't speak French, you can hire an English-speaking guide (see page 54). For regional visits, you can hire an English teacher from a local school to translate for you.

Enagnon Dandan is an NGO based in Lissezoun, near Bohicon. They run an orphanage, library, and computer center, and provide microfinancing to local businesses. They often host short-term foreign volunteers. You can reach the President, Mathieu Hozounon, at 97.52.55.23 / 95.81.98.05. To get there from Bohicon, take a zemidjan to Chez Dahissiho in Lissezoun.

The **YETEN Center** is a well-run and locally-funded orphanage located in Gbozounme, near Porto-Novo. Two retired teachers founded the orphanage, which houses about 60 orphans and stresses education while giving the kids a safe, orderly, and caring environment. The orphans are known as the smartest and most polite students at the local schools, and in their spare time they help raise crops and animals, which the orphanage sells to pay for the kids' lodging and school fees.

You can volunteer at the center, and even stay in one of their private guest rooms. Reach the president, Jean, at 97.54.22.23 / 97.47.14.77. To get there from Porto-No-vo, take a zemidjan to Gbozounme (pronounced BO-zo-may).

Femmes, Enfants, et l'Environnement pour le Développement (FEE-D) is an NGO based in Péhunco, in the Atakora *département*. The name means "Develop-ment through Women, Children, and the Environment." They engage in a variety of work, including contract work for foreign aid organizations such as USAID (the U.S. Agency for International Development) and PSI (Population Solutions Interna-tional), as well as projects they develop themselves. A few recent projects include building preschools in rural villages, spraying houses and villages to protect against mosquitoes, and ensuring that school cafeterias are clean and can charge affordable prices. To inquire about visiting or supporting the NGO, contact its direc-tor, Lucien Sorokou Mama, at 96.24.43.66 or feed_dev@yahoo.fr.

Bethesda Benin is an NGO based in Cotonou that works in partnership with German Evangelical Development Services. It is divided into three departments: Health, Environment, and Microfinance. Since its establishment in the 1990s, Bethesda has initiated significant projects in each of these domains: they've constructed the Besthesda Hospital in Cotonou, led recycling workshops, and conducted waste management projects. *Website: bethesdabenin.org*

International

The **Benin Education Fund (BEF)**, established in 1998, is a U.S.–based not-for-profit that provides scholarships and educational support to students in Benin's Atakora region. More than 450 students have been able to stay in school because of this program. The BEF is primarily funded by donations from individuals in the U.S. and Canada, with material support such as school supplies and office space donated from individuals and organizations in Benin. For $300 a year, you can sponsor a high school student. This donation includes public school tuition and fees, supplies, uniforms, books, tutoring when needed, and housing assistance for those who must leave their villages to attend high school. Smaller donations are also welcome. *Website: benineducationfund.org*

Peace Corps Partnership Program (PCPP) Check out projects that Peace Corps Volunteers in Benin are currently undertaking. Run by the Peace Corps, the PCPP allows Americans to donate online to Volunteers' projects in a secure and account-able way. The Peace Corps focuses on projects that are community-initiated and respond to pressing needs, with at least 25% of funding for each project coming from the local community. You can donate to a specific project, or to the Benin country fund. *Website: donate.peacecorps.gov*

Kiva aims to connect people through lending for the sake of alleviating poverty. It is the world's first person-to-person micro-lending website, allowing individuals to lend directly to unique entrepreneurs around the globe. Starting at US $25, you can contribute to a loan for an individual in Benin and then receive updates on the progress of his or her projects. *Website: kiva.org*

Hands Around the World is a UK–registered charitable trust that seeks to help vulnerable children around the world, encouraging enthusiastic and well-prepared short-term volunteers to offer practical help, skill-sharing, support and friendship. *Website: hatw.org.uk*

The **Solar Electric Light Fund (SELF)** is an American NGO active in Benin. They focus on using solar energy to improve the lives of people who don't have access to electricity—as is the case for much of Benin's rural population. *Website: self.org*

The **Online Volunteering Service** is one of the United Nations Volunteers (UNV) program's corporate tools to mobilize volunteers for development. It connects volunteers with organizations working for sustainable development. *Website: onlinevolunteering.org*

The Hunger Project is a global, non-profit, strategic organization committed to the sustainable end of world hunger. It has been working in Benin since 1997 and is currently empowering over 31,000 partners in 11 epicenter communities to end their own hunger and poverty. *Website: thp.org*

Atlantique & Littoral

This is Benin's most urban and cosmopolitan region. Cotonou is the only city in the country that resembles a major Western city and offers a range of Western-style amenities. The climate here is hot and muggy, the traffic is anarchic, the streets are congested, and the pace of life is fast.

The Littoral *département* comprises only the city of Cotonou, while the Atlantique includes the surrounding towns of Abomey-Calavi (home to Benin's leading university, the University of Abomey-Calavi), Allada, and Ouidah.

Cotonou

Cotonou began as a small fishing village at the mouth of the Ouémé River. Under the Kingdom of Dahomey, it became a major slave-trading port, earning it the Fon name *Cotonou*—meaning "the mouth of the river of death," a reference not to a literal river

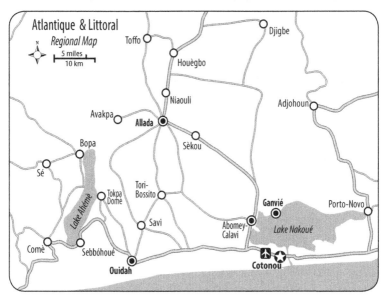

Atlantique & Littoral
Regional Map
N
5 miles
10 km

Toffo
Houègbo
Djigbe
Niaouli
Adjohoun
Avakpa
Allada
Bopa
Sèkou
Sé
Tori-Bossito
Tokpa-Domè
Savi
Ganvié
Porto-Novo
Lake Ahémé
Lake Nakoué
Abomey-Calavi
Comè
Sebbóhoué
Ouidah
Cotonou

but to the slaves' voyage into the oblivion beyond the sea. The French sporadically controlled Cotonou beginning in 1851, giving them a foothold from which to eventually colonize the entire region. Cotonou also provided a port for the French navy, allowing them to keep tabs on British forces based in nearby Lagos.

Today, Cotonou is Benin's main city. With an estimated 700,000–1,000,000 inhabitants, it is four times larger than any other city in the country. While Porto-Novo is the official capital, Cotonou holds the Presidential Residence and most of the ministries of the Government of Benin. It is also the country's economic engine. The Port of Cotonou allows trade with Europe and Asia—not just for Benin, but for the landlocked countries of Niger and Burkina Faso, who import and export manufactured goods and raw materials through Cotonou. The seemingly infinite Dantokpa Market is among the largest open-air markets in West Africa, with over a billion FCFA, or two million U.S. dollars, changing hands every day.

The city rests on a sliver of land between Lake Nokoué to the north and the Atlantic Ocean to the south. A canal, dug by the French in 1855, splits the city and connects the lake to the ocean. The hot, humid weather combines with significant pollution to create a grimy, muggy atmosphere.

For a visitor, Cotonou offers everything from Western-style lodging and dining to more local experiences, including cuisine from throughout West Africa and the largest artisans' market in the country. Since it houses Benin's only international airport, it will probably be the start and end point of your trip. However, its indescribably chaotic streets and markets can easily overwhelm the uninitiated, and after a few days you'll probably be ready to see the rest of the country.

GETTING THERE AND AWAY

Bus/Taxi

Buses heading north depart Cotonou each morning at 7am sharp from the Place de l'Étoile Rouge. Others take off from Carrefour St. Michel or Gare de Jonquet (see *Neighborhoods* on page 86). You can buy tickets in advance at the bus company's office—most companies have their offices at Étoile Rouge—but, unless you're traveling around a major holiday such as Easter or Christmas, you can usually get a seat by simply showing up half an hour before the bus leaves. Seats are more expensive on newer, air-conditioned buses, such as those operated by ATT and La Poste.

Since 2012, the deteriorating condition of the Cotonou–Bohicon road has forced bus companies to reroute their buses. Most buses now reach Bohicon via Porto-Novo. Taxis, which are small enough to dodge potholes, still take the direct road to Bohicon.

For information on travel to bordering countries from Cotonou, see *Getting There – Land* (p53).

Airport Information

Cotonou's international airport, named after Cardinal Bernadin Gantin in 2008, is the only international airport in Benin. It's located at the west end of town. Once you get off the plane, a doctor will be waiting to check your proof of vaccination (see *Health* on page 75), and then officials will check your passport to confirm that you have a valid Beninese visa (see *Getting There* on page 49). After that, you will go to baggage collection. Porters in blue uniforms will swarm you, offering their services. It's a good idea to hire one: not only can they help you extract your bags from the chaotic room, but they're friendly with the *gendarmes* who man the exit, and can dissuade them from giving you any problems. Pay your porter FCFA 1,000 once you get your bags safely outside. While problems aren't common, take note of the number painted on the back of your porter's uniform—if he absconds with your stuff, you can report him to the airport police.

There is a currency exchange bureau at the airport. You may get a better rate if you change money at a bank in the city center (see *Money* on page 59).

If you're staying at a high-end hotel, the hotel may provide a complimentary shuttle from the airport. Ask them about this when you make your reservation. Otherwise, you'll need to get a taxi or zemidjan. Taxis are the best option, especially if you have a lot of luggage. You'll find taxis waiting just outside the terminal. If your hotel is in the city center, it should cost FCFA 2,500–5,000 to get there. If you want to take a zemidjan, avoid the group that waits just beyond the parking lot. They'll attempt to charge you astronomical rates, and they've been known to have associates down the street who are waiting to steal your bags. You'll find more trustworthy *zems* if you walk down the street for a few minutes—however, if it's after dark, this isn't the safest option either.

Bernardin Gantin

Cardinal Bernardin Gantin, after whom Cotonou's airport is named, was born in the village of Toffo in 1922. He joined the seminary at age 14 and achieved priesthood in 1951. He then went to Rome to study theology and was named archbishop of Cotonou by Pope John XXIII in January 1960. For over a decade he worked from his home country to promote the founding of religious schools and support catechism in the diocese. In 1971, Gantin was called back to Rome, where he participated in the Second Vatican Council. Pope Paul VI made him a cardinal in 1977. He worked for 30 years with the Roman Curia in a variety of positions and was the first black African cardinal to hold such high appointments in the Vatican. He retired and returned to Benin in 2002, where he continued to work with the Catholic Church until his death in 2008.

GETTING AROUND

Cotonou's streets fulfill many stereotypes of the urban Third World. Few traffic rules apply, with cars and semi-trailer trucks careening through the chaotic streets and traffic circles, passing within inches of each other, and motorcycles weaving through it all. In market areas, pedestrians join the mêlée. Salesmen often wait at intersections and, once the light turns red, rush the helpless occupants of stopped cars and motorcycles, urging them to buy a pack of Kleenex or a wall clock or a guitar before the light turns green.

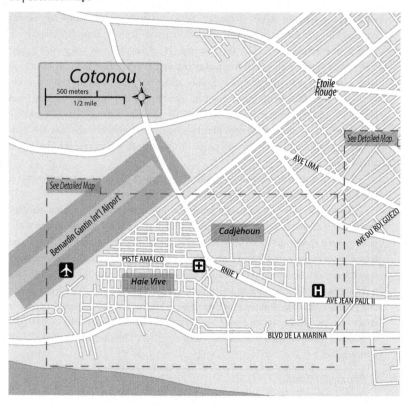

Zemidjans in Cotonou wear yellow shirts and can be found on every corner, at any time. You'll be relying on them: there are no city buses in Cotonou, and taxis are available only by appointment (see recommended taxi drivers below). A zemidjan ride within the city should cost FCFA 150–400, but if you appear to be a foreigner, *zem* drivers will usually attempt to charge you 2–3 times the normal price.

Some of Cotonou's major intersections are *La Place de l'Étoile Rouge*, whose name, meaning Red Star, hearkens back to the Communist era; St. Michel, located by the church of the same name; *Le Stade d'Amitié*, the national stadium; and *Carrefour Godomé*, the junction between the highways heading north and west.

TAXI DRIVERS IN COTONOU

These are some recommended taxi drivers. You can call them for a simple pick-up and drop-off within the city, hire them for the day, or have them take you to nearby attractions such as Porto-Novo, Ouidah, and Ganvié. Maximum four passengers.

Alexandre Adjakale 95.56.32.31 / 90.91.17.42 / 97.22.25.14

Norbert Ahouansou 93.03.99.59 / 94.31.73.07 / 66.99.48.39

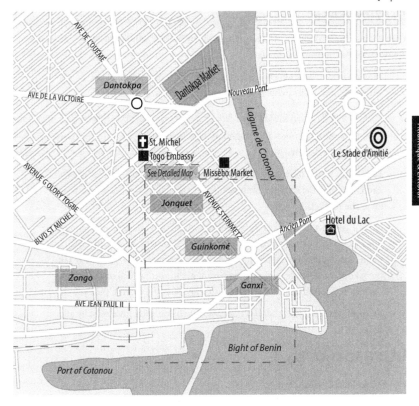

Raymond Atchadé 97.57.82.29 / 95.11.80.87

Roger Dagba *95.21.93.76*

Richard Edo Tchodo 96.88.11.01 / 95.16.13.20

Zemidjans in Cotonou

These are some recommended zemidjan drivers. You can hire them for short trips within Cotonou, either for a single trip or by the hour. After nightfall, zemidjan prices go up significantly, usually to about double the daytime price.

Jean Victor Pedros Marcos 97.77.54.59

Claude Padonou 95.42.78.88

Théophile Adjimon 95.60.72.00

Saturnin Ayanou 97.26.48.13

Guenolé 95.02.07.25

Erik 98.82.80.67

STAYING SAFE

Crime issues in Cotonou are similar to those in any big city around the globe. Here are a few particular precautions to take:

Muggings are common on the beach. Don't go to the beach alone, do stay within sight of other people, and never go to the beach after sunset.

Women should be careful in clubs and bars at night, especially if out alone.

Avoid traveling on foot after nightfall, especially alone, and do not walk down dark or deserted streets.

Keep close watch on your valuables in congested areas such as the Missèbo and Dantokpa markets—or, even better, leave them in a safe place before you go to the market.

Do not get on a motorcycle with someone who doesn't have an official zemidjan shirt with a registration number painted on the back, especially at night. Foreigners have fallen victim to violent organized muggings after taking fake *zems*. If you're going somewhere at night, you can call one of the recommended zemidjan or taxi drivers listed above and have him pick you up.

Be careful in the area around St. Michel, which can get a little sketchy after dark.

NEIGHBORHOODS

Haie Vive and Cadjehoun

Located close to the airport, these upper-class neighborhoods are where many expatriates reside. The Piste Amalco, the paved road running down the center of the Haie Vive neighborhood, stems from the Carrefour Cadjehoun, a traffic circle marked by its green water tower advertising the MOOV cell phone company. This area boasts a high concentration of high-end European and Asian restaurants, grocery stores, and internet cafés. The quiet, chic neighborhoods present a surreal contrast to the rest of the city: palatial villas and walled concessions decorated with bougainvilleas line the peaceful streets, all of it protected by an army of private security guards. A group of Touareg vendors set up shop next to the Livingstone's restaurant, with a brilliant display of fine silver jewelry and stone carvings. Pricier handicrafts and souvenir shops can be found along Piste Amalco, such as Farafina and Bric a Brac.

Jonquet and Guinkomé

These two neighborhoods border each other and house many small hotels, pleasant and reasonably priced restaurants, bars, and dance clubs. The main strip in Jonquet is lively day and night, lined with kiosks, food stands including rotisserie chicken, and Nigerian money vendors. You can find taxis heading to the Mono-Couffo region in the Jonquet taxi station. There's a large mosque and a Catholic church near one another on Avenue Proche. The Ganxi Market is within easy walking distance of Guinkomé.

Atlantique & Littoral

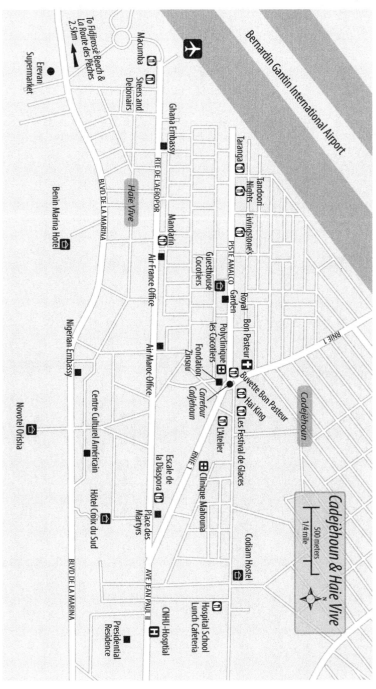

Bernardin Gantin International Airport

To Fidjrosse Beach &
La Route des Pêches
2.5km

Macumba

Erevan
Supermarket

Steers and
Debonairs

Ghana Embassy

RTE DE L'AEROPOR

Taranga

BLVD DE LA MARINA

Haie Vive

Benin Marina Hotel

Tandoori
Nights

Livingstone's

Mandarin

Air France Office

PISTE AMALCO

Guesthouse
Cocotiers

Royal — Bon Pasteur Garden

Polyclinique
les Cocotiers

Fondation
Zinsou

Carrefour
Cadjèhoun

RNIE 1

Buvette Bon Pasteur

Hai King

les Festival de Glaces

Cadjèhoun

Nigerian Embassy

Air Maroc Office

Novotel Orisha

Centre Culturel Américain

L'Atelier

Clinique Mahouna

Escale de
la Diaspora

Place des
Martyrs

RNIE 1

Hôtel Croix du Sud

Codiam Hostel

BLVD DE LA MARINA

AVE JEAN PAUL II

Presidential
Residence

CNHU-Hospital

Hospital School
Lunch Cafeteria

Cadjèhoun & Haie Vive

500 meters
1/4 mile

N

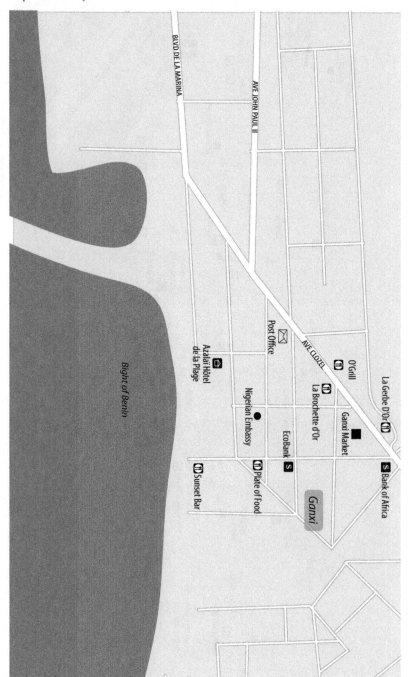

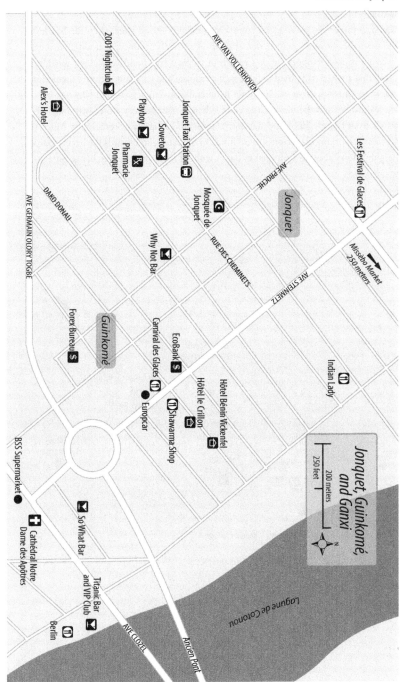

Jonquet, Guinkomé, and Ganxi

Ganxi

Ganxi, pronounced *ganhee*, is a commercial neighborhood situated by the beach. It has a smaller covered market that specializes in fresh produce, seafood, and meat. Vendors beckon shoppers with a wealth of tropical fruits and vegetables, including those that are normally hard to find, such as squash and eggplant. Around the perimeter of the market, other vendors offer handicraft souvenirs, CDs, and Nigerian bootleg DVDs. Beyond the market, there are Lebanese-run grocery stores with imported goods from Europe, book and stationary stores, and a variety of restaurants. Much of Cotonou's working class comes to eat lunch in the cafeterias towards the beach. Ganxi neighborhood also has a number of banks with ATMs and money exchange bureaus.

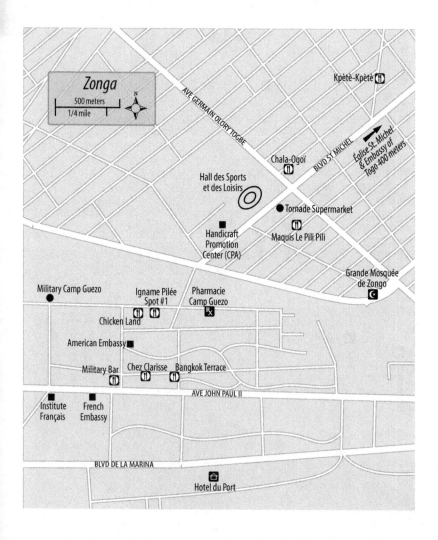

SIGHTS AND ACTIVITIES

Dantokpa Market

Dantokpa means "snake out of water" in Fon. That is all you need to know. The utter chaos of this 100–acre open-air market defies the descriptive powers of the English language. However, it is worth a visit: among the anarchy, you'll find the sense of action and vitality that can both overwhelm and allure visitors to Benin. Nearly anything, either imported or produced in Benin, can be found here—the locals say that if you can't find it in Dantokpa, you can't find it in Benin.

As with any large market, petty theft is common here. Avoid carrying valuables such as your passport or large amounts of cash, and be wary of invitations to more secluded areas of the market.

> If you're in central Cotonou, you'll probably see Camp Guézo, the main base of the Beninese army. Its name honors the military exploits of Dahomey's King Guézo.

Missèbo Market

Located near Dantokpa, this giant second-hand clothing market is a whirlwind of aggressive vendors and a great place to find amazing deals. If you're patient, you can find brand name clothing and shoes at great bargains. Missèbo is also home to many boutiques run by Indians and Middle Easterners selling textiles, miscellaneous household items, and groceries in bulk. There's a wide range of Beninese fabric of all colors and patterns throughout this market.

Le Stade d'Amitié
Friendship Stadium

Catch a football match at Cotonou's main stadium. This is the home of the Squirrels, Benin's national football team, and there are matches between regional Beninese teams as well. It also hosts other athletic events and the occasional outdoor concert. *Location: northwest of the city center. All zemidjans know where it is. Taxis usually stop here on their way into and out of Cotonou.*

Cathédrale de Notre Dame des Apôtres
Cathedral of Our Lady of the Apostles

This eye-catching red-and-white striped church is commonly known as the *Cathédrale de Cotonou*. It houses a book store that sells books by West African authors, as well as text books. The cathedral is the seat of the Roman Catholic Archdiocese of Cotonou. Bernardin Gantin was the Cardinal of this church from 1960 to 1971, followed by Marcel Honorat Leon Agboton. In 2011, Pope Benedict XVI conducted mass in the cathedral during a short visit to Benin. *Location: Ganxi neighborhood, near the Ancien Pont.*

Centre de Promotion Artisanal (CPA)
Handicraft Promotion Center

This touristy artisan center consists of a village of bungalows full of sculptures, paintings, vases, glass and silver jewelry, Batik drapes, colorful hand-woven fabrics, masks, bronze pieces, and much more. You can see the artisans at work in the common court-yards behind the bungalows. Vendors here routinely propose astronomical prices to tourists—sometimes over ten times the "real" price of the item—so be ready to bargain like mad. (See a list of real prices above.) For some bargaining tips, see *Money* on page 59. Stop in here on the last day before your flight home, so you don't end up lugging your souvenirs all over Benin.

Institut Français
French Institute

The Institut Français, which has replaced the earlier Centre Culturel Français, is a common meeting place for French expatriates and Beninese artists. The French library includes Parisian magazines and newspapers from the day before. The entrance gallery always has art exhibits, and the center organizes numerous cultural performances in the outdoor theater such as plays, concerts, and dance galas. Contact the center for information on upcoming events. *Hours: 8am–6pm. Closed Sundays and Mondays. Tel: 21.30.08.56 / 21.30.74.79. Location: on Avenue Jean-Paul II, next to the Embassy of France.*

Centre Culturel Américain
American Cultural Center

The cultural center provides a library and other resources to expats and to Beninese who are interested in American culture. It subscribes to several English– and French-language magazines, which you can peruse in their reading room. The center is often a testing site for collegiate and English language tests. It also offers English classes, internet access, movie nights, and an American education counseling office. *Hours: Mon–Thurs 8am–12:30pm and 1:30–5pm, Friday 8am–1:30pm. Tel: 21.30.06.50. Location: off Avenue de France.*

"Real" Prices for Popular Handicrafts

Painting: FCFA 5,000–12,000, depending on size

Mask: FCFA 3,000–10,000, depending on size

Drum: FCFA 6,000–15,000, depending on size

Sculpture: FCFA 2,000–10,000, depending on size

Replica king's scepter: FCFA 5,000

Small clay necklace: FCFA 1,500

Glass bead necklace: FCFA 3,500

Ebony keychain: FCFA 500

Indigo dyed fabric: (1 pagne): FCFA 4,000

Small patchwork tapestry: FCFA 4,000

Fulani leather sandals: FCFA 1,500

Batiks: FCFA 2,000 (small), FCFA 10,000 (large)

La Fondation Zinsou

Started by the Zinsou family in 2005, this private foundation is dedicated to the promotion of traditional and contemporary African art. It displays photography and paintings by prominent Beninese artists in order to allow the public to appreciate contemporary Beninese artistic culture. With continual exhibits from local art collectors, a shuttle to bring children to the museum, a children's art program called *Les Petits Pinceaux*, and a "Free Wednesdays" program at the Museum of Abomey, the Fondation Zinsou is making headway. *Hours: 10am–7pm. Closed Tuesdays: Location: at Carrefour Cadjéhoun.*

Fidjirossè Beach & La Route des Pêches
The Fishing Road

La Route des Pêches, or The Fishing Road, is a sand road that follows the coast from Fidjirossè Beach all the way to Ouidah, about 30 kilometers west of Cotonou. The road is lined with coconut palms and beachside, makeshift cabins that are available to rent for a picnic. On Sunday afternoons the beach is packed with working class Beninese and expatriates alike enjoying a picnic. There are several *buvettes*, restaurants, and a growing number of hotels at Fidjirossè. Some even have sea-water swimming pools.

SUPERMARKETS

Erevan is by far the largest supermarket in Cotonou and in Benin. In range and selection of Western merchandise, it resembles Target in the United States or LeClerc in France. Since it mainly serves Cotonou's French expatriate community, it has a particularly impressive wine and cheese selection. However, if you can find what you're looking for in one of Cotonou's other supermarkets, it's best to buy it there— prices run high at Erevan. *Location: near the beach, west of the city center. Zemidjans usually know it by name. A zemidjan ride from the city center should cost FCFA 400.*

BSS This is Cotonou's second-largest supermarket, after Erevan. It's centrally located in the Ganxi neighborhood and offers a wide selection of groceries, household products, and some electronics. *Location: near Marché Ganxi, on the main boulevard toward the cathedral and the overpass.*

Abomey-Calavi

This northern suburb of Cotonou is along the road leading to Parakou. It houses the University of Abomey-Calavi, the main campus of Benin's national university, which was founded in 1970. There are over 16,000 students enrolled here, of which less than one-quarter are women. The university has 19 departmental schools and six campuses. The second largest campus is in Parakou. A taxi ride to Abomey-Calavi from the center of Cotonou costs FCFA500–600.

The tourism office for the stilt village of Ganvié (p102) is also located in Abomey-Calavi. Since many tourists head straight for Ganvié via Lake Nokoué upon arrival in Abomey-Calavi, a curious visitor might well be the only yovo in town.

Tornade is a smaller shop with a limited selection of Western and Middle Eastern groceries. They do have Haagen-Das ice cream and a decent cheese selection. *Location: down the street from the Hôtel de l'Union, near the Artisanal Center.*

Ganxi shops Several smaller supermarkets and bakeries line the wide boulevard running through the Ganxi commercial district. A few shops here specialize in electronics. If you need to replace earbuds or any similar item, go to one of these shops rather than buying the low-quality merchandise of the vendors in the market.

EATING AND DRINKING

Cotonou houses significant populations of European, Asian, and Middle Eastern expatriates, and its excellent dining options give each of them a taste of home. Here you'll find the largest selection of both African and non-African cuisine in Benin. The numerous Lebanese restaurants are notable for *schwarma*, a kind of Mediterranean burrito that's a good midrange dining option. Western-style spots serve pizza, sandwiches, salads, hamburgers, pasta, seafood, and ice cream. The city even has two South African fast-food chains, Steers and Debonairs. A few Chinese, Indian, and Thai restaurants complete the selection of international cuisine. You can also find cuisine from throughout West Africa, ranging from pricier restaurants to roadside stands.

Dining in Cotonou is generally more expensive than in the rest of the country. Local cuisine, while still cheap, costs about twice as much as elsewhere. If you're eating European, American, Asian cuisine, plan on spending around FCFA 5,000 per meal, without drinks. At the upscale foreign restaurants, beer and soda cost 2–4 times what they cost at a normal *buvette*. If a restaurant has both an air-conditioned indoor dining room and a terrace, they may charge you slightly more if you sit in the dining room—basically a surcharge for the air conditioning.

High-end

⊗ **Livingstone's** This is perhaps the closest you'll get in Benin to a European pub, and consequently it's a major hangout for Cotonou's European and American expatriate community. Visit in the evening to check out this community that exists within Cotonou, yet remains remarkably cut off from the rest of the city. The restaurant serves excellent European-style pizza, pasta, and sandwiches. To drink, choose from carafes of wine, beer on tap, and a liquor bar. On Saturday evenings, there are happy hour specials. *Meals: FCFA 4,000–10,000. Drinks: FCFA 800–2,000. Hours: 11am–midnight. Open daily. Tel: 21.30.27.58. Location: on the Piste Amalco, in Haie Vive. If you're coming from Carrefour Cadjehoun, it'll be on your right. Zemidjans usually know it by name.*

⊗ **Berlin** While the competition is fierce, many hold that this place serves the best pizza in Cotonou, in addition to other excellent European dishes. The restaurant overlooks the wide canal that divides Cotonou. *Meals: FCFA 4,000–9,000. Drinks: FCFA 800–1,500. Hours: 11am–11pm. Open daily. Location: in Ganxi, along the canal and near the Ancien Pont, directly across the canal from Hôtel du Lac.*

Hôtel du Lac Come here to get away from the chaos of Cotonou's streets. At the in-house restaurant, you can sit on a peaceful terrace overlooking the canal and eat pizza cooked in a wood-fired oven. You'll also find seafood, a range of European cuisine, and an impressive liquor bar. Non-guests can swim in the hotel pool, located next to the restaurant terrace, for FCFA 2,500. *Meals: FCFA 5,000–10,000. Drinks: FCFA 1,000–2,000. Hours: 11am–1pm. Open daily. Location: along the water on the east side of the canal, near the Ancien Pont. Zemidjans know where it is.*

Macumba Here you'll find a range of Mediterranean and European cuisine, ranging from pizzas to Greek salads to steak sandwiches. Lebanese expats like to hang out on the terrace, smoking shisha and watching music videos or football matches on the large outdoor projection screen. Since it's just a couple minutes' walk from the airport, this is a good place to eat before or after a flight. It sometimes turns into a nightclub in the evening. *Meals: FCFA 4,000–8,000. Drinks: FCFA 800–1,500. Hours: 11am–11pm. Open daily. Location: by the airport. If your zemidjan doesn't know the name, say "le restaurant à côté de l'aéroport."*

⊗ **Taranga** Home to arguably the best burgers in Cotonou. Their burgers aren't exactly what you'd find in America, but they fulfill the basic requirements: they're large and drowning in cheese and sauce. They do come with cole slaw on them, but you can move it to the side if it bothers you. The restaurant also offers a range of European and Lebanese dishes, and they have Castel beer on tap. *Meals: FCFA 3,000–7,000. Drinks: FCFA 1,000–2,000. Hours: 11am–11pm. Open daily. Location: Piste Amalco, in Haie Vive. If you're coming from Carrefour Cadjehoun, it's on your right, just past Livingstone's.*

Royal Garden If you're craving Indian cuisine, eat here. The food and service are excellent. *Meals: FCFA 4,000–9,000. Drinks: FCFA 800–1,500. Hours: 11am–11pm. Open daily. Location: on the Piste Amalco, the main street in the Haie Vive neighborhood.*

⊗ **Bangkok Terrasse** Come here for delicious Thai cuisine. They have a very pleasant—and very East Asian–themed—dining area, as well as friendly staff. *Meals: FCFA 4,000–12,000. Drinks: FCFA 1,000–2,000. Hours: 12pm–10pm. Closed Wednesdays. Tel: 21.30.37.86. Location: a couple blocks south of Pharmacie Camp Guézo, on the road leading to the Avenue Jean-Paul II.*

Hai King For Chinese cuisine, this is hard to beat. It's centrally located across from the Bon Pasteur *buvette* and steps away from Haie Vive. The upper balcony dining room overlooks Carrefour Cadjehoun. *Meals: FCFA 5,000–10,000. Drinks: FCFA 1,000–2,000. Hours: 11am–11pm. Open daily. Tel: 21.30.60.08. Location: at Carrefour Cadjehoun.*

L'Atelier This is a classy French-owned restaurant that serves very high-end African cuisine with French influence. The restaurant also serves as an art gallery with exhibition space open to Beninese artists. *Meals: FCFA 7,500–16,500. Drinks: FCFA 1,000–3,000. Hours: 12pm–3pm, 7–11:30pm. Closed Sundays. Tel: 21.30.17.04. Location: Carrefour Cadjehoun, behind the SONACOP gas station.*

Midrange

⊗ **Secret Schwarma** You have to walk down a dirt alley to get there, but this place serves arguably the best schwarma in Cotonou. You can get lamb, chicken, or vegetarian schwarma, plus a side of French fries—though they also put fries directly in the schwarma. It's delicious and filling and popular with both locals and Lebanese expats. Maybe it's not so secret now that we've told you about it. *Meals: FCFA 1,000–2,000. Drinks (non-alcoholic only): FCFA 500. Air-conditioned indoor or patio seating. Hours: 11am–9pm. Open daily. Location: hard to find, hence the secrecy. Go to Hôtel Concorde, on Avenue Steinmetz, near Ganxi. If your zemidjan doesn't know the hotel, tell him "La Grande Direction MTN" (the big MTN headquarters), and when facing the MTN building, turn right and walk until you see the hotel's sign. When you're facing the Hôtel Concorde, turn left and take the first right. This will be a dirt road. Go down the road about 30 meters and you'll see the restaurant on your right.*

⊗ **Chicken Land** Yes, it's called Chicken Land. This small establishment serves chicken and fries, chicken kebabs, and sometimes rabbit. Their salads are of the quality you normally find at high-end restaurants for triple the price. The servers are extremely friendly and attentive. If you hang around long enough, some Peace Corps Volunteers will probably show up. *Meals: FCFA 1,000–2,000. Drinks: FCFA 250–700. Shaded outdoor seating. Hours: 10am–9pm. Location: Across the street from Camp Guézo, in the direction of Pharmacie Camp Guézo.*

Mandarin Despite its name, this is a Lebanese restaurant. For Middle Eastern cuisine (excluding schwarma), Mandarin offers one of your best options in Cotonou, and the price is right. The place is clean and air-conditioned, with fast service. Try one of the varieties of *manaquiche* with a side of hummus and pita bread. They also sell some Lebanese groceries. *Meals: FCFA 1,500–5,000. Drinks (non-alcoholic only): FCFA 500–700. Air-conditioned indoor seating. Hours: 11am–10pm. Location: Avenue Jean-Paul II, next to the office of Air France. If your zem doesn't know it by name, say "le bureau d'Air France."*

Tandoori Nights This comfortable restaurant serves a fusion of Indian and Lebanese food, reflecting Cotonou's historically large Indian and Lebanese expatriate communities. Portions tend to be a bit smaller than other Lebanese or Indian restaurants in Cotonou. They have a well-stocked (and expensive) bar and often have football matches playing on TV. They also have wifi. For a delicious and inexpensive meal, try the Indian schwarma for about FCFA 2,000. *Meals: FCFA 2,000–7,000. Drinks: FCFA 1,000–2,000 for soda and beer, FCFA 2,500 and up for liquor. Indoor (air conditioned) and patio seating. Hours: 11am–midnight. Open daily. Location: the western end of Haie Vive.*

Plate of Food This nickname refers to two similar eateries located across the street from each other. They both offer big plates with your choice of chicken or fish, fried plantains, French fries, peas, basic salad, and brown rice. A good choice if you're looking for an affordable, filling meal that blends Western and local cuisine. Eat it there, or get it to go and take it down the street to Sunset Bar. *Meals: FCFA 1,500–2,000. Drinks: FCFA 250–1,200. Covered patio seating. Hours: about 12pm–9pm. Location: If you're coming from the main boulevard of Ganxi, it's just past Ecobank Ganxi, about 100 yards from the beach.*

Maquis Pili Pili This higher-end African restaurant is quite popular among both Beninese and expatriates. It offers an extensive and varied menu; the roast chicken is particularly delicious. *Meals: FCFA 4,500–6,500. Drinks: FCFA 1,000–2,000. Hours: 11am–5pm, 7pm–midnight. Open daily. Tel: 21.31.29.32. Location: northwest of the town center, off the paved road near Boulevard St. Michel.*

⊗ **La Gerbe d'Or** The ground floor is a bakery and grocery store, selling fresh baguettes, croissants, and exquisite pastries such as eclairs, rum babas, fruit tarts, and custard from around FCFA 500. Upstairs, a restaurant lounge is perfect for a hearty dinner. *Meals: FCFA 4,500–6,000. Restaurant hours: 5–10pm. Closed Mondays. Tel: 21.31.42.58. Location: on Avenue Clozel, across from the Ganxi Market.*

Chez Clarisse This restaurant specializes in high-end French, Beninese, and West African cuisine. The ventilated dining room is comfortable and tastefully decorated, with professional and attentive servers. This is a great place for fresh grilled fish with rice and *moyo* sauce, or *escargots* with garlic and herbs. *Meals: FCFA 3,000–15,000. Drinks: FCFA 1,000–2,000. Hours: 11am–3pm, 7–11pm. Open daily. Tel: 21.30.60.14. Location: behind the American embassy.*

⊗ **Festival des Glaces** This is a popular bakery, pizzeria, and ice cream parlor. The meal portions are a bit small, but there's a delicious variety of gelato-style ice cream flavors. The air-conditioned dining room is blissfully cool, a pleasant place to escape the heat and humidity of the city. Taking ice cream outside to eat reduces its price; there are tables available at the front door. *Meals: FCFA 5,000–10,000. Hours: 8am–10pm. Open daily. Two locations: on Avenue Steinmetz, past the Missèbo Market; and at Carrefour Cadjehoun.*

Steers and Debonairs These two South African fast food chains offer beef, chicken, or vegetarian burger combos with fries. Debonairs specializes in pizza, which can be ordered to deliver. This is the place to go for a change of taste and style if the Beninese meals are too hard to digest. *Meals: FCFA 3,000–5,000. Hours: 11am–9pm. Open daily. Location: next to Macumba, near the airport.*

Carnaval des Glaces This Indian-managed restaurant and ice cream parlor was established to resemble the wildly popular Festival des Glaces. The ice cream isn't exactly what one hopes, but the burgers and fries coupled with a relaxed ambience provide for a good meal. *Meals: FCFA 3,000 and up. Hours: 9am–10pm. Open daily: Location: on Avenue Steinmetz.*

Budget

Igname Pilée Spot #1 At this hole-in-the-wall eatery, a few women prepare a variety of good local cuisine: pâte rouge, igname pilée, fried fish, chicken, and even wagasi cheese—a rarity in the south. It's a good place to have your first taste of Beninese cuisine after arriving in country. If you want igname pilée, be prepared to wait a bit: they have to pound the yams first. *Meals: FCFA 400–1,000. Drinks: FCFA 250–1,200. Indoor and covered patio seating. Hours: lunch only, about 11am–2pm. Location: Across the street from Camp Guézo, in the direction of Pharmacie Camp Guézo, next to Chicken Land.*

Igname Pilée Spot #2 If you're just looking for igname pilée, come to this place—it reportedly serves the best igname pilée in Cotonou, along with a green sauce called tchiayo that you won't find anywhere else in the city. The sauce is so good that you'll want to drink it. *Meals: FCFA 700–1,200. Location: at the Place de Trinité, near the Place de l'Étoile Rouge, next to the Avenue St. Jean.*

Challa-Ogoï This open-air *buvette* has stand-up service, with a great selection of Beninese cuisine such as *igname pilée*, *pâte*, *pied de beouf*, fried chicken and fish, and salads. *Meals: FCFA 1,000–3,000. Hours: 10am–11pm. Open daily. Location: Avenue St. Jean, across from the Hall des Sports and near the Boulevard St. Michel.*

Kpètè-Kpètè This large outdoor dining and beer-drinking area is surrounded by food vendors offering grilled meats, fish, fried plantains, and salads. The atmosphere is lively—it's a great place to enjoy the evening breeze and experience local nightlife. *Meals: FCFA 500–2,000. Hours: noon–midnight. Open daily. Location: off Boulevard St. Michel, around the southwest corner of l'Église St Michel and close to Petit Babo Hotel.*

⊗ **Escale de la Diaspora** Sandwiches, burgers, and spaghetti are served from a bright yellow mini-bus located at the edge of a large public square, under the shade of Néré trees and parasols. The tables are on a raised concrete platform, away from the noise of the traffic. Soft drinks, beer, and select liquors are available. *Meals: FCFA 1,000–2,000. Hours: noon–midnight. Open daily. Location: Place des Martyrs, along the Avenue Jean-Paul II.*

Indian Lady in Missèbo A former cook for an Indian family named Madame Eugenie Guinnakou serves authentic Indian meals in an upstairs salon. The experience, though at first awkward because it seems to be in her living room, is absolutely beautiful. There's a cool breeze and a laid-back atmosphere. Madame Guinnakou also sells bottles of wine for about FCFA 2,000, a perfect accompaniment to the meal. *Meals: from FCFA 2,000. Tel: 97.57.23.76. Location: near Missèbo Market.*

Lunch Cafeteria by the Hospital School One of Cotonou's best kept secrets, this outside food court is open only at lunchtime. Each vendor prepares and sells her specialty; simply ask what's inside the cauldrons and coolers. Tailored for the medical students and researchers, the food and dining area are kept very clean. You can find beans and gari, rice and boiled vegetables, *pâte*, *igname pilée*, fish, chicken, beef, *wagasi* cheese, *ignames frites*, omelets, spaghetti, fresh pineapple juice, soda, beer, instant coffee, and tea. *Meals: around FCFA 1,000. Hours: 10am–4pm. Open Mon–Fri. Location: within the walls of the Hospital School compound.*

Buvettes

The following places mainly serve drinks—which, in Benin, usually means beer and soda.

Bon Pasteur This large open-air *buvette* borrows its name from the church next door. It's located on the border between normal Cotonou and Haie Vive, the surreal expatriate quarter, so it draws an unusual mix of foreign expats and ordinary Beninese. Come here before or after a dinner in Haie Vive to escape the inflated price of drinks at the expat restaurants. It's most active after dark, when vendors circulate through the crowded tables peddling anything from toothpaste to CDs of Nigerian music. Street performers sometimes set up shop, balancing tables on their noses and so forth. In the evening you can find a variety of street food, including grilled turkey and goat meat. *Drinks: FCFA 250–1,200. Open-air seating. Hours: about 11am–4am. Open daily. Location: the western side of the Carrefour Cadjehoun. Zemi-djans know it by name.*

Sunset Bar A small, somewhat run-down *buvette* on the beach near Marché Ganxi. It's earned its nickname because it's a good place to enjoy a drink while watching the sun set over the ocean. You can also watch freight ships coming in to the nearby Port of Cotonou and, if you're lucky, spot a navy boat patrolling for Nigerian pirates. They sometimes serve local cuisine, but it's a better bet to bring food in from Plate of Food (p96)—the servers won't mind. *Drinks: FCFA 250–1,200. Covered patio seating. Hours: about 12pm–9pm. Location: At the end of the road leading from the main boulevard of Ganxi toward the beach, past Ecobank Ganxi.*

Military Bar The nickname comes from the army officers and policemen who are always hanging around, but they don't seem to mind if civilians drink here too. You can sit on the patio, or on absurdly comfortable sofas and armchairs inside. Prices for most beers are, for some reason, slightly lower than at other buvettes. They sometimes serve akassa and fish in the courtyard, but there are better dining options in the area. *Drinks: FCFA 250–1,000. Indoor and patio seating. Hours: about 12pm–11pm. Location: Between the American and French embassies, just off the Avenue Jean-Paul II and across the street from the ORTB building.*

NIGHT LIFE

Cotonou's night life primarily takes place in the **Jonquet neighborhood**, appropriately nicknamed "*Quartier Rouge*" or the Red Light District. The main strip is lined with *buvettes*, Nigerian money vendors, kiosks, and a multitude of prostitutes and gigolos. There are several rather decadent bars in the area which are open all night, including **Playboy**, **Soweto**, and **2001** (*Deux mille-et-un*). All are located off of Rue des Cheminots, in the heart of Jonquet. There is usually no cover charge, and the atmosphere is booming with music and filled with women offering their nightly services. For those tough-skinned travelers in search of the real Beninese nightlife experience, this is the place. Jonquet, however, is dangerous at night with frequent muggings. To avoid any potential incidents yet still catch a glimpse of the action, visit during the day as it is just as busy and entertaining during the light hours.

Nearby ***Quartier Guinkomé*** also provides streetside bars and food stands that come to life in the early evening. **Hotel Accropole** is in this neighborhood, next door to **Le Repaire de Bacchus**. Other restaurants here are **Restaurant L'Amitié** and **Le Laurier**. For the more familiar version of a nightclub with disco balls, mirrors on the walls, and even karaoke, try **Hotel Le Chevalier**, or **Cristal Palace** at **Alex's Hotel**. Admission is about FCFA 3,500. The **Why Not Bar** is a very popular 'basement' club off of Avenue Proche where one can dance all night to European and African beats. The cover is FCFA 4,000, with drinks around the same price.

Ganxi and Avenue Steinmetz

Foley's Jazz Club, off Steinmetz Boulevard, has a comfortable, easy ambiance with live bands most nights and good mixed drinks. **So What! Bar** is a very popular place at the town center, near the Nouveau Pont and not far from Hotel le Crillon. This bar often has live West African music, and drumming lessons can be arranged here. The cover is usually FCFA 3,000–4,000 on Fridays, Saturdays, and nights when a live band is playing. **Titanic Bar** in Ganxi is across the lagoon from Hotel du Lac and provides a pleasant distraction with a great view of the water. There are live bands on Fridays and Saturdays. The **VIP Club** is next door, with a FCFA 7,000 cover charge that includes a drink.

Cadjehoun and Around the Airport

The Marina Hotel's club, **Le Téké**, has complimentary admission for hotel guests and is busiest on weekends or holidays; weeknights here are pretty quiet.

ACCOMMODATIONS

Cotonou offers the widest range of accommodation of any city in Benin, from backpacker hostels to international luxury hotel chains. Most high-end hotels accept Euros and major credit cards; midrange and budget places will probably require you to pay in FCFA.

Although Cotonou is Benin's most developed city, power and water cuts are common. Most hotels keep a plastic bucket of water in each bathroom so you can manually flush the toilet or take a bucket bath if the water's cut. If the bucket isn't full when you arrive, make sure to fill it and keep it filled. High-end hotels have their own generators and water reserves, so they generally aren't affected by cuts.

High-end

Benin Marina Hotel If the Queen of England visited Benin, she would stay here. Part of a multinational chain, this place offers two pools, three tennis courts, a soccer field, a nine-hole golf range, a sauna and massage parlor, landscaped gardens, shops, a business center, restaurants, bars, a casino…you get the idea. They accept Euros and major credit cards. *Single-occupancy FCFA 81,000–88,500, double-occupancy FCFA 93,000–100,500, bungalows FCFA 130,345, suites FCFA 228,595–333,395. A/C, satellite TV, telephone, wifi, minibar, in-room safe, hot water, private bathroom. Meals: FCFA 16,500. Tel: 21.30.01.00. Website: benin-marina-hotel.com. Location: Boulevard de France, west of the city center.*

Hôtel du Port This French hotel is charming and tastefully decorated with traditional and contemporary West African art. The hotel surrounds a courtyard and a 25-meter pool. A bar and restaurant covered by a thatched roof serves European and African cuisine, including wood-oven pizza. The hotel also boasts an underground nightclub that's popular on the weekends. Next door, a lively salsa dance club offers dance lessons and is open to the public in the evenings. *FCFA 46,000–100,000. A/C, satellite TV, telephone, minibar, hot water, private bathroom. Tel: 21.31.44.43. Website: hotelduportresort.com. Location: Boulevard de France, next to the Port of Cotonou.*

Azalaï Hôtel de la Plage Now part of the West African Azalaï hotel chain, Hôtel de la Plage is one of the oldest high-end hotels in Cotonou. The colonial-style architecture, pool, and private beach make for a pleasant experience. The room rate includes breakfast. Non-guests can use the pool for FCFA 1,000. *Standard rooms FCFA 104,500–144,000, suites FCFA 169,000–269,000. A/C, satellite TV, wifi, hot water, private bathroom. Tel: 21.31.72.00. Location: on the beach near the Ganxi Market.*

Novotel Orisha Novotel is a high-end hotel catering to foreigners and well-off Africans. It has 100-plus rooms, a beautiful pool, and a classy French restaurant. Non-guests can use the pool for FCFA 3,000. Major credit cards are accepted. Internet access is available at the hotel business center. *FCFA 90,500–96,000. A/C, satellite TV, telephone, minibar, in-room safe, hot water, private bathroom. Tel: 21.30.41.77. Location: Boulevard de France, west of the city center.*

Midrange

⊗ **Hôtel du Lac** This is a great place to indulge in some luxury without burning through all your money. The hotel offers clean, spacious, and luxurious rooms, as well as a pool, sauna, massage salon, bar, and restaurant. At the restaurant, sit on the terrace overlooking the canal and enjoy excellent European cuisine, including seafood, hamburgers, and pizza cooked in a wood-fired oven. The hotel can arrange tours to Ganvié for FCFA 7,000–9,500 per person, depending on the size of your group. *Standard rooms FCFA 44,000–48,000, suites FCFA 50,000–60,000, extra bed FCFA 10,000. A/C, satellite TV, telephone, in-room internet, in-room safe, hot water, private bathroom. Meals: breakfast FCFA 4,500, lunch and dinner FCFA 5,000–10,000. Tel: 21.33.19.19. Website: hoteldulac-benin.com. Location: along the water on the east side of the canal, near the Ancien Pont. Zemidjans know where it is.*

Alex's Hotel This classy multiple-story hotel also has a hopping nightclub and karaoke bar called Cristal Palace. *Single-occupancy FCFA 45,500, double-occupancy FCFA 52,500, suite FCFA 83.500. A/C, TV, hot water, private bathroom. Tel: 21.31.25.08. Location: Jonquet neighborhood. It's a tall building with a big sign saying "ALEX'S" on top.*

Hôtel Bénin Vickenfel This centrally-located hotel offers small but comfortable rooms, with good-sized bathrooms. For this level of comfort, Vickenfel is one of the best deals in town. *Single-occupancy: FCFA 19,000, double-occupancy FCFA 23,000. A/C, TV, wifi, private bathroom. Tel: 21.31.38.14. Location: on Avenue Steinmetz, near Le Crillon.*

Budget

Guesthouse Cocotiers This recently-opened hostel offers cheap beds in a four-bed dorm as well as private rooms. It's located on a quiet street in the heart of Haie Vive, just steps away from many of the high-end restaurants listed in this book. You can use their wifi for FCFA 1,000 per day, and they offer airport pickup for FCFA 5,000—though, since it's so close to the airport, you might get a better price from one of the taxi drivers waiting at the airport terminal. *Double-occupancy private room with private bath: FCFA 15,500. Double-occupancy private room with shared bath: FCFA 8,500. Bed in four-bed dorm: FCFA 5,500. Contact: you can make a reservation on Hostelworld.com. Location: just off the Piste Amalco, the main road running through Haie Vive.*

CODIAM This budget place is within walking distance of surrounding upscale shops and restaurants in the Haie Vive and Cadjehoun neighborhoods. Rooms and bathrooms are very basic. Avoid the cheaper rooms—they're often mosquito-infested and the hotel doesn't provide mosquito nets. Bonus points if you can get somebody to tell you why CODIAM is always capitalized, whether it is an acronym, and, if so, what it stands for. *FCFA 6,500–8,500 with fan and shared bathroom, FCFA 11,000–12,500 with A/C and private bathroom. Tel: 21.30.37.27. Location: down the street from Camp Guézo, in the direction of Haie Vive. Zemidjans know where it is.*

⊗ **Le Crillon** This is a small and usually clean hostel. Sometimes the sheets are questionable, but the price is right. It's located near the travel agency Evénémenciel and the "Secret Schwarma" restaurant. *FCFA 5,500 with fan, FCFA 10,000 with A/C. Private bathroom. Tel: 21.31.51.58. Location: off of Avenue Steinmetz, across from the restaurant Carnaval des Glaces.*

Ganvié

Ganvié, sometimes known as the Venice of Africa, is a vast fishing community located in the lagoon waters of Lake Nokoué, just north of Cotonou. It was established by the Tofinu people as a way to elude Dahomeyan slave-hunters. Custom forbade the Dahomeyans from fighting battles in or on water, so the Tonifu were safe as long as they stayed on the lake.

> In the Tonifu language, *vié* means "community" and *gan* means "we are saved," hence *Ganvié*.

While slave-hunters are no longer a major concern, this community continues to thrive on the lake. Villagers live in stilt houses, attend stilt churches, send their children to stilt schools, and sell their goods in stilt markets. They get around the village in small dugout canoes. You'll see vendors paddling around, their canoes laden with fish, fruit, and vegetables for sale. You'll also see canoes weighed down with black canisters, which are full of gasoline pirated from Nigerian pipelines. The villagers breed fish within barricades of trees and branches surrounding the village.

> Some guides and tour operators may be able to arrange unofficial tours of Ganvié. See *Tours And Travel Agencies*, p54.

Unfortunately, Ganvié has become a major tourist trap, perhaps the worst in Benin. Visitors often report that the tour feels more like a scam than a cultural experience. If you take a tour through the official office, your guide will be mostly interested in dragging you into souvenir shops—he gets a cut of any purchases you make.

GETTING THERE

Tours begin at the Ganvié tourist office in Abomey-Calavi, a suburb northwest of Cotonou. A bush taxi ride from the Dantokpa taxi station in Cotonou to the tourist office should cost about FCFA 500. A *zemidjan* from central Cotonou should cost FCFA 300–400, while a taxi from the Place de l'Étoile Rouge should cost FCFA 100–200. The tourist office is at a jetty, a short walk from the main road.

If you're staying at a higher-end hotel in Cotonou, your hotel may be able to arrange tours beginning and ending at the hotel. This will cost more than going to the tourist office yourself, but the convenience might be worth it.

THE TOUR

A tour of Ganvié takes about two hours in a motorized boat. It includes a five-kilometer ride to the village, plus stops at souvenir shops and refreshment stands. At least one of the guides can give tours in English. Here are a few tips:

▷ Try to get a covered boat. It beats roasting in the sun.

▷ Try to visit early in the day, also to avoid roasting in the sun.

▷ The locals will ask for money if they see you taking pictures of them. To avoid getting ripped off too badly, have your guide negotiate the price with someone before you take their picture.

If you're looking to buy Beninese crafts and artwork, buy them from one of the artists or at one of the artisan's markets listed in this book. In the shops in Ganvié, you'll probably be paying tourist prices for tourist-quality items. Take any recommendations from your guide with a grain of salt: he gets a percentage of any purchases you make here.

TOUR PRICES

You can take a tour in a motorboat, or in a dugout canoe with a sail or paddles. A guide and a driver will accompany you. While their services are technically included in the tour price, think about tipping them a couple thousand francs. Tour price you can expect to pay:

Size of party: price per person for motorboat / canoe

1 person: FCFA 7,050 / FCFA 6,050

2–4 people: FCFA 5,050 / FCFA 4,050

5–9 people: FCFA 4,050 / FCFA 3,050

10+ people: FCFA 3,050 / FCFA 2,550

Allada

Allada is the site of one of the three kingdoms formed by the descendants of the Adja who migrated to present-day Benin from Tado, Togo. Today, it remains a bustling town along the semi-paved Cotonou–Bohicon highway. One dirt road leads southwest to Ouidah and was the original slave route used by slave-traders from the Kingdom of Allada. A second dirt road leads to the royal palace of the 16th king of Allada, located in the village of Togoudo. The royal palace is open to visitors, and the King's assistants can arrange a tour of the grounds and perhaps a visit to the King. A donation of FCFA 1,000–5,000 is expected. Guides at the palace can also set up a visit of Togoudo's sacred forest, home to several *fétiches* and the site of many Vodoun ceremonies. An impressive Italian-run Catholic cathedral, complete with a decorated bell tower and a private radio station, adorns the hillside just south of Allada. The backdrop to the cathedral's altar features magnificent mosaic tiles from Italy, and majestic frescoes painted by Beninese artists adorn the palatial walls. Many taxi drivers stop in Allada to fill up on gas and buy food. Roadside vendors carry baskets and trays of giant grilled snails and crispy *agouti* legs with hot pepper purée. The region is known for its savory pineapples, especially those from the agriculture technical school at Sékou, just south of Allada.

GETTING THERE

A taxi from the Place de l'Étoile Rouge in Cotonou should cost around FCFA 800, while a taxi from Abomey should cost around FCFA 2,000. Due to the abysmal condition of the Cotonou–Bohicon road, most bus lines no longer pass by Allada.

Ouidah

Perhaps more than anywhere else in Benin, Ouidah embodies Benin's turbulent history and diverse cultural roots. If you want to discover and understand Benin's history and the impact of this region on Europe and the Americas, you have to come here. It's also one of Benin's cleanest and most pleasant towns, displaying its colonial and Brazilian heritage while providing Western-style accommodations and restaurants. You'll want to take some time off from sightseeing to simply appreciate this unique town.

Ouidah was once a small village called Gléwé within the Kingdom of Xwéda. The villagers subsisted on agriculture, hunting, and fishing in the coastal lagoons. The Europeans first arrived here in the 16th century and began trading slaves with the Kingdom of Xwéda at the end of the 17th century. The powerful Kingdom of Dahomey, based in Abomey to the north, soon recognized the economic value of the slave trade. Dahomey seized control of Ouidah in 1727 and took over trading with the Europeans. The Portuguese, Danish, French, and English all participated in slave-trading here. In 1818, the King of Dahomey installed the Brazilian Francisco Felix de Souza, known locally as Chacha, as the manager of the slave trade in Ouidah.

Ouidah is also the Vodoun capital of Benin, if not the world. It hosts important ceremonies, with the grandest festivities taking place on January 10, the national celebration of traditional religions. The city offers a wealth of

Bruce Chatwin's *The Viceroy of Ouidah* (1980), set in Ouidah, is a fictional account of the life of Francisco Felix de Souza and the slave trade with Brazil.

tourist attractions, including fortresses built by the early Europeans, the slave route leading to the Gate of No Return, Vodoun temples, and a selection of hotels along the palm-lined beaches. Knowledgeable guides at the historic Portuguese Fort can take you on a city-wide circuit to explain the history and legends behind each monument and landmark.

GETTING THERE

A taxi from the Place de l'Étoile Rouge in Cotonou costs FCFA 1,000. To catch a taxi back to Cotonou, the best place to wait is the side of the road near the restaurant Hank Pete.

BANK

Ecobank has the only ATM in town. It's located in the center of town, near Hôtel Kpassè.

SIGHTS AND ACTIVITIES

Le Musée d'Histoire de Ouidah – Fort Portugais
Ouidah History Museum – Portuguese Fort

The Portuguese fort, built by Joseph de Torres in 1721, originally served as a missionary and slave-trading base. The Portuguese retained control of the fort during the French colonization of the country. In 1961, the government of the newly-independent Republic of Dahomey annexed the fort and expelled the Portuguese. Although the Portuguese burned the fort before leaving, many of their maps, illustrations, and antique objects were recovered during the fort's reconstruction in the mid-1960s. Today, recognized by its surrounding white walls, the Portuguese Fort–turned–History Museum covers one hectare and contains the Portuguese representative's residence, a chapel, and military barracks. Most of the permanent collection is arranged by themes in the residence, covering the history of the fort, the Kingdom of Xwéda, the Kingdom of Dahomey, the slave trade, Vodoun, and the cultural links between Benin and the regions of the Americas where slaves were shipped. The chapel houses temporary exhibits, and the museum has a boutique as well as a little craftsmen's village for souvenir shopping. *Hours: Mon–Fri 8am–12pm and 3pm–6pm; Saturdays, Sundays, and holidays 9am–6pm. Entry fee: FCFA 1,000 for foreigners, FCFA 500 for Beninese nationals. Entry fee includes a guided tour, and some guides speak English. Tel: 22.34.10.21. Website: museeouidah.org. Location: Rue du Général Dodd, east of the marketplace.*

La Route des Esclaves
The Slave Road

The four-kilometer sandy track leading from Ouidah to the beach was the route taken by captives boarding ships bound for the Americas. A trip down the slave road is a sad but important reminder of the price millions of Africans paid for the growth and prosperity of Europe and the Americas.

The road begins at the **Slave Auction**, also called **Place Chacha**, located in front

---

Festival de Films – Ouidah Film Festival

This film festival is usually held in January, linking the sister-cities of Ouidah and Melun, France. The festival is meant to promote new, original, and pertinent films on multicultural dialogue. Films in the festival comprise long works, such as movies or television shows, and shorter works of fiction, as wells as documentaries.

Jean Odoutan, who initiated this festival, also founded the Institut Cinematographique de Ouidah (ICO), the Cinematographic Institute of Ouidah, which is the first free African school of image, sound, and animated film. For more information on the festival, see www.festival-ouidah.org.

of Francisco Felix de Souza's residence. Here, European merchants selected slaves, chained them, and marched them down the road to the **Arbre de l'Oublie**, the Tree of Forgetting. Here, they branded the slaves according to the mark of their purchaser and forced them to walk around the tree to symbolically forget their homes and families. Men were made to circle the tree nine times, and the women seven. Today, the tree has been replaced by a statue of the vodoun goddess Mamiwata.

The next stop on the route is the **Arbre du Retour**, the Tree of Return, planted by Dahomeyan King Agadja. Slaves circled the tree three times to ensure that their souls would return to their homeland after death. Before continuing to the ships, the slaves were kept for days or weeks in the tight quarters and darkness of the **Zomaï Cabin**, whose name means "where the light does not go." Many died there and were buried in a mass grave, today marked by the six-meter-high **Mur de Lamentations**, the Wailing Wall.

From here, the slaves finished their trek to the beach, where they were loaded into longboats and piled inside the ships. This final stage is marked by an arched gateway covered in murals erected by UNESCO and known as the **La Porte du Non Retour**, the Gate of No Return. Two statues of Vodoun Revenants, representing the spirits of the dead, await the return of the dead slaves' souls to their homeland. In 2003, **La Porte du Retour**, the Gate of Return, was built further west on the beach in honor of the returned descendants of slaves. A museum there displays photographs and posters about the slave trade and the Diaspora. The entry fee is FCFA 1,000.

Le Temple des Pythons
The Python Temple

As proof of the peaceful coexistence of religions in Benin, and also as a reminder of the struggle between natives and the early missionaries, the Python Temple sits directly across from Ouidah's Catholic cathedral. The priests of the serpent deity Dangbé oversee the temple, which is shaded by towering sacred trees inundated with

---

Twins

For the Beninese, the birth of twins is an extraordinary sign of blessing. Twins are believed to share a powerful bond that must be both celebrated and respected. Twins are always welcomed, no matter what the family's financial situation might be. There's a coconut tree grove along the Route des Esclaves in Ouidah where families with twins celebrate their good fortune. An annual celebration is held there on the first Sunday in October.

In Benin, both twins must always be treated with absolute equality. If one of the twins dies as a child, the surviving twin is informed that the other has gone to search for wood. From that point on, this twin will carry a doll representing his or her lost sibling. The doll is given gifts and food in keeping with the custom that the twins are to be treated equally. If both twins should die, the mother carries two dolls with her. She hides the dolls in her pocket or within the wraps of her wraparound skirt. Beninese tradition also demands that a mother with twins must have another child, to close the "gap" formed by the double birth.

fruit bats. In commemoration of this venerated reptile, the temple houses dozens of languid pythons inside a dark circular room. Visitors can enter the room and stand among the pythons; the more daring can have a snake draped around their necks for a photo. *Hours: 9am–6pm. Open daily. Entry fee: FCFA 1,000. Location: across from the cathedral.*

Musée de la Fondation Zinzou
Zinzou Foundation Museum

Opened in November 2013, the Zinzou Museum is the first and only museum of contemporary African art that's actually located in sub-Saharan Africa (outside of South Africa). Displaying paintings, sculptures, and mixed-media works by artists from all over the continent, the museum is the latest endeavor by the Zinzou Foundation, which has promoted popular appreciation of contemporary Beninese art for several years through its headquarters in Cotonou. The museum is located inside the newly-restored Villa Ajavon, a mansion built in 1922 by a wealthy merchant from Togo. Its distinctive Afro-Brazilian architecture recalls Ouidah's diverse history and makes the villa an impressive work of art in its own right. The museum maintains a team of French- and English-speaking guides who can show you around. Budget about an hour to see the exhibitions. Admission to the museum, and to all Zinzou Foundation venues and events, is free of charge. *Hours: Wed–Sun 10am–7pm; Tuesdays 3–7pm. Closed Mondays. Free admission Tel: 21.30.99.25 / 21.30.99.26. Website: fondationzinzou.org (currently in French only). Location: in the Villa Ajavon, a sand-colored two-story building northeast of the Basilica.*

Célébration des Religions Traditionelles
Celebration of Traditional Religions

January 10 is a national holiday dedicated to traditional religions in Benin. Since Ouidah is Benin's Vodoun capital, the festivities are most pronounced here. You'll find related ceremonies and rituals around Ouidah during the weeks between Christmas and mid-January. While Vodoun is practiced in Ouidah year-round, this timeframe offers the most opportunity for visitors to witness authentic Vodoun rituals. To see the most interesting traditions, avoid the official political ceremonies and seek out less-publicized ceremonies.

Other than an increase in drunk driving, the period around January 10 poses no particular security risks to foreigners. But, as always, stay alert in large crowds and ask permission before taking pictures.

La Maison du Brésil
The Brazil House

The former residence of the Brazilian Governor, this beautifully restored house showcases temporary art exhibits of Vodoun culture and the African diaspora. *Hours: 8am–7pm. Open daily. Entry fee: FCFA 1,000. Location: Avenue de la France, on the west side of town.*

La Forêt Sacrée de Kpassè
The Sacred Forest of Kpassè

The sacred forest displays sculptures and woodcarvings that illustrate the history of the territory. The forest was named after King Kpassè of the Xwéda Kingdom, who is said to have fled from his Dahomeyan enemies and turned himself into an Iroko tree that still stands there today. *Hours: 9am–7pm. Open daily. Entry fee: FCFA 1,000. Location: about one kilometer from the town center. Zemidjans and drivers know it by name.*

La Route des Pêches
The Fishermen's Road

La Route des Pêches is a sandy road leading from western Cotonou to Grand Popo, passing by Ouidah. If you have a private car, the road is a scenic seaside drive, and it provides opportunities to watch local fishermen at work. Remember to ask the fishermen before taking pictures of them.

EATING AND DRINKING

⊗ **Attiéké de Sonia** Attiéké is a cassava-based couscous dish from Côte d'Ivoire, served with beans, fish, plantains, beans, and pasta. You can include or omit as many of the sides as you like, but this is a great place to stop for a filling and cheap lunch. FCFA 300–400 is a good portion to start with, and you can always order more if you're still hungry. *Meals: FCFA 200 and up. Drinks: FCFA 500. Hours: 9am–6pm. Open daily. Location: across from the Poissonnerie Sol des Anges on the main road.*

⊗ **Hank Pete** If you like pork, this is the place to go. The meat is grilled and served with lots of onions and hot peppers as well as a delicious sauce. You can choose to add *piron* as well. The cost varies depending on how much meat you buy, but a good portion is FCFA 600 of meat and FCFA 100 of *piron*. *Meals: FCFA 600 and up. Drinks: FCFA 300–1,000. Hours: 8am–7pm. Closed Mondays. Location: off the main highway, near the unofficial taxi stop.*

Restaurant L'Amicale With its bright red and yellow walls, this friendly restaurant is hard to miss. They serve schwarma, salad, attiéké (a kind of couscous from Côte d'Ivoire), hamburgers, sandwiches and pizza. They also have plenty of cold drinks, yogurt, and pastries if you would rather snack. You can choose to sit inside with the fans or outside under their shady umbrellas. *Meals: FCFA 1,000–2,500. Drinks: FCFA 500–1,000. Hours: 10am–11pm. Open daily. Indoor or cover patio seating. Location: next to the Catholic Church.*

La Détente Renovée This food stand serves typical Beninese street food. You can choose between pâte or rice with a tomato sauce, but the thing to try here is the spicy vegetable sauce full of cooked leafy greens. Accompaniments include fish, eggs, local cheese, or balls of melon seeds that are known as "sesame." *Meals: FCFA 300-2,000. Drinks: FCFA 300-500. Hours: 9am-10pm. Closed Tuesdays. Location: across the street from Hôtel Kpassè.*

Restaurant Escale des Arts Stop here for a local meal or cold drink while traveling the Slave Road. They serve decent rice and pâte dishes along with the usual accompaniments of fish, chicken, eggs, or beef. You may also find handicrafts for sale here, including jewelry, Batiks, and wooden sculptures. *Meals: FCFA 2,000–3,000. Drinks: FCFA 300–900. Hours: 11am–10pm. Open daily. Location: Inside the Village Artisanal de Ouidah, along the Slave Road.*

ACCOMMODATIONS

⊗ **Casa del Papa** This hotel is as club-med as it gets in Benin. It's a great place to unwind and be pampered after a back-country trip through Benin. The restaurant serves quality international and local cuisine. It's best to have a personal vehicle if you're staying at this hotel, since zemidjans don't come this far and you'd have to walk a few kilometers down the sandy road to get back to town. A hired zem from Ouidah's town center costs about FCFA 1,000. If driving a rented vehicle, be aware that the road between the Gate of No Return and Casa del Papa is sandy and vehicles commonly get stuck in sand pits. Chauffeur lodging is provided at the hotel for FCFA 10,000 per night, including meals at the chauffeur cafeteria. *FCFA 35,000-68,000. Bungalow, oceanfront or lagoon-side rooms, A/C, complementary continental breakfast, three pools, private beach, tennis courts. Tel: 95.95.39.04 / 95.95.09.11. Website: casadelpapa.bj. Location: on the Route des Pêches, seven kilometers from the Gate of No Return.*

⊗ **Le Jardin Secret** In 2008 Pascal came to Ouidah from France on his motorcycle, crossing the Sahara on two wheels. He then set up this charming six-room inn in Ouidah, where he welcomes guests and also serves up a delicious three-course meal at his restaurant. You can rent bikes here—a convenient way to get around town. *FCFA 10,500-13,500. Meals: breakfast FCFA 1,200-2,000, à la carte FCFA 2,500, full meal FCFA 3,500. Fan and private bathroom. Tel: 96.66.90.14. Email: jardinsecretouidah@gmail.com. Website: lejardinsecretouidah.net. Location: behind Radio Kpassé, near the Ouidah History Museum.*

Hôtel DK While this German hotel rests within a large and modern complex with a swimming pool, it's a bit far from town and sits directly on the highway, making noise a problem. *FCFA 15,500–25,500. A/C, hot water, and satellite TV. Tel: 97.72.38.30 / 90.91.62.43 / 21.05.34.36. Location: on the Cotonou–Togo highway.*

Le Jardin Brésilien / Auberge de la Diaspora The rooms at the Jardin Brésilien are set in attractive thatched bungalows. A restaurant serves international and local cuisine. The private beach with palm trees makes a beautiful and peaceful setting, and it is a cheaper alternative to the less accessible Casa del Papa for those without a private vehicle. *FCFA 10,500–25,500. Fan or A/C, private bathroom. Tel: 21.10.12.26 / 97.20.03.09. Location: on the beach near the Gate of No Return.*

Hôtel Kpassè This is the most central hotel in Ouidah, and the most conveniently placed for travelers without a vehicle. The manager is also the chef, and can provide good meals with advance notice. There's a lively bar on the ground floor. *FCFA 9,500–20,500. Single or double occupancy, Fan or A/C. Tel: 21.34.10.91. Email: ouidahoasis@yahoo.com. Location: about 300 meters west of the Portuguese Fort, toward the Python Temple.*

Mono & Couffo

This region stretches north along the Mono River, which forms the border with Togo. It's mostly populated by the Adja, Mina, Fon, Kotafon, and Watchi peoples. The Mono *département* was one of the first areas in present-day Benin to have significant contact with French colonists, and you may see churches and schools dating back to the first missions in the 1880s.

As in much of Benin, the landscape here has mostly lost its native vegetation. The gallery forests along the Mono River give you an idea of the woods that used to cover this area; today, it's mostly covered by cultivated fields, savanna grasses, and secondary-growth forests. Farther north, in the Couffo *département*, you'll find gentle hills and distinct red earth. Here, cotton is the main cash crop, while people sustain themselves by growing corn, cassava, and beans.

The whole region is often referred to as "Adja," after one of the main ethnic groups here.

Mono & Couffou
Regional Map

5 miles
10 km
N

Azovè
Aplahoué
Dogbo
Doukounta
Lokossa
Bopa
Sé
Athièmè
Tokpa Domè
Possotomè
Lake Ahèmè
TOGO
Comè
Sebbôhoué
To Cotonou (60km)
Grand Popo

Grand Popo

Grand Popo is perhaps Benin's most popular beach town. It was once a major slave-trading hub and remained an important port into the 19th century, until the French sent it into decline by building a deep-water port in Cotonou. You can still see some of the colonial ruins, though much of the old town has fallen into the sea.

Today Grand Popo is a small, tranquil village. Its population of about 2,000, mostly of the Mina ethnicity, is spread widely along the beach. They make a living through farming, tourism, and selling goods along the Cotonou-Lomé highway. Grand Popo is the second-largest onion producer in Benin, after the northeastern town of Malanville. Surprisingly, the village's many fishermen are mostly not locals, but rather Ghanaian immigrants. You can watch them hauling in enormous nets full of fish on the beach.

For a visitor, Grand Popo's quiet, palm-lined beaches and numerous low-key beachside resorts make it an ideal place to unwind. However, the locals have got tourists figured out: standard items like street food and beer will cost more here, and you'll likely have to pay if you take a picture of anybody.

GETTING THERE AND AWAY

From the Place de l'Étoile Rouge in Cotonou, a taxi to Grand Popo should cost FCFA 3,000–3,500. You can ask your taxi driver to drop you off at your hotel, or take a zemidjan there once you reach Grand Popo.

SIGHTS AND ACTIVITIES

Grand Popo is a great place for a peaceful day lounging at the beach. While exploring the town, be sure to catch a soccer or basketball game at the local school or public stadium. Head over to the main drag to shop for souvenirs in the various handicraft cabins, especially **Aux Beaux Arts** near the Auberge and Farafina Boutique. The calabash lamps at Aux Beaux Arts are particularly interesting. The Grand Popo market is located at the base of the bridge crossing the Mono River, but it is fairly small since it is so close to the larger market of Comé. The **Villa Karo** is a Finnish-African cultural center which provides film nights, concerts, dance and language lessons, a museum, and a library.

For some insight into local life, go down to the beach before sunset to watch the fishermen pulling in the day's catch. Be aware that if you start taking pictures, they may ask for money. Avoid a confrontation by asking them beforehand if you can take pictures and negotiating the price.

While the sea off Grand Popo's beaches may appear calm, it hides powerful undercurrents and rip tides that can overcome the strongest swimmer. Local fishermen regularly drown in the currents, which may run very close to shore. It's best to avoid swimming in the ocean altogether.

Fishing Villages on the Coast

A series of coastal fishing villages sheltered by tall coconut trees stretch along the beach to the Togo border. The beachfront here is practically deserted during the day, and the waves are quite intense. An hour before sunset the fishermen return from the day's work, fighting the waves to reach the shore. Sometimes their canoes overturn, and children waiting on the beach chase after fallen items like nets, buckets, and other lost gear. Once they reach the shore, everyone helps pick the fish out of the nets, pull the canoes onto the beach, and roll up the nets. Women from the market, or those just buying for the evening's meal, await the fishermen to barter for fresh fish.

La Bouche du Roi

A tour of the older, colonial-era part of Grand Popo and a boat trip to *La Bouche du Roi*, the King's Mouth—the local name for the mouth of the Mono river—can both easily be organized through the **Auberge de Grand Popo** (p113). The tour of the old town goes through several small villages and beautiful mangroves along the river. On the river tour, pay attention to the tremendous currents, especially when swimming. For a tour, you should pay FCFA 2,500–5,000 per person.

Nonvitcha

Grand Popo is the place to be for Pentecost, known as *Nonvitcha* in Mina, which takes place 50 days after Easter. Hundreds to thousands of visitors attend the weekend-long party and celebrate throughout the village. There are parties all Saturday night, with a Catholic mass befitting the size of the party. After mass, the celebrants and everyone else find a corner of the beach to have a picnic lunch—the beach is packed and it's a great time.

Across the Border

Grand Popo rests on a small tongue of land sticking into Togo; the Mono River here runs parallel to the coast before emptying into the ocean on the east side of the village. You can cross into Togo via a ferry to reach Agbannakin, a small village with colonial ruins and calm *buvettes*. This is reportedly the site of the Mina people's last stand against the Fon in the time of the slave trade. The name *Agbannakin* is a shortened version of the true name of the town, a phrase representing how difficult it was to conquer the Mina: "one cannot make *pâte* in a calabash."

Togo Border Crossing

The official Togo border crossing, about 30 kilometers west of Grand Popo, is popular for its 'tax-free' zone with many products such as music CDs for FCFA 500, yovo vegetables, meat, bread, and other treats. Togolese taxis to Lomé cost about FCFA 2,000 from this point. Before entering Togo via the official border crossing, you must obtain a Togolese tourist visa from the Togolese consulate in your country or in Cotonou.

EATING AND DRINKING

Auberge de Grand Popo The hotel restaurant serves high-end European cuisine with local influence. They serve cocktails as well as the usual beer and soda. *Meals: à la carte FCFA 4,500–5,500, three-course meal FCFA 8,500. Drinks: FCFA 600–1,500, cocktails up to FCFA 4,000. Location: on the beach east of the village center.*

Awalé Plage Like the Auberge, this hotel's restaurant serves high-end European dishes with local influence. *Meals: à la carte FCFA 4,500–5,500, three-course meal FCFA 10,500. Drinks: FCFA 600–1,500. Location: near the main intersection, on the road to Togo and just past the gendarmerie.*

Bar Restaurant Bel Ibis This place serves spaghetti and omelets, making it an ideal stop for those tired of *pâte*. *Meals: FCFA 600–1,000. Drinks: FCFA 250–1,200. Hours: 9am–10pm. Open daily. Location: right at the intersection of the brick road and highway, next to the zemidjan station.*

Blue Moon This chic restaurant provides upscale service and excellent European cuisine. *Meals: FCFA 3,000–7,000. Drinks: FCFA 600–1,500. Hours: 12pm–10pm. Open daily. Location: on the road towards Togo, before Awalé Plage.*

Sous les Nimes (Under the Neem Trees) This reputable buvette is ideally located, with an outdoor dining area under the shade that is degrees cooler and perfect for lunching. Try the fresh grilled fish with a side of rice and sauce. *Meals: FCFA 500 and up. Drinks: FCFA 250–1,200. Hours: 11am–10pm. Open daily. Location: beneath a stand of Neem trees between the brick road and the highway.*

Sea Turtles

From July to March, sea turtles come to the beach side near the Bouche du Roi. A local environmental organization collects the eggs each season. On January 9th, they release the baby sea turtles at the beach. Visitors in the region at this time have a great opportunity to see conservation at work in Benin.

ACCOMMODATIONS

Lion Bar If you're looking for a cheap beachside Bob Marley–themed inn run by a bunch of Rasta dudes, we've got some good news for you. Despite the low price, this place is friendly and reasonably comfortable. They offer parasols and beach mats for lounging in the sand, and you can get soda, beer, and cocktails at the bar. If you order in advance, they can prepare food for FCFA 1,500–2,500. They also have a chauffeured vehicle—painted red, green, and yellow, naturally—that you can rent for tours in the region. *Single or double room FCFA 5,000, triple FCFA 7,000, camping FCFA 2,500. Fan, shared shower and toilet. Tel: 95.42.05.17. Location: about 50 feet off the brick road. Look for the red, green, and yellow sign.*

Auberge de Grand Popo This beachfront guest house is set far back from the paved road and has a calm atmosphere. The colonial-style Auberge has a restaurant overlooking the ocean, a swimming pool, and lounge chairs both on the beach front and poolside. Rooms are located either in the main building or in private bungalows. They're clean but a little cramped. The restaurant serves excellent French cuisine with local influence. The staff can help organize various tours and can also arrange private drum lessons. The Auberge is French-owned and is the first of a chain of hotels located in major towns across Benin. *Single occupancy: FCFA 16,000–23,500. Double occupancy: FCFA 18,500–27,500. A/C and private bathroom. Meals: continental breakfast FCFA 2,000; full breakfast FCFA 3,800; three-course meal FCFA 8,500. Drinks: FCFA 600–1,500. Tel: 22.43.00.47 / 64.16.64.36. Location: on the beach east of the village center.*

Awalé Plage This guesthouse rests in the middle of a tropical garden, with a private beach and swimming pool equipped with lounge chairs. You can stay in a room or in a private bungalow. The open-air restaurant serves high-end European cuisine. *Room with fan: FCFA 20,500–25,500. Bungalow with A/C: FCFA 25,500–30,500. Deluxe bungalow with A/C: FCFA 50,500–60,500. TV, private bathroom. Meals: breakfast FCFA 2,000–3,500, lunch and dinner FCFA 4,500–10,500. Tel: 95.50.29.15 / 97.48.00.12 / 95.86.78.29 / 97.48.00.17. Email: awaleplage@yahoo.fr. Website: hotel-benin-awaleplage.com. Location: near the main intersection, on the road to Togo and just past the gendarmerie.*

Hôtel Bel Azur This German-owned hotel opened in 2005. It offers a swimming pool and a private beach equipped with lounge chairs and parasols. Rooms are spacious and have balconies with views of the sea. The restaurant serves European and Beninese dishes. Located out of town, toward Togo, this hotel is designed more for those with personal vehicles or a hired taxi. Though it has a business-style atmosphere, there's a great nightclub that's hopping on holidays and decent on an average Saturday night. *FCFA 15,000 with fan, FCFA 25,000–38,000 with A/C, FCFA 80,000 for suite. TV, private bathroom. Nightclub cover: FCFA 3,000. Location: on the far west end of town, on the highway toward Lomé.*

Comé

The predominantly Mina town of Comé is a significant commercial hub with a bustling market. It's an important transport junction for the southwest of Benin, and taxis will usually stop here before continuing either west toward Togo or north to Lokossa. From Cotonou, a taxi should cost around FCFA 800; from Lokossa, FCFA 600–700; and from Grand Popo, FCFA 500. Comé is most notable for its *ablo*-vendors, who chase relentlessly after slowing vehicles with their baskets full of food. These women often have children strapped to their backs and a load of *ablo* (steam-baked corn bread), fish, and fried snails balanced on their heads as they race to be the first to sell. Cafeterias and food stands also line the road, making for a convenient lunch stop.

Sé

The village of Sé is the next stop after Comé, for FCFA 200–300 more in a taxi from Cotonou, and is notable for its pottery market. Visible from the highway at the southern edge of town, many roadside stands display clay pots of various sizes. You'll find vases for holding a day's worth of water, tea mugs, ashtrays, and many other objects. For a cold drink or a local meal, stop at the **Pole Nord**, a two-story open-air *buvette* on the northern edge of town.

Possotomé and Lake Ahémé

Possotomé will be a familiar name once you arrive in Benin: it's the name of a ubiquitous brand of bottled water sold throughout the country. It's also the name of the lakeside town where the water is bottled. This lakeside fishing community has become a popular destination for visitors seeking the beauty and ecological diversity of Lake Ahémé.

GETTING THERE

The best way to get to Possotomé is to first take a taxi to Comé. (Taxis for Comé depart from the Place de l'Étoile Rouge in Cotonou.) From there, take the asphalt road that goes directly to the lakeside village. A zemidjan ride should FCFA 500–1,000, depending on how much luggage you have. Renting a whole taxi from Comé to Possotomé costs about FCFA 5,000. The ride is very pleasant, with passing scenery of lush green groves and small villages.

SIGHTS AND ACTIVITIES

Ecobenin Tours

Ecobenin is a non-governmental eco-tourism organization based in Abomey-Calavi that arranges tours at popular eco-tourist sites across the country, including the wildlife parks in the north. Their regional office in Possotomé is very active and coordinates numerous activities, from biking through lakeside villages and participating in community festivities, to exploring the local sacred forests and viewing the monkeys and bird life that inhabit them, to visiting Possotomé's many artisans and learning about their crafts. Ecobenin also runs a small guesthouse and can provide local meals (see *Accommodations* below). *Price: FCFA 3,500–5,000 per tour. Tel: 67.19.58.37. Website: ecobenin.org. Office location in Possotomé: at the Gîte de Possotomé, about 150 meters from the water-bottling plant.*

Other Tours

Some local fishermen also offer tours in their dugout canoes. You can arrange a tour through the **Palais des Jeunes**, **Chez Théo**, or the **Hôtel Village Club Ahémé** (see "Accommodations," below). You may also be able to go fishing, but recent overfishing of the lake means that you might not catch anything.

EATING AND DRINKING

The hotels listed below house the only formal restaurants in town. However, you can find street food and *buvettes* around town. The local specialty is smoked prawns and fried bush rat, served with *eba*, which is *gari* cooked in palm oil.

ACCOMMODATION

Gîte de Possotomé This is the local headquarters of Ecobenin (see above). They offer basic accommodations, and can provide local meals with advance notice. *Single-occupancy FCFA 4,500–9,000, double-occupancy FCFA 7,000–12,500. Private or shared bathroom. Tel: 67.19.58.37. Location: about 150 meters from the water-bottling plant.*

Hotel Village Club Ahémé This hotel has 46 rooms of different categories surrounded by a lush garden full of birds. There is a high-end restaurant and bar, a swimming pool, and internet access for hotel guests. Lake tours can be organized by the staff. *FCFA 12,500–22,500. A/C, private bathroom. Email: villageaheme@yahoo.fr. Location: on the lakeshore.*

Chez Théo This hotel is a wonderful retreat with a clean and calm courtyard of flowers, trees, and a garden kitchen. At the restaurant, you eat on a vast and beautifully constructed covered wooden deck over the water. *FCFA 10,000–18,000. Fan or A/C, private bathroom. Location: on the lakeshore, northeast of Hotel Village Club Ahémé.*

Mono & Couffo

Palais des Jeunes This is the cheapest inn in Possotomé, offering clean, basic rooms set around an open courtyard. The restaurant makes food to order. The staff is friendly and helpful in coordinating lake tours and providing information on the local markets. *FCFA 5,000. Private bathroom. Meals: about FCFA 1,000. Email: palais-desjeunes@yahoo.fr. Location: just beyond the village center and close to the lake.*

Lokossa

Lokossa is an important regional market town and the capital of the Mono region. It was originally called *Irokosa*, meaning "under the Iroko tree" in the Kotafon language. Dominated by the Kotafon ethnicity, the *commune* of Lokossa has a population of about 70,000, with about 40,000 people residing in the town itself.

GETTING THERE

Here's what you should pay for a taxi between Lokossa and the following destinations:

Place de l'Étoile Rouge, Cotonou: FCFA 2,000–2,500

Comé: FCFA 1,000–1,500

Athiémé (by zemidjan): FCFA 500

Dogbo: FCFA 600–1,000

Doukounta: FCFA 1,000

COMMUNICATIONS

There are a number of internet cafés in Lokossa. They're constantly moving or closing, with new ones often popping up. A few recommended internet cafés are La Madeleine Hotel, the Ciel Ouvert (across from the market), and the Centre Songhaï (behind the Maison du Peuple). Western Union services are available at the Ecobank in Lokossa.

SIGHTS AND ACTIVITIES

If seeking to experience life in a typical bustling Beninese town, then there are some key areas to see in Lokossa. Tour the market area and eat some of the fried snack foods sold throughout. Baobab juice, lemonade, and other chilled juices are sold out of calabashes by the market. Saturday and Sunday mornings, especially after church service, the women and children tend to gather in the city center wearing their best outfits. A small market profits from this informal congregation as the women purchase items for dinner while they socialize.

The cathedral, the largest Catholic church in the region, decorated beautifully with floor-to-ceiling art behind the altar, is worth a visit. This church was consecrated in 2005, and since has served the Catholic population of Lokossa every Sunday, and the Mono-Couffo regional population on holidays with visits by high-ranking church officials. The courtyard wall is lined with statues of the Stations of the Cross. There is an affiliated book store next door that sells religious artifacts and school books.

Doukounta – Hippopotami in Lake Doukon

Visit the small fishing village of Doukounta, found about five miles northwest of Lokossa, and take a boat tour of Lake Doukon. Guided by local fishermen, you can observe a hippopotamus family that lives in this small lake. It's best to visit just after sunrise or just before sunset. After the lake visit, continue to the village for a ceremonial shot of *sodabi* and interact with the villagers. The guided tour costs FCFA 2,000, which you should pay at the end of your visit.

The Hippos of Doukounta 👣INSIGHT

The small Lake Doukon is filled by periodic flood water from the Mono River. During one of these floods several years ago, a very small hippopotamus population secluded themselves in the lake: two females and a male. One day, a pregnant hippopotamus was crossing the road in search of food. At the same time, a woman with her baby strapped on her back was walking along the road. A large truck rushed past the hippo and spooked the animal into a stampede, ultimately trampling the woman and her baby. Outraged, the community killed the pregnant hippopotamus. Years later, when the community had recovered from the accident, a Peace Corps Volunteer and a local non-governmental organization initiated an eco-tourism project on the lake. Tourists came to observe the hippos, guided by the local fisherman who understand the hippos' behavior. At the beginning of 2008, the remaining female hippopotamus gave birth. The male died of natural causes later in the same year, leaving a protective mother and her playful hippo-puppy as the main attraction for the profitable eco-tour activity in an otherwise simple fishing village.

To get to Lake Doukon, ask a zemidjan or taxi driver in Lokossa if he can take you to the village of Doukounta to visit Lake Doukon. Your driver will need to wait for you while you take the hippo tour, since there is very little traffic along this dirt road. A full taxi should cost about FCFA 2,000, while a zemidjan should agree to FCFA 500–1,000 for the entire trip. Pay your driver FCFA 1,000 extra for each hour he spends waiting for you.

Kpinnou Bird Lake

Kpinnou is a small village located along the highway in the *commune* of Athiémé. The small lake next to the village creates an ideal bird habitat. You'll find an impressive variety of birds on this lake, including ducks and other water fowl. A great way to get out on the lake is to schedule a tour by contacting the local *Chef d'Arrondissement,* at the *Mairie* (town hall) in Athiémé, or with the manager of the Hunger Project in Kpinnou. Typically, a fisherman offers visitors the front, unused portion of his boat while he checks his nets from the back. Be sure to arrive at daybreak for the tour. Not only is it the best time to see the birds, but this is when fishermen usually check the day's catch. The tour should cost FCFA 500.

If you get a zemidjan from Lokossa rather than Athiémé, you'll have to pay more because of the distance—FCFA 1,000 or more. A taxi from the Lokossa or Athiémé intersection should cost FCFA 200–300. Ask the driver to drop you off at the Kpinnou Hunger Project building, a locally-recognized landmark, and ask there about a tour of the lake.

EATING AND DRINKING

La Cachette This place serves plates of rice or *pâte* and your choice of chicken or *wagasi* cheese. The price is right, the sauce is good, and the drinks are always cold. *Meals: FCFA 500. Drinks: FCFA 300–900. Location: down the dirt road, right before the Belgium Environment Company. You can walk, or take a zemidjan for FCFA 150.*

Café-Bar du Coin This casual eatery serves cold drinks and a nice leaf sauce with tender rabbit or *wagasi*, along with a choice of chicken, goat, or eggs. It's an excellent spot to have a meal and a cold beer, watching the day's business wind down and the evening crowd gather. *Meals: FCFA 1,000–2,000. Drinks: FCFA 250–900. Hours: 11am–10pm. Open daily. Locatoin: at the corner of the central intersection in Lokossa.*

Restaurant Ambiancer Delicious *igname pilée* is sold here under a thatched roof. The dining area is small, but the restaurant's straw structure cools the place nicely. The manager and owner's charisma livens up the place. *Meals: FCFA 700–2,500. Drinks: FCFA 300–800. Hours: 11am–10pm. Open daily. Location: up the street from the Maison du Peuple and across the side street of the fabric factory.*

Supermarché Bel-Air Buvette Enjoy a cold drink are at this open-air buvette, where tables and chairs are set out each evening on the sandy yard. The good music and crowd are a wonderful means of relaxation on clear, warm nights. *Drinks: FCFA 300–800. Hours: 11am–10pm. Open daily. Location: past the cathedral, 50 meters to the left at the paved roundabout.*

Bar Restaurant Les Collines Les Collines, named after the region that's well-known for its *igname pilée*, is one of the cleanest restaurants in Lokossa. Enjoy some of the best *igname pilée* in southern Benin, with comfortable private dining among dividers made of woven palm leaves. Their selection of drinks is sometimes limited. *Meals: FCFA 700–1,700. Drinks: FCFA 300–900. Hours: 11am–11pm. Open daily. Location: past the Supermarché Bel-Air along the dirt road.*

Bar Restaurant Mefils This local spot serves cold drinks and various grilled meats including turkey, chicken, fish, and bush rat. Salads are also available. Everything is prepared by a local woman and her family. The service is usually great, but can be slow on busy nights. *Meals: FCFA 1,000–2,000. Drinks: FCFA 300–800. Hours: 11am–10pm. Open daily. Location: up the dirt road, straight past the supermarket.*

Les Marmites de Grand Frère Catering more for planned parties and events, the staff will need advance warning to provide special dishes, though they do prepare basic plates daily. Grand Frère, the chef and owner, is by far the best cook (for Beninese and Western dishes) in all of Lokossa. *Tel: 93.46.62.72 / 93.66.69.51. Location: about 50 meters down a dirt road directly across from the cathedral.*

FanMilk Depot FanMilk is always good for a cold treat. This place has nearly all flavors available. The manager is a gentleman and provides great service. *Hours: 9am–7pm. Open daily. Location: next to the market.*

Markets

There are two markets in Lokossa: the typical market held every five days and the small *yovo* market where less common goods such as carrots, cabbage, eggplant, lettuce, and, canned vegetables are usually found daily.

For more Western goods, go to **Supermarché Bel-Air**, located behind the cathedral. It sells a range of goods, including yogurt, butter, milk, and a selection of wines and spirits.

ACCOMMODATION

Hôtel La Madeleine La Madeleine is the newest hotel in town, and fairly impressive. There are a number of rooms, some air-conditioned and others with a fan. The restaurant, while expensive, serves decent Western and Beninese dishes. There is an internet café with quality computers connected to the hotel. Satellite televisions in each room offer many French, Ghanaian, and Nigerian channels. This hotel sits right next to the market and along a bustling thoroughfare to neighboring towns and villages. Despite its location, noise is generally not a problem. *FCFA 10,000 and up. Fan or A/C, satellite TV, private bathroom. Location: the far end of the market, headed out of town along a gravel road.*

Hôtel le Baron This hotel is a landmark in Lokossa. It has a swimming pool, which non-guests can use for FCFA 5,000. The restaurant is equal to or better than that of La Madeleine, and a lot cheaper. The food here can be hit or miss, though, depending on the night of the week and the chef. *FCFA 7,000 and up. Fan or A/C, private bathroom. Tel: 22.41.18.80 / 22.41.14.64. Location: well off the highway, on the southern edge of town in the neighborhood known as Chez Pedro. Zemidjans know where it is.*

Athiémé

The charm of Athiémé is in the air of the Mono River and the colonial ruins. Athiémé was the colonial capital of the Mono region beginning in the early 1900s, when it was economically and politically more important than Cotonou or Lokossa. A railroad transported produce, creating commerce and ethnic diversity from Accra, Ghana, through Togo, to Athiémé and Grand Popo in Benin (then Dahomey). The railway lines were removed when the trade collapsed during the Communist era, but the remaining path serves as a road between Athiémé and Grand Popo, linking many villages in between.

The international commerce during the first half of the 1900s induced strong diversity resulting in five different ethnic groups, each with their respective language, within the jurisdiction of the Athiémé commune. The Mina people, also called Guin, are descendants from Ghana and dominate the town, while the Kotafon people tightly surround Athiémé. Six kilometers northwest of Athiémé reside the Watchi, and eight kilometers to the east a form of Adja is heard. Fon, the dominant language in the south, is spoken throughout the region.

Mono & Couffo

Disputed History

Athiémé has a unique history in that its founder is disputed! Ancestry is the root of belonging in Beninese culture, thus varying settlement stories are sensitive topics. According to legend, a man named Adity Donou fled tribal wars between the Fon people in the 1800s and settled an area he named *Adanlokpé*, meaning "Where the Anger Stops." His nephew, Akoubalaty, followed him and settled an area closer to the river, in the Samba trees. "In the Samba trees" translates to *Atihéweme in Mina*, the area now known as Athiémé. The French colonists arrived via the river in the mid 1880s, thus finding Akoubalaty and his settlement first. The disagreement lies in which of the two founders should be credited for the establishment of the town. Today, Adanlokpé is a neighborhood of Athiémé. The residents of any neighborhood are sure to recount some version of this story, depending on where their alliance lies.

GETTING THERE

From the taxi station in Lokossa, a zemidjan ride to Athiémé costs FCFA 500.

From the Place de l'Étoile Rouge in Cotonou, take a taxi toward Lokossa, which drivers often refer to as "Adja." The driver will stop at Zounhoué; the trip should cost FCFA 1,500. A zemidjan will complete the four kilometers on the dirt road to Athiémé for FCFA 300.

SIGHTS AND ACTIVITIES

Visit the river at the west end of town. In Athiémé, the river is a popular site for catching a bit of fresh breeze, doing laundry, or participating in any other river-side activity. A few families live on the Togo side of the river and cross the water regularly for school and business. You can explore the Togo side of Athiémé by taking one of the readily available canoes for a small donation (FCFA 100–200 should suffice).

There is an official river crossing point located past Athiémé and through the neighboring villages of Agniwedji and Lokossavi. Many local merchants traverse the Mono River here to buy goods in Lomé, Togo. The crossing fee is FCFA 100–200. There is a small Togolese town and market farther down the road. Show identification to the border guards and explain the visit. On the return trip, be sure to bring a small gift for the guards since technically a Togo visa is required (see *The Togo Border* on page 122). An Italian development organization has promised to construct a bridge at this river crossing.

Be sure to ask permission to take pictures and say hello to the passers-by, for Athiémé has great personality. Soccer games and political rallies are dear in this town. If either are manifesting, take care to pay attention for at least the entertainment it brings.

Where's the Pâte?

Don't expect to find pâte for sale at lunch or dinner time, as legend forbids that it be sold in Athiémé. Reportedly, Adity Donou asked for pâte one day upon returning from work in his fields. When the vendor asked him to pay for it, Donou was appalled and declared that neither he nor any of his descendants should ever have to pay for pâte in their own town. Akassa and pâte rouge are sold instead.

EATING AND DRINKING

Bar Restaurant Les Delice de la Berge At this casual restaurant, you can chill out on the banks of the Mono River, enjoy the view, and have a cold beer or soda with some local cuisine. They serve rice, akassa, piron, and fish. *Meals: FCFA 500. Drinks: FCFA 250–900. Tel: 95.25.02.16.*

Cafeteria Chez Casi It has been reported that this place has the best spaghetti omelettes in Benin. (Spaghetti omelettes being a Beninese concoction involving an omelette on top of a pile of spaghetti.) They also have beer, soda, and hot or cold instant coffee. *Meals: FCFA 350. Drinks: FCFA 250–900, coffee FCFA 150.*

Azové

Known by locals as *Azovi*, this bustling town is the commercial capital of the Couffo, due to its location along the highway and its junction leading to Abomey. The market is scheduled in coordination with the Lokossa, Klouékanmè, and Dogbo markets. Internet access remains elusive in this town, though hotels, restaurants, and *buvettes* provide plenty of distraction for locals and visitors.

GETTING THERE

The road between Abomey and Azové is not frequently traveled. It's much easier to find transportation from Azové to Abomey, rather than the other way around. Taxis and zemidjans for Abomey await passengers at the northwestern-most intersection in Azové. Vehicles fill rather quickly on market days. The taxis are in poor condition and make vehicles bound for Cotonou appear luxurious—a sign of this region's economic status. The road toward Abomey passes through lengthy spans of unpopulated forests and farm-land, making for a pleasant two-hour ride. There are only a few small villages lining this section of highway, so patience is the virtue-of-all-virtues if your vehicle breaks down.

From the Place de l'Étoile Rouge in Cotonou, a taxi to Azové should cost FCFA 3,000.

SIGHTS AND ACTIVITIES

Azové's main attraction is the vast market in the center of town. Market day takes place every five days and boasts a large textile section, with an endless selection of fabrics on display. From Azové, there are several possible excursions or day trips to discover surrounding villages.

Local Villages

A great way to experience the rural life of the Couffo region is to explore the local villages and towns, which tourists seldom visit. **Djakatomé** is a small town south of Azové with an even smaller heritage museum. Though there are no official guides, in-formal village tours are available with a polite request. **Klouékanmè** is located well off the main highway between Azové and Abomey and has a substantial regional market worth visiting.

The Togo Border

Azové is located near the border with Togo, which is reached via a road leading through the village of **Aplahoué**. As in many border communities in Benin, the locals here cross the border frequently and with a minimal amount of monitoring by the authorities. However, it is illegal for foreign visitors to cross borders without showing a valid visa and getting their passports stamped at an official border crossing, such as the checkpoint west of Grand Popo (p112). While the authorities may not notice or care if you cross the border for a short amount of time, they may also take the opportunity to hassle you. See *Safety And Security* (p71) for information on legal issues for foreigners in Benin.

EATING AND DRINKING

You'll only find local cuisine in Azové. At the various food stands and buvettes lining the streets, you can find *pâte*, beans with *gari*, and a regional specialty called *klouik-loui*—dry, crunchy rings of fried peanut butter, usually eaten with *gari* or corn *bouille*. If you prefer to avoid street-side stands, the restaurant at Hôtel Le Plateau (see below) offers basic meals.

ACCOMMODATION

Hôtel Le Plateau A simple hotel with basic amenities, Le Plateau is located within walking distance of Azové's market. Its in-house restaurant offers basic fare such as fried chicken, rice, and omelettes, though the menu selection on any given day depends on ingredient availability. They also offer coffee and cold drinks. *FCFA 8,500 with fan, FCFA 12,500 with A/C. TV, telephone, private bathroom. Meals: breakfast FCFA 1,500, lunch and dinner FCFA 2,500–3,000. Tel: 22.46.52.26 / 22.46.54.26. Location: on the road toward Aplahoué and the Togo border, northwest of the intersection for Abomey.*

Dogbo

Dogbo is an important commercial town. Oranges are a popular produce in the market, as well as red palm oil, *sodabi*, and beautiful hand-dyed indigo fabrics (ask for the "*tissu bleu de Toviklin*"). The hustle and bustle of the market makes it an exciting place to be, though the traffic has a particularly bad reputation. It has been reported that at least one accident happens every market day.

GETTING THERE

A taxi from Lokossa should cost FCFA 600–1,000. From Azové you should pay around FCFA 400.

SIGHTS AND ACTIVITIES

On a day trip to Dogbo, you can tour the market, followed by a visit to the small village of **Dogbo-Ahomé**, where the King of Dogbo resides. Here, the continuous runoff from an artesian well has created a unique wetlands ecosystem adjacent to a sacred forest. The forest is forbidden to outsiders, but the artesian well, the spectacular flowers, and an opportunity to see the king make the trip worthwhile. A zemidjan ride from the Dogbo market to Dogbo-Ahomé costs about FCFA 200.

Zemidjans at the Dogbo market can also give tours to the neighboring village of **Midangbé.** A former iron smelting site, this village is characterized by large piles of ore deposits and rudimentary smelting tools. There are caves which are said to have been used for sleeping, storage, or for hiding from various slave raids. Some old men in the village have attempted to mine mercury by hand. Not all zemidjans can conduct a proper tour of Midangbè; one way to check is to ask them is they are familiar with the story of *les trous des hommes à queue,* or "the holes of the men with tails."

What's in a Name?
The town name of 'Dogbo' is an onomatopoeia. According to legend, a giant calabash fell from the sky and landed at the top of a hill (near the current mayor's office). As it rolled down the hill, something inside the calabash made the sound dogbodgobdog-bodogbo. At the bottom it cracked open against a large tree, releasing a man and a woman, each with one arm and one leg. The couple worked together to build a home. Hunters who traveled through the region were so well received by the couple that they settled there and eventually built a town.

EATING AND DRINKING

The food stalls in the Dogbo market serve chickpeas in palm oil, a highly recommended local specialty. A plate costs about FCFA100–200. More established *buvettes* and restaurants are located past the market on the paved road toward the high school and mayor's office.

The Holes of the Men with Tails
One day foreigners began selling iron tools at the Dogbo market. Thought to have come from the north or perhaps Ghana, they arrived at the marketplace before everyone else, and they were always the last to leave. Villagers thought this behavior was odd and began to investigate the area of the market where the iron tool sellers set up shop. They discovered holes in the ground and assumed that these strange foreigners must have tails that they hid in the holes while sitting down. To unveil their secret, the story goes that the villagers filled the holes with red palm oil to attract fire ants. As expected, the "men with tails" screamed, jumped up, and ran out of the market.

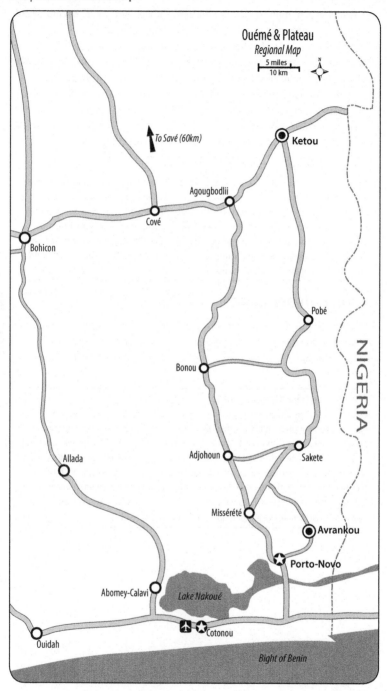

Ouémé & Plateau

Bordering Nigeria, the most populous and economically important country in West Africa, this region is important to international commerce and transport. Its largest city, Porto-Novo, is an historical and political hotbed, and also the capital of Benin. It's dominated by the Gún people.

As you travel from Cotonou to Porto-Novo, you'll cross the Ouémé River, which reportedly feeds the third most fertile valley in Africa. It begins in the Atakora Range, in the far northwest of Benin, and empties into the Atlantic Ocean at Cotonou.

Farther north, in the Plateau *département*, the Yoruba and related ethnicities dominate. This is a mixing bowl for cultures, languages, and traditional religions from Nigeria and from Benin. It's also the area where the Oro fetish (p25) is most strictly observed.

Porto-Novo

Porto-Novo, once called Hogbonou, began as one of the three kingdoms created during the split of the Adja of Abomey. It was a tributary state of the Oyo Kingdom, based in present-day Nigeria, and served as an important trading port for the Portuguese, who gave the town its current name. In 1863, King Toffa I responded to the threat of a British attack by signing a treaty with France that made Porto-Novo a French protectorate.

Today, you can see Porto-Novo's rich cultural heritage throughout the city, from the Portuguese and French colonial architecture to the Afro-Brazilian cuisine brought back by the descendants of slaves who were sent to Brazil. The city's primary ethnic group, the Gún (pronounced "goon"), trace their roots to both the Adja people of medieval Abomey and the Yoruba of the Oyo Kingdom, and their language reflects this diverse heritage. The languages, cultures, and traditional religions of both the Fon and the Yoruba thrive here.

While the Presidential Residence and most government ministries are in Cotonou, Porto-Novo is technically the capital of Benin. Awkwardly, it is also ground zero for opposition to current President Yayi Boni. Adrien Houngbedji, Yayi's main rival in the 2006 and 2011 elections, comes from Porto-Novo, and the city often witnesses spirited political demonstrations. As you walk around the city center, you'll probably see graffiti proclaiming "*À bas Yayi Boni!*"—Down with Yayi Boni!

In the city center, colonial buildings, parks, and villas line the cobblestone roads. It still feels like a city, but without the utter anarchy of Cotonou's streets. The town's museums and historical sites make it worth a visit for anyone looking to explore Benin's history and heritage.

GETTING THERE AND AWAY

Taxis and minibuses regularly leave for Porto-Novo from the taxi station at the Dantokpa Market in Cotonou. Just tell a zemidjan that you want a taxi to Porto-Novo, and he'll take you there. As in the rest of the Dantokpa Market, chaos rules here. As soon as you get off the *zem*, porters will mob you and try to take your baggage to their car. Hold on to your stuff and choose a vehicle that appears to be almost full, so you won't have to wait as long to depart. A minibus should cost FCFA 500–600, while a sedan costs around FCFA 700–800. You can also take a zemidjan from Cotonou to Porto-Novo for about FCFA 2,000, but the long ride can be tiring, especially with a bag on your back.

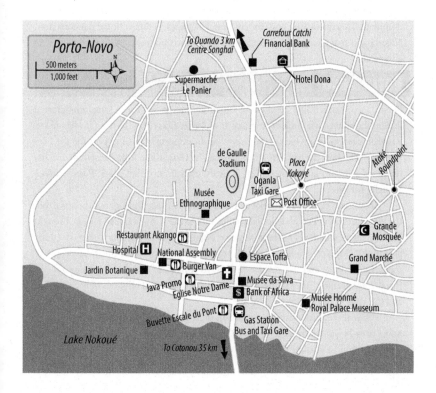

Taxis drop off passengers at various locations in Porto-Novo. The most central place to get off is the main taxi station, just north of the town center. Many taxis coming from Cotonou continue from the station all the way to the Ouando Market (pronounced "wando"), on the outskirts of town. If you accidentally end up in Ouando, just take a zemidjan back to the town center.

Zemidjans here wear blue shirts and, as in Cotonou, they are everywhere. A ride around the town center should cost FCFA 100–200, while rides to outlying areas like Ouando or the Songhaï Center will cost FCFA 200–300.

To get a taxi back to Cotonou, tell a zemidjan that you want a Cotonou taxi and he'll take you to one. Taxis to Kétou and Abomey depart from the Ouando Market and cost around FCFA 1,500.

INTERNET ACCESS

Porto-Novo's best internet café is located in the **Songhaï Center**. You can use one of their computers or bring your own. Numerous other internet cafés around town offer internet access at varying degrees of speed and reliability. At any internet café, access should cost around FCFA 500 per hour, or less if you purchase several hours at a time.

SUPERMARKETS

Porto-Novo's two best supermarkets are **Champion** and **Supermarché Dupont**. Champion, located on the Boulevard Extérieur toward Carrefour Catchi, is the larger of the two. Dupont, affiliated with the Dupont supermarket in Cotonou, is more upscale and located next to the Ecobank by the mosque in Ouando. For something more local, there's a produce market held every four days near the Great Mosque.

SIGHTS AND ACTIVITIES

The city can be divided into four main parts: the old, with its colonial buildings and narrow roads at the town center; the commercial, which contains the **Grand Marché (main market)** and many businesses, and extends toward the lagoon on the southwestern side of town; the administrative, with government offices on the west side; and the new residential districts along the eastern outskirts of town. The **Église Notre Dame**, in front of the Espace Toffa, is a beautiful church established by the first colonists in the late 1880s. The **Jardin Botanique (Botanical Garden)** is also worth a visit with its displays of native plant species, sacred trees, and monkeys. These botanical gardens are located on the west side of town, near the hospital. The entrance fee is FCFA 300, guided tours cost around FCFA 1,000, and the gardens are closed on Mondays.

Centre Songhaï
Songhaï Center

The Songhaï Center's motto is "L'Afrique relève la tête!"—Africa stands up! Founded in 1985 by Father Godfrey Nzamujo and six teenage high-school dropouts, the cen-

> The Songhaï Center's name comes from the medieval Kingdom of Songhaï, which once controlled much of West Africa.

Ouémé & Plateau

ter aims to improve the lives of ordinary Africans through efficient and sustainable agriculture and entrepreneurship. Their activities range widely: experimental farming, pisciculture, beekeeping, and animal husbandry, to name a few. It has expanded from its base in Porto-Novo to four satellite agricultural and training centers throughout the country. Visit the Porto-Novo center to see a thriving organization, founded and run by Beninese, that creatively responds to local needs and goals. You can also buy a range of products from their shop, use their internet café, eat at their excellent restaurant, or stay at their hotel (p131). *Location: on the paved road toward Ouando. Zemidjans know it by name.*

The National Assembly 🐾INSIGHT

As you enter Porto-Novo from the direction of Cotonou, you'll notice a massive concrete structure along the lagoon to your right. This is the new National Assembly building. It will someday replace the current National Assembly building, a colonial-style structure in the city center. It was meant to be completed in time for the 50th anniversary of Benin's independence in 2010, but in 2014 it stands far from finished and astronomically over budget—a monument to the corruption that plagues Benin's government.

YETEN Center

For a rewarding local experience, visit this orphanage in a village near Porto-Novo. You'll get to see a well-run organization that's working for a better future for Benin. A few years ago, two retired teachers founded the orphanage, which houses about 60 orphans and stresses education while giving the kids a safe, orderly, and caring environment. The orphans are known as the smartest and most polite students at the local schools, and in their spare time they help raise crops and animals, which the orphanage sells to pay for the kids' lodging and school fees. You can volunteer at the center—gardening, tutoring the students, helping prepare meals, and so on—and even spend the night in one of their private guest rooms (p132). For more details, see *Development Organizations Active In Benin* (p78). *Contact: the director's name is Jean and you can reach him at 97.54.22.23 or 97.47.14.77. Location: the village of Gbozounme (pronounced BO-zo-may), located just north of Avrankou. A zemidjan from Porto-Novo should cost about FCFA 750.*

Musée Ethnographique de Porto-Novo
Porto-Novo Museum of Ethnography

Established in 1962 and housed in an old colonial building, this museum focuses on the culture of the Yoruba people, who originally come from present-day Nigeria but have heavily influenced central and southeastern Benin, including Porto-Novo. It displays masks, musical instruments, weapons of war, and traditional tools, as well as divination boards and items employed by traditional priests and masks used in the famous Guélédé ceremonies. *Hours: 9am–12pm and 3:30–6pm. Open daily. Entry fee: FCFA 1,000. Location: on the west side of town, next to the Charles de Gaulle Stadium.*

Musée Da Silva des Arts et de la Culture
Da Silva Museum of Art and Culture

A superb example of Afro-Brazilian architecture, this building was built in 1890 as the residence of a family of returned descendants of slaves from Brazil. It houses a collection of miscellaneous remnants from the Da Silva family and other returning Afro-Brazilians, including photographs and old cameras. *Hours: 9am–6pm. Open daily. Entry fee: FCFA 1,000. Location: Rue Toffa, near Bank of Africa.*

Musée Honmè de Porto-Novo
Royal Palace Museum

Set within the royal palace of the former Kingdom of Hogbonou, the museum displays the residence of the kings and tells the story of the kingdom, focusing on the last sovereign king, King Toffa. King Toffa established the first relations with the French before colonization.

The museum showcases the *alounloun* musical instrument, which is used to play *adjogan* music, unique to the Porto-Novo area. This instrument and its music date to the founding of Hogbonou and its first king. Initially used as a symbol of the king's power, the alounloun's evolved into a musical instrument played to honor Porto-Novian royalty, living or deceased. The instrument is made of copper-clad iron and is about a meter long. It's played by sliding metal rings along the instrucment. Today the *alounloun* is still used in royal ceremonies. *Adjogan* music is also played in the Catholic churches in the area, though in this situation the emblem on the instrument is changed from the bird crest to a Christian cross. *Hours: 9am–12pm and 3:30–6pm. Open daily. Entry fee: FCFA 1,000. Tel: 20.21.36.66.*

Église Notre Dame
Church of Our Lady

In the 1880s, French colonists built this impressive church to serve Porto-Novo's Catholic population. Since it's centrally located, just in front of the Espace Toffa, you can't miss it while exploring the town center.

La Grande Mosquée
The Great Mosque

This impressive Afro-Brazilian mosque stands out in the city, with its faded shades of yellows, reds, and blues. With permission from the Mullah and for a small fee, visitors can climb the tower and view the city of Porto-Novo and the Nokoué Lagoon from above. *Location: by the marketplace, on the northeast side of town.*

O.N.G. Vie Pour Tous
"Life for All" Non-Governmental Organization (NGO)

One of the first things a tourist will notice in Benin is the omnipresent black plastic bags littering the gutters, streets, fields, and trees. A small group of women decided to transform these eyesores into works of art. After collecting and washing the discarded bags, the women, using methods of crocheting and knitting, began to create dolls, hats, place mats, purses, and pretty much anything else they could think of to sell.

Ouémé & Plateau

Based on their success, the NGO Vie Pour Tous inspired similar creative businesses in the neighborhood. There is a metal recycling shop where craftsmen transform spark plugs into insect figurines and tin cans into lamps. *Location: near the post office in the Oganla neighborhood.*

Espace Toffa

This large park features a statue of the last sovereign king of Porto-Novo, Toffa I. It's located at the intersection Place de Jean Bayol, named after the first governor of the French colony of Dahomey. There's a botanical garden nearby, created from the remains of the sacred forest of Porto-Novo. Biology students once used the garden to study the rich diversity of this area's indigenous plants. Most of Porto-Novo's markets and museums are within easy walking distance of the Espace Toffa. *Location: at the intersection Place de Jean Bayol, near the entrance of town.*

Le Stade Charles de Gaulle
Charles de Gaulle Stadium

Named after Charles de Gaulle, who, as president of France, granted independence to Benin and to France's other African colonies, this stadium is very popular among Porto-Novians. You might catch a game of basketball, handball, volleyball, or bocce ball, among other sports. Entrance is free and spectators are welcome.

Adjarra Market

The village of Adjarra, just outside Porto-Novo, has a nice market held every fourth day. Apart from the typical market items, it offers traditional pottery, musical instruments—including lots of drums—and various voodoo objects. Adjarra also houses a Vodoun water temple called Zekpon. The village is popular with Porto-Novians for its eateries, especially those serving pork. *Location: about 10 km northeast of Porto-Novo. A zemidjan from Porto-Novo should cost about FCFA 500.*

EATING AND DRINKING

Restaurant Akango International This place serves salads, sandwiches, and a large variety of fish, chicken, and steak dinners. They also have various desserts and a long cocktail list. *Meals: FCFA 1,000–3,500. Drinks: FCFA 500–1,200, cocktails FCFA 1,000–2,000. Hours: 12pm–10pm. Open daily. Indoor or patio seating, with an air-conditioned formal dining room available upon request. Location: near the Ministère des Enseignements Maternel et Primaire (Ministry of Preschool and Primary Education). If you're facing the National Assembly building, turn left down the paved road until you reach a dead end at the Ministry. The restaurant is on your left.*

⊗ **Java Promo** This is one of Porto-Novo's best options for Western cuisine. Their meals include pasta, fish and chicken dishes, and steak and potatoes. Local musicians play live on Sundays. *Meals: FCFA 1,500–4,000. Drinks: FCFA 300–1,200. Covered patio seating. Hours: 11am–midnight. Open daily. Location: opposite Casa Dansa, kitty-corner from the park that houses the National Assembly building. Most zems know it by name, or say "l'Assemblée Nationale." Tel: 20.21.20.54*

Burger Van Sit at a picnic table in the park in front of the National Assembly building and eat surprisingly good hamburgers. The food is served out of a grey van that's perpetually parked here—though, oddly enough, they provide table service. You can also get a soda or beer. *Meals: FCFA 3,000. Drinks: FCFA 700–1,000. Location: in front of the National Assembly building, and across the street from Java Promo.*

⊗ **Espérance Maquis** Specializing in African and European cuisine, this restaurant is popular with both visitors and locals. The service is excellent. Try the schwarma, served with a unique sweet sauce and available vegetarian or with meat. It's a great place to stop upon arrival in Porto-Novo, or after a trip to the Ouando Market. *Meals: FCFA 500–1,500. Drinks: FCFA 250–800. Open daily. Tel: 64.30.44.09 / 66.07.20.15. Location: inside the Ouando taxi station.*

⊗ **Chez Houssou** The village of Adjarra, near Porto-Novo, is famous for its pork—Porto-Novians often come here for lunch or dinner. This restaurant serves its pork with *piron*, raw onions, and three types of hot sauce: a red sauce made of dried chiles, a green sauce made from fresh green chiles, and a brown sauce made from peppercorns, ginger, and garlic. If you're more adventurous, try the blood sauce. Like other pork places in Benin, they cook all parts of the pig. If your plate comes out with pieces of skin or liver, just ask and they'll replace it with real meat. *Meals: FCFA 600–1,200. Drinks: FCFA 250–800. Hours: 11am–6pm, but they run out of food later in the day, so go around noon. Open daily. Location: next to the main market in Adjarra, 10 km outside Porto-Novo. A zemidjan from Porto-Novo should cost FCFA 500.*

Resto de Bonne Viande de Lapins Braises Also in Adjarra, this place is similar to Chez Houssou, except that it serves grilled rabbit instead of pork. *Meals: FCFA 600–1,200. Drinks: FCFA 250–800. Hours: 11am–6pm, but they run out of food later in the day, so go around noon. Open daily. Location: next to the mayor's office ("La Mairie") in Adjarra.*

ACCOMMODATIONS

⊗ **Centre Songhaï** Overall, this is the best place to stay in Porto-Novo. Rooms are clean and simple, the restaurant serves excellent food at reasonable prices, and you can enjoy the beautiful natural surroundings of the Songhaï Center. The restaurant offers local and European cuisine, with much of the food produced right there at the Center, while the tranquil open-air *buvette* overlooks a small lake. They also have the best internet café in town. While it's not centrally-located, a zemidjan ride to anywhere in the town center shouldn't cost more than FCFA 200–250. Whether you stay here or not, be sure to visit to check out their innovative agricultural projects and to visit their boutique, where you can buy their soaps, syrups, juices, and baked goods. *FCFA 7,500–12,500 with fan, FCFA 15,500–30,000 with A/C. Private bathroom. Meals: breakfast FCFA 2,800–3,200, lunch and dinner FCFA 1,500 and up. If you're staying in an air-conditioned room, breakfast is complementary. Tel: 20.24.68.81 / 20.24.60.92. Location: on the paved road leading from the town center toward Ouando. Zemidjans all know where it is.*

Musée da Silva Hotel The museum offers clean rooms, though it is beginning to look run-down. Because it is on a busy street, noise can be a problem. *FCFA 8,500. Private bathroom, A/C. Tel: 20.21.50.71. Location: Rue Toffa, near the Bank of Africa.*

Ouémé & Plateau

YETEN Center This orphanage (see SIGHTS AND ACTIVITIES) offers clean, basic private rooms to visitors. Located in a village near Porto-Novo, it's a good out-of-the-way choice: you'll get to visit the orphanage and see what life is like outside the city. You can choose to volunteer for a couple hours during your stay—gardening, tutoring the students, helping prepare meals, and so on. They play soccer on Sunday afternoons. Despite the village location, the center has electricity and running water. *FCFA 5,000. Fan, private bath and shower. Contact: the director's name is Jean and you can reach him at 97.54.22.23 or 97.47.14.77. Location: Gbozounme, a village located just north of Avrankou. You can get there by zemidjan.*

Avrankou

Originally called *Avlankou*, this village was named after a local plantain picker named Avlan. (The word *kou* in the Gún language means death.) As with several other town and city names in Benin, the French later altered the word to 'Avrankou' so that it was easier to pronounce. Located on the paved road between Porto-Novo and Nigeria, the village and its surroundings hold several sacred forests where traditional festivities take place. There is a large Catholic cathedral on the northern edge of the village, which was decorated by Beninese artist Félix Agossa (p39), who also painted frescoes in the cathedrals of Lokossa, Allada, Dassa-Zoumé, and Godomé in Cotonou. Street stands and cafeterias can be found at the town center for a cheap Beninese meal. There are no lodging options in Avrankou, so it's best to plan on staying in Kétou or Porto-Novo when visiting this area.

Kétou

Kétou is a predominantly Yoruba town with a rich spiritual history. It was once linked to the Oyo Kingdom, a powerful Yoruba state based in present-day Nigeria, and Yoruba traditional religious practices called *Orisha* thrive here. Kétou is also famous for its pile of trash. Known as **Aitan Ola**, this sacred garbage pile is a small mountain of waste that tells a fabulous tale of religious customs unique to the town (see following Sights and Activities section for more information on Aitan Ola).

GETTING THERE

Paved roads connect Kétou to Porto-Novo to the south, and to Bohicon to the west. The paved roads in the Ouémé-Plateau region are in much better shape than the road leading directly from Cotonou to Bohicon. While it's a bit of a detour, passing through this area can be a more comfortable way to get to the north.

To get to Kétou from Cotonou, take a taxi at the Dantokpa taxi station. It should cost around FCFA 2,500. From Porto-Novo, taxis leave frequently from the Ouando taxi station and cost about FCFA 2,000. Kétou-bound taxis usually find passengers faster in Porto-Novo; in Cotonou, you may be waiting a while for the taxi to fill up with passengers.

There are three taxi stations in Kétou: one near the market for people heading south to Porto-Novo and Cotonou, one on the west side toward Bohicon, and another on the southern road that heads to Pobé. Taxis from Kétou to Bohicon cost about FCFA 2,000, and local *zemidjan* rides should not cost more than FCFA 150.

SIGHTS AND ACTIVITIES

The Royal Palace of Kétou

The palace houses the current king and is open to visitors. There is no official entry fee or tourist office, but guides are always available in the vicinity. A donation of about FCFA 1,000 is expected. Visitors must remove their shoes before entering certain parts of the palace and ask permission to take photographs. There are many fetishes and shrines throughout the palace, each with its own history and sacred significance. For etiquette to observe when visiting kings, see *Etiquette* (p32). *Open daily. Location: about 200 meters down a dirt road on the north side of town.*

The Sacred Door Akaba Idenan

This sacred doorway was once the only entrance to Kétou. It's fortified with traditional military walls and ditches. It is also the center for the Orisha cult of Kétou, and the area is full of shrines, statues, and ceremonial sites. Because this site is sacred, it's important for visitors to first seek permission or find a local guide before approaching and taking photographs. The best way is to ask the king at the royal palace. He will ask for a fee of about FCFA 500–1,000 and provide a guide.

Aitan Ola - The Sacred Trash Pile

Located near the Royal Palace, this Orisha shrine was established in the early days of Kétou's history. The mound of garbage sits over a sacred charm, said to offer protection to the Kétou Kingdom in time of war. When it was first buried, locals were given strict instructions to cover the charm with anything they could find—hence the garbage.

Kétou Markets

Kétou has three markets: the main market held every five days, a smaller market held two days after the main market, and a daily market located near the western taxi station. The lively main market attracts vendors and shoppers from throughout the region. You can find the typical foods and market items, as well as many intriguing Vodoun objects, such as the protection ring. Made from metal, these common vodoun rings can be bought at the market and "charged" to protect the purchaser from sickness and curses. Other items include plant seeds, pulverized animal bones, and rodent skulls. Many of these items are used to appeal to deities and spirits through sacrificial ceremonies. The ingredients used in a particular ceremony vary depending on the deity concerned and the reason for the sacrifice.

EATING AND DRINKING

Kétou's specialty dish is *lafou,* a type of *pâte* made of cassava and corn flour. You can find it in food stalls and restaurants throughout town.

Ave Maria This is the best place to eat in town. The owner is a very welcoming woman who loves foreigners. She makes akassa, amiwo, chicken, salad or just about anything with advance notice. *Meals: FCFA 500–1,000. Drinks: FCFA 300–800. Hours: 11am–10pm. Open daily. Location: on the road to Porto-Novo, halfway between the high school and the customs checkpoint.*

Maquis La Détente This bar and restaurant serves Beninese cuisine, including a good selection of fried fish. Salads are also available depending on ingredient availability. *Meals FCFA 500–1,500. Drinks FCFA 300–800. Hours: 11am–10pm. Open daily. Location: on the southern edge of town.*

Food Stall The woman here prepares excellent local dishes such as akassa, amiwo, and eba. Her cooking attracts people from all over town, especially at lunch time. *Meals: FCFA 300–800. Hours: 9am–8pm. Open daily. Location: across from the old city hall.*

ACCOMMODATIONS

Auberge de la Cité Auberge de la Cité prepares dishes such as grilled chicken, fish, couscous, and fries. The cook will make a hearty salad too, if requested a couple days prior. The rooms have shared bathrooms, or a private bathroom for a little extra. *FCFA 3,000 and up. Fan, TV, shared or private bathroom. Meals FCFA 600–1,800. Drinks FCFA 300–800. Location: just down the road leading from the taxi station south toward Pobé.*

Zou & Collines

Abomey, capital of the pre-colonial Kingdom of Dahomey and administrative center of the present-day Zou–Collines region, houses much of Benin's cultural heritage. You can still visit the palaces of what was once one of West Africa's most powerful kingdoms and discover its vibrant culture and violent history, including its generations-long participation in the slave trade.

When the French built the railroad from Cotonou to Parakou, the city of Bohicon sprang up as a liaison between the railroad and Abomey. Today, the railroad

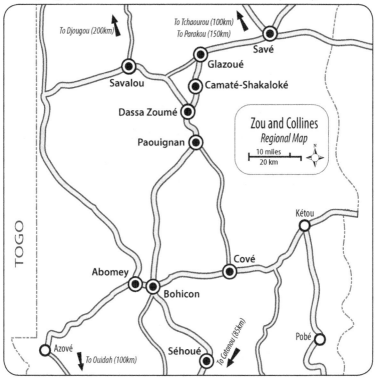

lies rusting, but Bohicon remains as a vibrant market town and a major crossroads between north and south.

As you move north into the Collines, you'll notice a shift in languages and cultures. Far from acting as the seat of a mighty kingdom, this region's history was shaped by refugees fleeing Dahomey's slave hunters. They sought refuge among the region's steep granite hills: *collines* means *hills* in French. You can still see that villages are often built right next to these steep hills. The refugees—including the Mahi and the Idaatcha—came into contact, and sometimes conflict, with the Nagot and Tchabé who already lived here. To this day, these ethnicities share the region, though they speak different languages and usually live in separate villages.

You'll also notice a change in landscape and climate. The gently rolling land of the Collines gives way to dramatic granite hills, which are often believed to house spirits that guard the nearby villages. Climb one to get a striking view of the landscape. The air is drier than in the south, but the dry heat can get more intense.

Sèhouè

Situated about halfway between Cotonou and Bohicon, this little town is renowned for its fruit vendors. You'll see cars and trucks stopped along the road as passengers stock up on pineapples, bananas, oranges, plantains, papayas, and tomatoes; prices further north in Bohicon are 2–3 times what they are here. Women and children carrying heavy baskets of produce instantly mob a slowing vehicle. Some of them are so enthusiastic that they'll shove their fruit through your car's open window, allowing you to appreciate its appeal at close quarters. This is a great place to purchase fresh pineapple before continuing to the arid north, where fruit is much harder to find—but keep in mind that in this climate, fruit will start to rot after a couple days. Some taxi drivers don't normally stop here, but will do so upon request.

Bohicon

Bohicon lies 130 kilometers north of Cotonou, just east of Abomey and along the north-south highway. The town was founded when the French constructed the Cotonou–Parakou railway in the early 20th century. A major marketplace grew up near the train station. Today, Bohicon lies at the crossroads of two major highways: the north-south road between Cotonou and Niger and Burkina Faso, and the east-west route running to Nigeria and Togo. Due to its crucial location, Bohicon has become a major crossroads of international trade. It is the third largest trade center in Benin, after Cotonou and Parakou.

While Bohicon isn't among Benin's most popular tourist spots, you'll pass through it on your way to nearby Abomey, the historical capital of the Kingdom of Dahomey. It's worth stopping in Bohicon to have a look at the vibrant market, and to check out the artisanal shops lining the road leading west toward Abomey. However, merchants and zemidjans tend to be quite aggressive here, and you may soon be ready to move on.

GETTING THERE

A bush taxi from the Place de L'Étoile Rouge in Cotonou costs FCFA 2,500, while a minibus costs FCFA 2,000–2,500, depending on whether you sit on the benches in the back or in the more comfortable front seats. A bus from Cotonou costs between FCFA 2,000–2,500, depending on the quality of the bus.

Taxis typically drop people off at various points in Bohicon. If you're visiting the city center, or staying at a hotel there, wait until the taxi reaches the station in the middle of the market before getting off. While teams of zemidjans in purple and orange shirts will crowd you as soon as you get out of the taxi, most hotels are within walking distance of the market.

Most bus companies no longer take the direct Cotonou–Bohicon road due to its deteriorating condition and massive potholes. (Taxis are less affected by this problem, since they're small enough to dodge most potholes.) Buses instead get to Bohicon via a long detour through Porto-Novo.

Taxi Rental

If you want to rent a bush taxi for a trip to or from Bohicon, call **Samuel Agbevanon** at 95.46.01.30. He's reliable, his prices are good, and his vehicle is in relatively good shape, though it's not air conditioned.

Zemidjans

Fidèle (tel: 94.61.00.90) and **Filiberto** (tel: 95.38.40.39) are a couple of reliable zems in the area. You can call them to arrange a pickup, or pay a fixed price to have them take you around for the day.

INTERNET

James Enterprise There are a few internet cafés in Bohicon, but this one is the best. It has a decent ethernet connection, as well as wifi. *Location: Second floor of the building across the street from Bank of Africa in the center of town.*

SIGHTS AND ACTIVITIES

Bohicon has a large daily market in the city center, and multitudes of food vendors and kiosks line the streets, especially the north-south highway, where they tempt travelers with fruits and snacks, including bags of oranges, fried corn cakes, soy biscuits, and bread of all sorts and sizes. On the road to Abomey you can find several banks, a large post office, cafeterias, a grocery store with European products, internet cafés, and the Great Mosque.

EATING AND DRINKING

Le Palmier For a break from local cuisine, come here. This French-owned restaurant serves a wide variety of excellent European cuisine, including *lapin braisé, poulet à la moutarde*, and pizza. They offer a liqueur bar, a selection of red and white wines, and local fruit juices, in addition to the standard beer and soda. *Meals: FCFA 2,500–4,000, pizza up to FCFA 6,300. Drinks: FCFA 500–1,000, higher for liqueur and bottles of wine. Hours: 8am–11:30pm. Closed Sundays. Tel: 67.88.52.57. Location: near Rond Point Dako.*

The Volcano This is Bohicon's first and, for the moment, only schwarma restaurant. The food is excellent, the price is right, and the owner, Sergio, provides good service and enjoys speaking English. *Meals: FCFA 1,000. Drinks: FCFA 250–900. Hours: 10am–midnight. Open daily. Tel: 98.55.75.18. Location: on the road to Abomey, across from the Moov store.*

Yam Plus This popular restaurant offers plates with chicken, fries, and salad for FCFA 1,500. Offerings for the more adventurous include cow stomach. It's best to go here for dinner. *Meals: FCFA 1,500. Drinks: FCFA 250–1,200. Location: on the paved road toward Abomey, near the big mosque.*

Super Paquita Another popular eatery in town, though this one is best for lunch. You'll find a variety of local cuisine—the chicken is particularly good. They run a major catering business, so their food is always fresh. *Meals: around FCFA 1,000. Drinks: FCFA 250–1,200. Location: on the paved road toward Abomey, next to the Maison des Jeunes.*

⊗ **Maquis Tanti Gabon** Conveniently located on the north-south highway, this restaurant is a popular lunch and dinner stop for travelers. The friendly Gabonese staff offers cauldrons of African dishes and a wide selection of cold beers and soft drinks. There are craft shops selling traditional wooden sculptures and mortars of all sizes in the vicinity. *Meals: FCFA 600–2,000. Drinks: FCFA 300–900. Hours: 11am–10pm. Open daily. Tel: 22.50.00.75 / 22.50.13.80. Location: at the south entrance of Bohicon, by the big traffic circle and across the street from Hotel Dako.*

Jardin de l'Hotel de Ville De Bohicon (City Hall Garden) This vast garden with tables in the shade offers a quiet escape from the noise and heat of the town. Togolese staff serve cold drinks and basic rice dishes. Street stalls nearby typically offer fried yams, plantains, and bean or wheat *beignets* at midday. *Meals: FCFA 1,000. Drinks: FCFA 300–800. Hours: 12pm–10pm. Open daily. Location: on the road to Abomey.*

Maquis Malodie Amid street stands heaped with pineapples and oranges, this casual eatery offers an affordable lunch of *igname pilée* prepared, as its sign says, "according to the Law of God." *Meals FCFA 500–1,000. Drinks FCFA 300–800. Hours: 12pm–4pm. Closed Sundays. Location: in the center of town, next to the (defunct) train station.*

Hôtel Dako Restaurant This is the place to go for a little splurge and a taste of international cuisine, or simply to enjoy a cold beer beneath the thatched shade structure while watching Beninese television. The restaurant staff is friendly, and can provide good advice on touring the region. *Meals: FCFA 4,000–6,000. Drinks FCFA 600–1,500. Hours: 8am–10pm. Open daily. Location: at the southern entrance of town, near the big traffic circle.*

ACCOMMODATIONS

Hôtel Dako The large hotel complex is hard to miss, with a pink-painted gateway and large signs. Hotel Dako offers dozens of spacious, clean rooms, a swimming pool, and night club. Due to Bohicon's central location within Benin, this hotel is often used for conventions and business conferences. The bar and restaurant, set under a thatched shade structure, offers international specialties. *FCFA 6,500–22,500. Private bathroom, TV, pool, fan or A/C. Tel: 22.51.01.38. Location: at the southern entrance of town, near the big traffic circle.*

Abomey

As the historic capital of the Kingdom of Dahomey, Abomey is one of Benin's premier tourist destinations. It's not to be missed by a visitor looking to explore Benin's rich and turbulent history. Today, despite its modest size, Abomey is the administrative capital of the Zou and Collines *départements*. While the people of the surrounding villages continue to live chiefly on agriculture, many inhabitants of the town specialize in handicrafts.

GETTING THERE

Abomey is situated 130 kilometers north of Cotonou. Whether you're coming from the north or the south, you'll have to go through Bohicon to get to Abomey. Almost any taxi going from Cotonou to Bohicon will continue to Abomey. (These taxis leave from the Place de l'Étoile Rouge in Cotonou.) It costs FCFA 500 extra to stay in the taxi until Abomey. Alternately, you can take a bus to Bohicon and then get a zemidjan to Abomey. A *zem* should cost FCFA 400 from the center of Bohicon, where taxis drop passengers off, or about FCFA 600 from the station on the outskirts of Bohicon where buses drop passengers off.

The condition of the Cotonou–Bohicon road has severely deteriorated in recent years. Most buses leaving Cotonou will take a lengthy detour through Porto-Novo rather than brave the direct road to Bohicon. However, taxis and minibuses still take the direct road. While the smaller vehicles are able to dodge most of the potholes, it's still a rough ride.

A taxi from Azové in the southwest costs FCFA 600. Vehicles headed to Adja-land from Abomey are not frequent and can take a long time to fill up. Many travelers take the quicker yet more expensive and much less comfortable option of hiring a zemidjan for the 45 minute ride to Azové. This costs around FCFA 1,500.

INTERNET

There is an internet café in the post office in the center of town. There are also a few places on the paved road leading out of Bohicon towards Abomey. As in the rest of the country, internet access here is ever-changing.

POLICE AND HOSPITAL

Both the police station and the hospital are located on the paved road between Bohicon and Abomey.

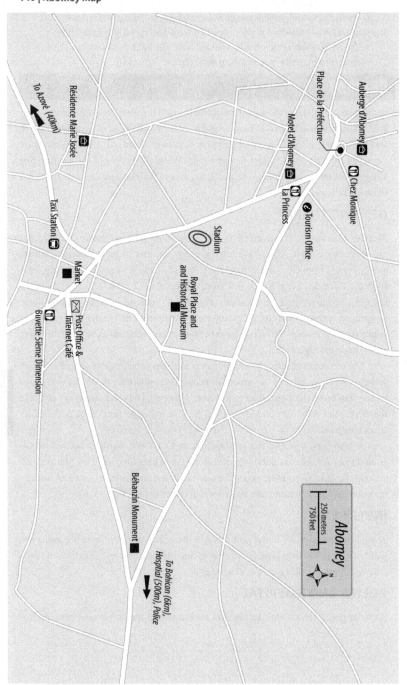

To Azové (40km)

Résidence Marie-Josée

Place de la Préfecture

Auberge d'Abomey

Motel d'Abomey

La Princess

Chez Monique

Tourism Office

Taxi Station

Stadium

Market

Royal Place and
and Historical Museum

Post Office &
Internet Café

Buvette 5ième Dimension

Béhanzin Monument

To Bohicon (6km),
Hospital (500m), Police

Abomey

250 meters
750 feet

N

SIGHTS AND ACTIVITIES

Béhanzin Monument

A towering statue of King Béhanzin, the last sovereign king of Dahomey, stands at Abomey's east entrance. His outstretched arm and open palm represent his fight to halt French expansion in the region.

Musée Historique d'Abomey
Royal Palace and History Museum

Situated in the heart of the ancient city, the red clay walls of the multiple kings' palaces built in the 17th century attest to the might of the Kingdom of Dahomey. The first palace was established by King Houègbadja in 1645. Each successive king built a new palace next to his predecessor's. When King Béhanzin added his residence in 1889, the twelve palaces encompassed an area of 44 hectares, entirely surrounded by a ten meter-high wall. Many of the palaces were destroyed in 1892 when King Béhanzin set fire to Abomey and fled as the French took control of the city and conquered the kingdom. In 1943 the French established the Royal Palace Museum within the best preserved remaining palaces, those of Kings Guézo and Glélé. In 1985, UNESCO designated the 44 hectares of palace remains as a World Heritage Site. Many international organizations have attempted to restore and protect the site. The museum is one of the best-organized tourist sites in the country.

Knowledgeable guides take visitors through the two hectares of historical buildings full of artifacts, wooden thrones, Vodoun statues, *fétiches*, decorated earthen huts, and objects of war while the guide recounts anecdotes of the centuries of events that occurred within these walls. The museum tour finishes in the craftsmen's courtyard. The kings of Abomey employed their own craftsmen within a series of workshops attached to the royal palace. Today, you can buy ornate brass sculptures, royal patchwork tapestries, handwoven drapes and hammocks, and other art objects here. The craftsmen use the same techniques and tools that their ancestors used centuries ago. *Hours: 9am–4:30pm. Open daily, except for national holidays. Entry fee (includes tour): Foreigners, FCFA 2,500 for adults and FCFA 2,000 for children; Beninese nationals, FCFA 1,500 for adults and FCFA 1,300–1,400 for children. Tours last about an hour. English- and French-speaking guides are available. Photos and audio recording forbidden. Tel: 22.50.03.14.*

EATING AND DRINKING

Motel d'Abomey This hotel restaurant serves both European and African cuisine, including fresh salads and chicken curry, in a dining room decorated with royal patchwork tapestries. *Meals: FCFA 2,500–7,000. Drinks: FCFA 600–1,500. Tel: 22.50.00.75 / 22.50.13.80. Location: north of the town center, near the Place de la Préfecture.*

Zou & Collines

Bar Restaurant Chez Monique Serving typical local cuisine, Chez Monique is best known for its fried *poulet bicyclette* (African free-range chicken). The *pâte rouge* and fries are great too. Food should be ordered in advance as it can take some time to prepare. *Meals: FCFA 2,500–3,500. Drinks: FCFA 300–800. Tel: 22.50.01.68. Location: near the Place de la Préfecture.*

Résidence Marie Joseé African and European specialties are served at this hotel restaurant. The garden atmosphere is relaxing and quite pleasant. *Meals: FCFA 2,000–4,500. Drinks: FCFA 500–1,000. Hours: 8am–10pm. Open daily. Tel: 22.50.02.89. Location: toward Lokossa, west of the market.*

La Princesse This open-air spot sits in a triangle between two roads. Vendors sell typical and budget Beninese food from their cauldrons, most often chicken and rice. If staying at the Motel d'Abomey located across the street, La Princesse is a good dining and drinking alternative from the more expensive hotel restaurant. *Meals: FCFA 700–1,500. Drinks: FCFA 300–800. Hours: 12pm–10pm. Open daily. Location: across the street from Motel d'Abomey.*

Buvette 5ème Dimension (The Fifth Dimension) This lively bar and restaurant is set in a pleasant garden. Loud music abounds. *Meals: FCFA 1,500 and up. Drinks: FCFA 300–800. Hours: 11am–12pm. Open daily. Location: near the market, in the town center.*

ACCOMMODATIONS

Auberge Chez Monique Chez Monique is a family-owned establishment that offers simple and clean rooms. It features a great nature scene, with pet monkeys, crocodiles, and small antelopes in the yard. Local artisans sell crafts and souvenirs in the shade of the large garden. There's even a makeshift ping-pong table and a bocce ball court. The bar and restaurant is an excellent spot for a refreshing drink after visiting the royal palace museum. *FCFA 7,500–8,500. Private bathroom and fan. Tel: 22.50.01.68 / 97.32.00.30. Location: near the Place de la Préfecture.*

Auberge d'Abomey This high-end hotel is part of a chain that also includes Auberges in Grand Popo and Dassa. It occupies two old colonial buildings built on garden-like grounds. The restaurant serves French cuisine with local influence. *FCFA 12,500–14,000 with fan, FCFA 17,000–20,000 with A/C. Private bathroom and satellite TV. Meals: continental breakfast FCFA 2,000; full breakfast FCFA 3,800; three-course meal FCFA 8,500. Drinks: FCFA 600–1,500. Tel: 95.82.80.28. Location: Across from the Préfecture.*

Motel d'Abomey This is a higher-end lodging option in town, with round bungalows split to form two spacious rooms. The lobby offers comfortable sofas and satellite television, and the elegant restaurant serves good European and African cuisine. The staff can assist in arranging a zemidjan tour of the city, including visits of the royal palace sites complete with stories about the Dahomeyan kings and the wars against the French. Prestige Nightclub is attached, with a FCFA 2,000 cover. *FCFA 12,500–60,500. Private bathroom, satellite TV, fan or A/C. Tel: 22.50.00.75. Location: north of the town center, near the Place de la Préfecture.*

Résidence Marie Joseé This is a shaded and calm retreat, far from the noise and bustle of the town center, with gardens and clean rooms. The hotel owners rent vehicles for day use and can organize guided tours of Abomey and surrounding areas. There is internet access available for FCFA 1,000 per hour. *FCFA 6,500–24,500. Private bathroom, some rooms with hot water and tubs, and fan or A/C. Tel: 22.50.02.89 / 97.72.09.16. Location: toward Lokossa, west of the market.*

Cové

Cové is a large village on the dirt road between Bohicon and Kétou. Its dominant ethnic group is the Mahi. The Mahi language is extremely similar to the Fon language: according to oral history, the Mahi originated as a rebel group from the Kingdom of Dahomey. Cové is known for the yearly Gèlèdé Festival celebrated by two of the region's other major ethnic groups, the Yoruba and Tchabé peoples. Beninese and foreigners come to watch the vibrant masked dancers depict daily activities that include honoring the role of women in their society. The Gèlèdé Festival is a tradition that dates to the 15th century, and the masked dances are only performed by village men who have been initiated through intricate rituals into the relevant secret society. These men play sacred ceremonial instruments and fall into a dancing trance as they personify the spirits and female characters being honored.

Environmental Concerns in the Collines ✊INSIGHT

The landscape of the Collines was originally wooded savannah, but the pressure of the increased population has resulted in deforestation at an alarming rate. Agriculture is the principal activity throughout the rural region. Cotton monocultures have been the main source of agricultural revenue, but climate change and over-cultivation have greatly diminished soil fertility and caused increasingly poor cotton harvests. In 2005, the Beninese National Assembly took into account this imposing agricultural problem as they evaluated each of the country's twelve *départements* for their economical values; the Collines department was designated as one of the key regions of interest for tourism.

Zou & Collines

Paouignan

As you enter the Collines *département* from the south, you'll soon see endless rows of towering plastic bags full of a thick white powder lining both sides of the highway. This village is called Paouignan, and the white powder (contrary to what you might be thinking) is *gari*, a rough flour made of dried cassava. For reasons that no one ever seems quite able to explain, this small and otherwise unremarkable village has distinguished itself as the best place to buy *gari* in the region, if not in the country. Travelers between Cotonou and Parakou regularly stop here to stock up. The price is better than elsewhere, and, if the vendors' hyperbolic signs are to be believed, so is the quality.

If you're hungry and don't feel like shoveling a bagful

Beninese often eat gari mixed with beans and drizzled with palm oil. Like other cassava products, it has a slightly bitter taste and little nutritional value. Its main asset is that it's cheap and gives you the feeling of being full.

of *gari* into your mouth, check out the **Paouignan Auberge**, just north of town and a little ways off from the highway. They serve chicken and fries, beer, soda, and fruit juices. However, be careful of stopping in Paouignon if you don't have your own transportation—it may take a while to flag down a taxi here and continue your journey.

Dassa-Zoumé

Like many towns and villages of the Collines, Dassa owes its existence to the slave trade. The dramatic hills around the town are where the Idaatcha people sought refuge from the Dahomeyan slave-hunters. It's said that a range

> Dassa's market is located up the hill, to the east of the main traffic circle. It takes place every five days and offers all the typical market items.

of 41 Sacred Hills in this region provided shelter for Idaatcha and Mahi refugees, a belief that probably owes more to the number 41—a sacred number in Vodoun—than to the exact number of hills. On some hills, you can still find the ruins of the refugees' settlements, hidden in the bush and protected by Vodoun spirits.

Today, the Idaatcha people, whose language is related to those of the Yoruba and the Nagot, still live mainly in and around Dassa. There's also a significant population of the Mahi, who descend from the Fon.

Dassa is a major crossroads. It lies about halfway between Cotonou and Parakou, and it's also where the paved highway coming from the south splits: one branch leads northeast to Malanville via Parakou, and the other leads northwest to Burkina Faso via Djougou and Natitingou. If you're traveling anywhere in the north of Benin, you'll almost certainly pass through Dassa.

GETTING THERE

From Cotonou, bush taxis and buses bound for Dassa from the Place de l'Étoile Rouge. Most buses leave at 7am. If you don't see a bus for Dassa, you can take a bus bound for Parakou, Djougou, Natitingou, or anywhere else in the north—they all pass through Dassa. When you get on the bus, let the porter and driver know that you'll be getting off in Dassa.

From Bohicon, bush taxis headed north line the right side of the highway leading north. If you can't find it, get a zemidjan and tell him you're looking for a taxi to Dassa. He'll know where to take you.

From Parakou, southbound taxis leave from Autogare Tchaourou, located on the main road south of the main Arzéké market. Buses leave from the offices of each bus company; there's no central location.

Buses and taxis drop passengers off at the main intersection in Dassa. Zemidjans in green and yellow shirts wait here for passengers. You shouldn't pay more than FCFA 300 to go anywhere within Dassa.

Destination to/from Dassa // Taxi price // Bus price:
Cotonou // FCFA 3,000–4,000 // FCFA 2,500–3,500
Bohicon // FCFA 1,000–1,500 // FCFA 1,000–1,500
Parakou // FCFA 4,000–4,500 // FCFA 3,000–4,000

Dassa-Zoumé

N

250 meters
500 feet

To Camate Shakaloke 15 km
Sokponta 20 km

Hôtel Miracle

To Maktub Farm 1.5 km

Auberge La Cachette

Hospital

Café-Restaurant
Chez Guy

Post Office

Dassa Market

Buvette Chez Angelo
La Fleur des Collines

Pharmacy

Internet Café

Royal Palace

Place Yaka

Okuta Site

To Glazoué 25 km
Parakou 200 km

Notre Dame d'Arigbo

Hôtel Chez les Soeurs

Bank of Africa

Hotel Arigbo

Bus/Taxi Gare

Hôtel Ave Maria
1/2 km
Auberge La Madeleine
1 km

Jeco Hotel Dassa

Auberge de Dassa

To Savalou 30 km
Djougou 225 km

To Bohicon 60 km

Zou & Collines

HOSPITAL

Dassa has a large regional hospital located on the dirt road leading northeast toward Camaté and Sokponta.

BANK

Dassa has a **Bank of Africa** branch that can conduct Western Union transfers. *Hours: 9am–12pm and 3–5:30pm. Closed Saturdays and Sundays. Location:* just up the hill from the Mayor's office (*la Mairie*), on the paved road leading from the main traffic circle to the center of town.

INTERNET

There's an internet café across the street from the two-story pharmacy, just off the main road. It costs FCFA 500 per hour. If you're staying in one of the higher-end hotels, you'll have wifi there, though the connection may be spotty.

SIGHTS AND ACTIVITIES

Royal Palace of Dassa

Although the King of Dassa holds no official governmental power, he is respected as a religious and local political figure. The palace is usually open for guided visits, though the current king, King Egbakotan II, does not reside there permanently. Guides present themselves at the palace entrance and give tours of the residence, including the throne room and a vast collection of patchwork banners representing each king who ruled in the long history of the Kingdom of Dassa. As with many royal palace tours, the guides recount colorful stories about the different kings and their reigns. *Open daily. Tour fee: FCFA 2,000–3,000. Location: at the center of town.*

Place Yaka and the Ogoun Divinity

Place Yaka is a highly sacred site located on the Hill of the Omandjagoun. Only direct descendants of original inhabitants of this mountain reside in the rocky hillside neighborhood. All visitors must seek permission from the residents to hike up the mountain and be escorted by a guide. French-speaking guides are available to take visitors through the neighborhood and up the steep slope to the main shrine of Ogoun, the Vodoun god of iron and war. The visit is rich in stories and breathtaking vistas of the town. *Tour fee: FCFA 3,000. Location: next to the Royal Palace and the Maison du Peuple.*

Notre Dame d'Arigbo

This giant basilica is hard to miss when arriving in Dassa from the south. It sits at the foot of a hill, surrounded by vast fields and peaceful, tree-lined paths. Tourists are welcome to visit the church, which has been brilliantly decorated by local artists. Behind the church sits a large shrine set in the granite boulders, where the Virgin Mary is said to have appeared. This shrine has become the destination of a yearly pilgrimage. Thousands of adepts congregate around the basilica each August, transforming all of

Dassa into a crowded religious camp. Behind the shrine, a stairway leads to a conclave of granite boulders with the Stations of the Cross installed in the rocks.

Okuta Site

This outdoor museum of rock sculptures is located at the base of the hill at the northeastern entrance of town. The site is run by the **Okuta Association**, established by local artist Felix Agossa in March 2008. Okuta, whose name means *rock* in Idaatcha, promotes cultural development and the collaboration of local artists. The Association has an office in the Maisons des Jeunes, a youth center located at the main traffic circle in town, where artists work together, exchange techniques, and train apprentices. In December 2008, Okuta launched the first major rock sculpture symposium in Benin. A group of artists from West Africa and Europe convened for three weeks to carve masks into the boulders at the main site. These works of art can be viewed at leisure, along with the contemporary monument and sculptures decorating the entrance.

Bétékoukou-Hippo River Tour

About 30 kilometers from Dassa, the village of Bétékoukou has a large-scale agro-pastoral farm. A bit farther east along the Ouémé River is a small fishing village and river crossing for merchants traveling to and from nearby Nigeria. This section of the river houses a significant hippopotamus population.

To visit, you can hire or a taxi or a zemidjan from Dassa to Bétékoukou, where local fishermen are available for a canoe tour of the Ouémé River. The tour costs FCFA

The Mystic History of Idaatcha-Land

The spiritual story of the region begins in western Nigeria. The Yoruba gods of Egba, Ilé Ifé and Abèokuta became angry with the local population for their lawlessness and neglect. Consumed with their material problems, the humans had abandoned the altars of the divinities. This prompted the gods to immigrate to more worthy and welcoming lands as they searched for a place with the right spiritual vibrations. Their exodus brought them to the region of Dassa. Pleased with the spiritual climate, they did not hesitate to settle there. Dassa became the promised land of the Yoruba divinities.

Four principal gods came to settle the region: Ogoun, god of iron and war; Arira, god of thunder and lightning; Sakpata, god of smallpox and maladies; and Arigbo, divine source of water, nativity, and old age. From Dassa, the gods continued their journey to discover cities and kingdoms in southern Benin, such as Abomey and Ouidah. They continued onwards in their voyage to Haiti and Brazil via the slave trade, where they evolved into the vodoun entities of Hèviosso, Ogoun and Sakpata. Meanwhile, the gods maintained their principal seat in Dassa.

In time, the Catholics also discovered the strong spiritual presence in this granite haven. At the base of the hill where the majority of the Yoruba gods chose to settle definitively, there was an apparition of the Virgin Mary. Dassa thus became the site of the largest pilgrimage in West Africa. The first Catholic population named this sacred site Notre Dame d'Arigbo, or Our Lady of Arigbo, representative of one of the local divinities. This site serves as an important symbol of the syncretic blend of traditional and Western beliefs that defines spiritual life throughout Benin.

3,000 per person and takes about two hours. It's best to go in the dry season during the early morning hours, when the hippos gather in the deeper parts of the river—making them easier to spot—and the fishermen have not left for the day. Once the fishermen find the hippos, they bang their paddle against the side of the *pirogue* to prompt the animals to stick their heads out of the water. The vibrations caused by the banging actually irritate and confuse the hippos, making them search for the source of the sound. The fishermen are accustomed to these dangerous creatures and know the importance of keeping a safe distance. It is crucial, however, to keep in mind that hippos are quite unpredictable and can swim very fast. If frightened or aggravated, they may attack. An alternative to the canoe tour is to view the hippos from land. Some zemidjan drivers in Dassa know the way to the best viewing spot along the river, but it's best to first go through the fishermen's village and seek permission in order to avoid any conflict or surprises.

Maktub Farm

This experimental farm, owned and run by a local biology teacher, offers education sessions on organic gardening, snail and rabbit breeding, painting, pottery, and traditional dance. You can also sleep and eat there (the following *Accommodations* section). *Tel: 97.71.27.96. Email: armandtbs@yahoo.fr. Location: on the outskirts of Dassa, in the furthest area of Quartier Ayedero. It's hard to find without a guide. Your best bet is to find a zemidjan who knows "La ferme chez Armand." The zem ride should cost FCFA 300–500.*

EATING AND DRINKING

Dassa's regional specialty is *igname pilée*, which you can find throughout the town. Restaurants also serve rice, *pâte*, or *akassa* with boiled eggs, fried fish, chicken, *wagasi*, beef, pork, or *agouti*. Popular sauces include spicy tomato, *gumbo*, peanut, sesame, and green-leaf, similar to spinach. Restaurants along the main road and the main traffic circle charge FCFA 1,000–2,000 per plate, while roadside stands in the town center charge FCFA 300–900 per plate.

> Bars or *buvettes* are found all around town, serving beer and sometimes fresh palm wine and *sodabi*.

Auberge La Madeleine There's a popular *buvette* attached to the hotel, and a cook prepares her legendary *igname pilée* nearby. You can get your choice of *wagasi*, rabbit, chicken, agouti, or antelope with peanut sauce. The crowds of locals who gather here at lunchtime testify to the quality of the cooking. *Meals FCFA 600–1,500. Drinks FCFA 250–800. Hours: noon–10pm. Open daily. Location: at the north entrance of town, on the highway leading to Parakou.*

Auberge de Dassa The hotel restaurant serves pricey French cuisine with local influence. If you're lucky, they'll be serving ostrich egg sandwiches or ostrich steaks. They have a full bar, which is expensive but the best place to go if you're looking for a mixed drink. *Meals: à la carte FCFA 3,000–5,000, three-course meal FCFA 8,500. Drinks: FCFA 600–1,500. Tel: 22.53.00.98 / 94.47.21.35. Location: at the main traffic circle, by the road leading to Savalou.*

Auberge La Cachette This restaurant and bar is cozy and inviting, with art and tapestries hanging from the walls. There is satellite television behind the bar. They specialize in grilled rabbit and rice, though other Beninese dishes are available. *Meals: FCFA 2,500-3,000. Drinks: FCFA 250-700. Hours: 11am-11pm. Open daily. Location: on the northeast side of town, off of the main dirt road leading to Camaté and Sokponta, just south of the CEG school.*

Buvette Chez Angelo – La Fleur des Collines (The Flower of the Hills) This former maternity ward from colonial times has been transformed into a marvelous buvette sprawled over a series of granite boulders. A modernized open-air thatched structure was recently built on top of the rocks. The buvette offers a pleasant view of the city and surrounding hills, especially at sunset. You can sit at the selection of tables and chairs around the grounds, or simply lounge on the flat rocks with a refreshing drink. *Drinks: FCFA 250–700. Hours: 10am–midnight. Open daily. Location: set deep in the middle of town, north of the paved road, behind the pharmacy.*

Café-Restaurant Chez Guy This restaurant and bar is at the center of the busiest crossroads in Dassa. The cafeteria and bar serves typical breakfast and spaghetti dishes, as well as beer and soft drinks. A woman serves good and cheap *pâte* and rice dishes from her food stand inside the restaurant. During the rainy season, she can also prepare salads upon request. *Meals: FCFA 300–700. Drinks: FCFA 250–750. Hours: 8am–midnight. Open daily. Location: across from the market.*

ACCOMMODATIONS

Jeco Hotel Dassa This is Dassa's newest and most high-end hotel. It has a swimming pool, which non-guests can use for FCFA 1,000, as well as a rooftop bar, lounge chairs around the pool, and a generally swanky atmosphere. *FCFA 30,000–41,800, suites FCFA 83,100–118,500. Satellite TV, wifi, private bathroom. Tel: 22.53.08.89 / 22.53.08.90 / 22.53.08.91 / 22.53.03.33. Email: jecohotel@jecohotel.com. Website: jecohotel.com. Location: entering Dassa from the south, it's after the church Notre Dame d'Arigbo, toward the main traffic circle.*

Auberge de Dassa Part of the French-owned Auberge chain, this hotel's rooms are in a U-shaped building with doors around the outside that open toward the restaurant. The restaurant and bar offer both indoor and terrace seating. There's a pleasant shaded patio with wooden tables and chairs—perfect for reading a book and enjoying a cold drink or coffee—as well as a garden with hammocks. *FCFA 12,500–14,000 with fan, FCFA 17,000–20,000 with A/C. Satellite TV (in some rooms), wifi, private bathroom. Meals: continental breakfast FCFA 2,000; full breakfast FCFA 3,800; three-course meal FCFA 8,500. Drinks: FCFA 600–1,500. Tel: 22.53.00.98 / 94.47.21.35. Email: aubergedassa@yahoo.fr. Location: at the main traffic circle, by the road leading toward Savalou.*

> The Auberge de Dassa has an ostrich farm in the fields behind the hotel. Most of the ostriches have been moved to a larger farm in a village ten kilometers south of Dassa, but a few are still around. The hotel restaurant sometimes serves ostrich-egg omelettes and delicious ostrich steaks.

Zou & Collines

Hôtel Arigbo Hotel Arigbo offers basic, budget rooms. The lobby has comfortable chairs in front of a satellite television often playing West African music videos. The hotel kitchen serves breakfast, lunch, and dinner with a European-style menu. *FCFA 6,000–12,000. Fan or A/C, private bathroom. Location: at the southern entrance of town, before the main traffic circle.*

Hôtel Miracle This three-story circular building was built in 2007, so the rooms are new, clean, and relatively luxurious. The rooms even have wifi. Each room has a name labeled on the door, such as Hope, Love, and Prosperity. The top floor provides pleasant views of the neighborhood. *FCFA 9,000. Fan, wifi, private bathroom. Tel: 22.12.01.15. Email: contact@miraclehotel.net. Location: on the northeast side of town, along the dirt road leading toward Camaté and Sokponta, north of the CEG school and the hospital.*

Hôtel Chez les Soeurs Set back from the paved road, this peaceful guesthouse is well-kept and run by the nuns of the cathedral next door. The rooms are quiet and spacious, with high ceilings. Breakfast is available, as well as cold non-alcoholic drinks. *FCFA 10,000. Fan or A/C, private bathroom. Location: behind the basilica Notre Dame d'Arigbo, at the south entrance of town.*

Hôtel Ave Maria Set apart from the town center, this hotel sits on a sandy path in a residential area. The rooms are simple and clean, with full bathrooms in each. There is a small food stand across the way, and the hotel kitchen can provide meals upon request. *FCFA 7,500–14,500. Fan or A/C, private bathroom. Location: on the north side of town, near the two paved roads leading to Parakou and to Savalou.*

Auberge La Madeleine The rooms here are rudimentary, but it's a good budget option if you're looking for a place set away from the town center. The attached restaurant and *buvette* get pretty lively at lunchtime. *FCFA 6,000. Fan and private bathroom. Location: at the north entrance of town, on the paved road leading to Parakou.*

Auberge La Cachette This hidden little restaurant and hotel has pleasant and basic rooms with friendly staff and a unique decor. The owner, Luc, raises rabbits and caimans, which he would be happy to show. *FCFA 8,000. Fan, private or shared bathroom. Location: on the northeast side of town, off the dirt road leading toward Camaté and Sokponta, just south of the CEG school.*

Maktub Farm Owned by local biology teacher Armand Tobossi, this paradisiacal eco-lodge is also a sheep and rabbit farm. The lodge offers rooms in modernized mud houses with thatched roofs and simple indoor plumbing, in addition to a new dormitory that can house up to 20 people. Meals are prepared upon request, and a delicious breakfast menu includes homemade cassava bread, preserves, and fruit juices. The kitchen is often well stocked with a variety of vegetables, and has cold drinks. Maktub Farm also organizes visits of the Dassa region, hikes in the hills, and festive musical gatherings under the straw huts in the evenings. *Rates are by donation, suggested at FCFA 5,000. Mosquito net, private or shared bathroom. Tel: 97.71.27.96. Email: armandtbs@yahoo.fr. Location: on the outskirts of Dassa, in the furthest area of Quartier Ayedero. It's hard to find without a guide. Your best bet is to find a zemidjan who knows "La ferme chez Armand." The zem ride should cost FCFA 300–500.*

Camaté-Shakaloké

This quaint village of about 2,000 inhabitants is a jewel hidden in the landscape ten kilometers northeast of Dassa-Zoumé. Situated at the foot of three rocky hills, the site is as beautiful as it is peaceful. The village was initially formed when three settlements of the Idaatcha peopls descended from hiding in the hillsides after the turbulent era of the slave trade. The three groups have since merged into one village, though they continue to distinguish themselves by neighborhood. Each is named after the hill they had once inhabited: Camaté, Shakaloké, and Oké N'la.

Local Income

Gravel-making is a primary economic activity in Camaté-Shakaloké. Walking down the main pathway, noise from the pounding of granite can be heard from all directions. Entire households labor with stone hammers at slabs of rock harvested from the surrounding hillsides. Piles of gravel lie at the village entrance, as the inhabitants await the next gravel truck in hopes of selling another load. If one adult works non-stop for two days, they can fill up an entire metal drum and sell it for the mere equivalent of US$2. Throughout the long dry season, this activity becomes the only constant source of revenue, and the hillsides have become heavily exploited quarries, augmenting erosion problems.

GETTING THERE

Camaté lies ten kilometers northeast of Dassa, accessible only by dirt road. A zemidjan ride from Dassa should costs about FCFA 700. Taxis generally do not take this route.

Camaté is 13 kilometers southeast of Glazoué. A zemidjan should cost around FCFA 800. Taxis run to and from Camaté on Wednesdays, which is Glazoué's market day, at a cost of FCFA 400. A zemidjan between Camaté and the village of Sokponta, 5 kilometers to the southeast, should cost around FCFA 400. Finding transportation out of Camaté, however, can be difficult, so it is best to arrange a pick-up in advance if following a tight schedule. You can pay a zemidjan to wait for you for about FCFA 1,000 per hour. Traffic is most frequent on Wednesdays (Glazoué's market day) and on Dassa's market days, held every five days.

SIGHTS AND ACTIVITIES

Connaitre et Proteger la Nature (CPN), les Papillons
Know and Protect Nature, the Butterflies

CPN les Papillons is a non-governmental organization located just outside the village. Founded in the year 2000 by two villagers, Léandre Onikpo and Hyacinthe Adamassou, the organization is a branch of CPN International, which promotes environmental education and protection. CPN les Papillons works actively with the village and surrounding schools to educate the community on the importance of environmental conservation, as well as the development of eco-tourism. You can see the organization's passion for nature in its tranquil and beautiful site. An abundance of trees, beds of plants and flowers, and colorful sculptures by local artists decorate the grounds.

CPN offers guest lodging and meals (see below). With its large pavilions and open spaces, CPN les Papillons is perfect for hosting retreats or family getaways.

The organization offers tours of the village, guided hikes in the area, and tours of Glazoué, Dassa, and Savalou. The tour of the village includes a visit to a blacksmith and to a soap-producing workshop. During the guided hikes, you'll climb one of the hills in the area, where you can see the ruins of centuries-old hilltop settlements. Other tours include hippo-spotting, visiting a traditional *Ifa* priest, and visiting local farms to check out their agricultural practices.

All tours are in French and cost FCFA 5,000 plus FCFA 1,000 per person, for up to five people. For the tours of Glazoué, Dassa, and Savalou, you'll also have to pay for transport. For more details, contact CPN directly with the contact information given above. *Tel: 95.42.34.28 / 97.32.00.95. Email: onikpol@yahoo.fr*

EATING AND ACCOMMODATIONS

CPN les Papillons Providing the only accommodations in the village, CPN les Papillons also has a restaurant serving quality local cuisine. The cook, Agathe (also known as *Inan-Jacques*), is known for her *igname pilée*. They also have a *buvette* serving locally-made fruit juices, as well as beer and soda at normal prices. They can make special arrangements for groups. *Bed in dormitory, fan, communal latrine and bucket shower: FCFA 2,000; private room with two small beds, fan, private bathroom: FCFA 5,000; private bungalow with one large bed, fan, private bathroom: FCFA 7,000; camping, access to communal latrine and bucket shower: FCFA 2,000. Breakfast: FCFA 1,000; lunch and dinner: FCFA 2,000. Meals at 7:30–9:30am, 12:30–1:30pm, and 7:30–9:00pm.*

Glazoué

Glazoué is an important international market town 30 kilometers north of Dassa, along the paved road to Parakou. The market takes place every Wednesday, with merchants traveling from as far as Togo and Nigeria to sell their produce. From Tuesday evening to late Wednesday afternoon, this sleepy town comes alive as trucks and taxis bring loads of vendors with produce and merchandise to sell in an otherwise empty marketplace. All types of goods can be found here, varying with the seasons. You'll find colossal quantities of yams and red hot peppers. There is a *shakparo* (the Idaatcha word for *tchoukoutou*, or locally-brewed millet beer) section, and several food stands offer delicious local cuisine. Near the paved road and next to the permanent boutiques at the edge of the market, a few women sell *atièkè*, a traditional dish from Côte d'Ivoire made of *gari*, hot peppers, onions, palm oil, and fried fish. In the middle of the taxi station, some women sell *baguette* sandwiches filled with avocado and fish for FCFA 200. There is a particularly large secondhand clothing section along the road, with vendors from Niger and other northern countries. The Glazoué market is also a perfect spot to see the Fulani people in all their splendor. These nomadic herders attend regional markets to sell their *wagasi* cheese, chat with the villagers, and, of course, drink *tchoukoutou*. Their elegant clothing, ornate jewelry, and overall style set them apart from Benin's other tribes. The un-betrothed girls wear especially bright fabrics full of pink, red, and blue hues. Colorful beads dangle from their hair, waists, and wrists, and their hands and feet are dyed magenta—a brilliant display for attracting prospective husbands.

GETTING THERE

It's best to go to Glazoué on a day trip from Dassa. A zemidjan between the two towns costs at least FCFA 1,000, but may be less on market days. Glazoué zemidjans wear purple and green shirts, in contrast to the yellow and green of those from Dassa. A taxi costs about FCFA 600. If traveling directly from Cotonou, a taxi from the Place de l'Étoile Rouge costs FCFA 3,500–4,000. From Parakou, the trip costs around FCFA 3,000.

Buses generally only stop in Dassa, but a stop in Glazoué could be negotiated.

EATING AND DRINKING

Pantagruel This European-style bakery and restaurant with shiny glass windows is impossible to miss. The bakery offers croissants, pastries, and fresh coffee. The lunch and dinner menu is a cross between French and African food, including fresh salads and sandwiches, but many of the items are not regularly available. The dining room is air-conditioned. *Meals FCFA 2,500–5,000. Drinks FCFA 600–1,200. Hours: 8am–10pm. Open daily. Location: on the paved road, just north of the marketplace.*

La Polygone This casual and often busy place serves a cheap and wide selection of *pâte*, rice, fish, chicken, eggs, and *wagasi*. They also have a nice selection of green leaf and tomato sauces. An air-conditioned dining room is available for a small fee. *Meals FCFA 300–700. Drinks FCFA 250–800. Hours: 11am–11pm. Location: next to the Maison des Jeunes.*

Savé

Savé is another railroad town, about 35 kilometers north of Glazoué on the road to Parakou and just 30 kilometers west of the Nigerian border. You'll recognize it from miles away by the three massive round hills of black granite that tower over the town. For obvious reasons, they're known as *Les Mamelles de Savé*—the breasts of Savé—and occasionally by less polite names as well.

Savé is the first Tchabé town you'll reach coming from the south. Unlike many of the other ethnic groups in the Collines, the Tchabé were here before the time of the slave trade. According to legend, they migrated from

> The Tchabé language is so closely related to Yoruba and Nagot that people from other parts of Benin often refer to them as Nagot, though they consider themselves a separate ethnic group with a unique history.

present-day Nigeria around 500 years ago and founded three villages: Kêmon, Kilibo, and Savé.

In the 17th and 18th centuries, Dahomeyan slave-hunters drove refugees of other tribes into territory controlled by the Tchabé, causing tension and sometimes conflict. In some cases, Tchabé kings would designate a site at a comfortable distance from their own villages where refugees could settle. You can still see the results today: throughout the region, the Tchabé and other ethnicities (mostly the Mahi) live near each other, but in separate villages and speaking different languages.

GETTING THERE

From the Place de l'Étoile Rouge in Cotonou, a taxi should cost FCFA 4,000–4,500. A taxi to or from Parakou should cost FCFA 2,500–3,000, while a taxi to or from Glazoué should cost around FCFA 500.

SIGHTS AND ACTIVITIES

The most interesting activity in Savé is hiking the hills. On a clear day, you'll get a spectacular view of the surrounding forest and be able to spot other hills—many of them located next to other villages—that are dozens of miles away. You can also visit the royal palace, located off of the road toward Nigeria, and pay your respects to the king.

ACCOMMODATION

Hotel Idadu The rooms are quite basic and the staff can provide information on visiting the town and hiking the hills. *FCFA 7,000–12,000. Fan or A/C. Location: at the center of town, at the Y intersection on the north-south highway.*

Toll Stop
On the highway to Parakou, a couple kilometers north of Savé, there's a toll stop and weighing station. Young women line the road by the toll booth, selling bags of sliced papaya, ronier palm roots with chunks of coconut, and large bags of roasted peanuts. The ronier and coconut mixture is a surprisingly tasty and very fibrous snack. The Beninese say that ronier roots are a sexual stimulant for men.

Savalou

Like many towns and villages in the Collines, Savalou traces its history to the days of the slave trade. The population of the town today is a mix of the descendants of refugees who came here fleeing the south, seeking to escape the slave-hunters, and the descendants of the people who were already here. The primary ethnic groups here are the Mahi, who are related to the Fon, and the Ifé, who are related to the Yoruba.

Today, Savalou is known for its excellent *igname pilée*—said to be the best in the country—and for its annual Yam Festival in mid-August. The main cash crop here is cashews, which are sold to foreign merchants and exported to India and Europe. Several kiosks and small shops in town sell bottles of roasted cashews, and even cashew butter.

Savalou sits at the foot of a large rock outcropping; the paved road goes around its base and continues north towards Djougou and Natitingou. A dirt road leads west to the Togo border.

GETTING THERE

A bush taxi from Dassa to Savalou costs FCFA 1,000. A taxi returning to Dassa can be difficult to find, especially later in the day. The best place to catch a southbound taxi is the traffic circle on the southern end of Savalou, a short zemidjan ride from the town center. You can also take a zemidjan to Dassa for around FCFA 1,500. A taxi from Savalou to Djougou costs FCFA 4,500.

INTERNET

The **STG Informatique Cyber** offers surprisingly fast internet via a satellite connection. You can use one of their computers or bring your own. *Hours: Mon–Sat 7:30am–10:30pm and Sunday 10am–10pm. Rate: FCFA 400 per hour. Location: behind the government building across from the Catholic Church.*

BANK

The **Ecobank** has an ATM that accepts Visa cards. *Hours: Mon–Fri 8am–5pm and Saturday 9am–1pm. Location: on the main paved road through town. It's on your right if you're coming from the south.*

SIGHTS AND ACTIVITIES

Annual Yam Festival

Each August, around the 15th, Savalou celebrates its traditional yam festival, marking the beginning of the annual yam harvest. The West African yam is one of the only domesticated crops that are native to West Africa, and they remain a major part of the local cuisine in central and northern Benin. During the festival, a large fairground is set up in the center of town, with performances from national and local music groups, as well as several stands selling handicrafts and snacks. In a traditional ceremony in front of the Royal Palace, the first of the year's yam harvest is sacrificed to the spirits of the ancestors.

Centre Songhaï

This is one of the satellite centers of the main Songhaï Center in Porto-Novo. You can buy their fruit juice and baked goods, or use their internet café. *Location: near the southern entrance of town, a couple hundred yards from the main paved road.*

Sacred Caimans of Todjitche

The village of Todjitche is home to various Vodoun shrines. If you ask nicely, the villagers may recount the significance of each one. It's a short zemidjan ride away from Savalou.

Fétiche de Dankoli

Located several kilometers east of Savalou, along the highway to Djougou, this is probably one of the most impressive (and reputedly the most powerful) Vodoun fetishes in the country. Based at the foot of a giant tree, the *fétishe* is adorned with hanging white sheets and grotesque mounds of organic matter including palm oil, animal parts, and blood. It is "open" every day to any believer who wishes to ask for help and guidance from the spirits. A priest is constantly on-site to assist in the ceremony. Those making a request to the gods must first buy a wooden peg from the priest and hammer it into the tree, all the while whispering the request to themselves, and promising the gods that once the wish is granted, they will return to make a sacrifice in thanks. Then, they must drizzle palm oil and spit mouthfuls of *sodabi* onto the fetish while they continue to whisper their requests. Finally, a donation of at least FCFA 1,000 is placed next to the wooden peg on the tree. The request is supposed to be granted within the year, after which the believer must remember to return and give thanks by sacrificing a chicken, sheep, goat, or cow.

EATING AND DRINKING

Maquis Le Zenith Specializes in *igname pilée* and serves other local dishes as well. *Meals: FCFA 500–1,000. Drinks: FCFA 250–800. Location: if you're coming down the paved road from Dassa, it's located on the right-hand corner just after Ecobank.*

Chez Maman Lucrece Offers *igname pilée*, white and brown rice, and *pâte* along with a wide variety of sauces, including sesame sauce, peanut sauce, legume sauce, and tomato sauce. *Meals: FCFA 500–1,000. Drinks: FCFA 250–800. Location: near the Maison des Jeunes. If you're coming down the paved road from Dassa, it's after the road turns right. You'll see it on your right-hand side. It has a prominent sign and the building is painted green.*

Merci pour l'Amour Serves excellent *igname pilée* and other local cuisine. Due to its large seating capacity and video projector, people sometimes come here to watch football matches on TV. Live DJ on Friday and Saturday nights. *Meals: FCFA 500–1,000. Drinks: FCFA 250–800. Location: it's the large yellow building along the paved road coming from Dassa, just before the road turns right and heads toward Natitingou.*

Le Gabonais This small eatery serves Beninese-style spaghetti, salad, couscous, and French fries. The owner and chef takes great pride in providing good food and service to his customers, and the price is right. It's open until 2am. *Meals: FCFA 300–800. Drinks: FCFA 250–800. Hours: 8am–2am. Open daily. Location: near the corner where the paved road from Dassa ends and connects with the road leading to Natitingou. It has a prominent sign, and the building is painted red with a Coca-Cola logo on its walls.*

ACCOMMODATIONS

Auberge de Savalou A former administrative office of the town, the Auberge de Savalou belongs to the chain of French-owned hotels also present in Dassa, Grand Popo, Parakou, and Kandi. They have a garden area, and outside terrace, and secure parking. The restaurant serves good but relatively pricey French and African cuisine. Preparing your meal may take a while. *FCFA 9,000 with fan, FCFA 13,000 with A/C. Private bathroom. Tel: 22.54.05.24. Location: near the hospital, off the paved road through town.*

Auberge SOHA This inn offers basic rooms and a garden featuring a collection of traditional statues. The restaurant serves European and African cuisine. There's only one air-conditioned room, so if it's taken you'll have to settle for a fan. *FCFA 8,000 with fan, FCFA 14,000 with A/C. Private bathroom. Tel: 97.54.14.39. Location: in Quartier Vodje. Various signs on the main paved road point you toward the inn, and zemidjans know where it is.*

Auberge La Perseverance This quiet but centrally-located inn offers clean rooms, as well as a restaurant and bar. *FCFA 6,500 with fan, FCFA 10,500 with A/C. Tel: 90.95.40.74. Private bathroom. Location: in Quartier Ahossedo, near the town center.*

Motel le Roseau This is a more low-end place for travelers on a budget. Rooms and services are very basic, and there is no restaurant on the premises. However, it's conveniently located near the center of town. *FCFA 4,000–5,000 with fan. Tel: 90.95.47.13. Location: next to the Songhaï Center, in Quartier Ahossedo.*

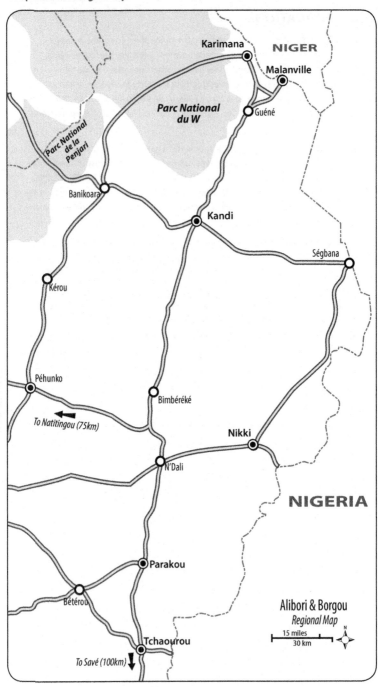

Alibori & Borgou

Welcome to the north. Getting off the bus from the south, you'll notice the drier air and slower pace of living. Even the larger towns often feel like they're simply big villages, not cities. The forests and farms of the south give way to the vast savanna, lightly wooded and thinly populated. The languages change too: instead of Fon and its sister languages, the people here mainly speak Bariba, Dendi, Fulani, Nagot, Tchabé, and many other dialects. Yams dominate northern cuisine, as do rice dishes, hot peppers, and a spongy cheese called *wagasi* that's hard to find in the south. You'll also find *tchoukoutou*, local millet beer, sold in small stalls made of thatch or clay, or in dedicated *tchoukoutou* markets.

You'll find much to like about the north. The people here tend to be friendlier toward foreigners, and negotiating with market vendors and *zemidjans* is less intense than in the south. You can discover the old cultural traditions that still thrive today among the northern tribes. However, Western-style amenities are few and far between outside Parakou, and the heat and dust can get intense, especially during the hot season from February to April.

Tchaourou

Located about 60 kilometers south of Parakou on the paved highway, Tchaourou is famous as the hometown of Benin's current president, Yayi Boni. In a way, the town has boomed since Yayi's election in 2006: while most of the population still lives in poverty, you'll see a conspicuous number of luxury cars and gated mansions. These are probably owned by the President's friends or family, many of whom hold lucrative government posts.

Along the highway just south of town, you can't miss the President's local residence—one of his many houses scattered throughout the country. In front you'll see the older house, a lavish white two-story structure surrounded by a pink fence, with a statue of a golden pot and a cowrie shell (the symbol of Yayi's political party) above the gate. Behind that stands a newer, even more impressive mansion that looks like it belongs in Southern California.

Alibori & Borgou

Tchaourou is a major market town. The market is located behind the rows of two-story shops next to the highway in the middle of town. Market day is Thursday, but there are plenty of vendors present throughout the week. The dominant ethnicities here are the Tchabé and Bariba; the Fon and Fulani also have a significant presence.

Parakou

The name *Parakou* comes from a Dendi phrase meaning "Everyone's city." You'll find dozens of ethnicities and languages from across Benin here, most prominently the Bariba, Dendi, and Nagot. Although it's one of Benin's largest cities, Parakou feels like a big village. Outside the bustling central market district, the town has the laid-back tempo and friendly population characteristic of rural northern Benin. Streets are far less congested than in Cotonou or Porto-Novo and buildings are interspersed with open fields and small farms.

Parakou is a good place to relax while traveling through northern Benin. You can find a limited selection of Western cuisine and Western-style accommodations, and you can also explore the town's numerous open-air markets and cultural venues.

GETTING THERE AND AWAY

Parakou is located 410 kilometers north of Cotonou and 315 kilometers south of Malanville, the main Benin–Niger border town. There's a semi-paved road leading northwest to Djougou, but it's so poorly maintained that the jarring 130–kilometer trip can easily take 4–5 hours. It may be faster and more comfortable to get to Djougou or Natitingou via Dassa, since the Parakou–Dassa and Dassa–Djougou roads are still in good shape.

The bus companies ATT, La Poste, Confort Lines, and Tunde each have an office in Parakou. There's no central bus hub, but if you tell a zemidjan the name of the bus company you want, he'll take you to their office, where you can buy tickets in advance and where buses depart from. Buses usually leave early in the morning and at midday.

Destination // Taxi price // Bus price:

Cotonou // FCFA 10,000 // FCFA 5,000–7,500

Dassa // FCFA 4,000 // FCFA 3,000–4,000

Djougou // FCFA 3,000 // –

Natitingou // FCFA 4,000 // FCFA 4,000–6,000

Kandi // FCFA 3,500 // –

Malanville // FCFA 4,500 // –

Zemidjans here wear yellow and green shirts and are easy to find, especially in the city center. Rides around the city cost FCFA 100–400.

Parakou has a dusty airstrip called *"l'Aéroport,"* but it's not currently used for public transport. President Yayi Boni's plane flies in once in a while.

HOSPITAL

Parakou's main hospital, a well-known landmark, is located on the road leading east from the Carrefour de la Colombe. See *Emergency Call Numbers* (p73) for details. In Parakou's many easy-to-spot pharmacies, you can find medicines for health problems that are common in Benin.

INTERNET

TerraCom, Parakou's most reliable internet café, offers a mostly consistent internet connection at a decent price. They have several desktop computers, along with tables and Ethernet cords to connect your laptop. *Hours: 8am–11pm Monday–Saturday, 9:30am-8pm Sunday. Location: On the first floor of a large building near Pharmacie Zongo. Most zemidjans know it either as "TerraCom," "le grand cyber," or "le cyber étage."*

BANKS

Ecobank, **Bank of Africa**, **SGBEE**, **Financial Bank**, and **Banque Atlantique** are all located in the town center. Ecobank and Bank of Africa are open through the lunch hour and can conduct Western Union transfers. Bank of Africa, SGBEE, Ecobank, and Banque Atlantique have ATMs that accept Visa cards.

SIGHTS AND ACTIVITIES

Hubert Maga Monument

As you enter Parakou from the south, you'll pass through a large traffic circle with a bronze statue in the middle. This is a monument to Hubert Maga, Parakou native and the first President of the newly-independent Republic of Dahomey. Maga was born in Parakou in 1916. His studies took him to Abomey, Bohicon, Porto-Novo, and eventually Dakar, Senegal. In his twenties, he converted from Islam to Catholicism—a rarity in those days. His educational background lent him credibility and influence among the uneducated masses, and he eventually founded the Northern Ethnic Group political party. In 1951 he was elected to the French National Assembly, where he rose to the position of Premier. He helped negotiate Dahomey's independence and became President in 1960.

Musée de Plein Air
Open-Air Museum

This museum showcases Bariba culture and displays the architecture and layout of traditional Bariba domiciles. A tour of the museum's round cement structures takes visitors through a series of themed rooms. You'll see exhibits of traditional Bariba clothing, an ancient loom, musical instruments, household pottery, and weapons The guide office has decorated calabash bowls and wooden sculptures for sale at typical tourist prices. It's a better bet to buy crafts from the artisans themselves (see *Artisans* on page 166). *Hours: 9am–5pm. Open daily, except for national holidays. Entrance fee: FCFA 1,500. Location: on the paved road toward Cotonou, near the southern entrance of town, between the Hubert Maga monument and the Arzéké Market. Zemidjans know where it is.*

Alibori & Borgou

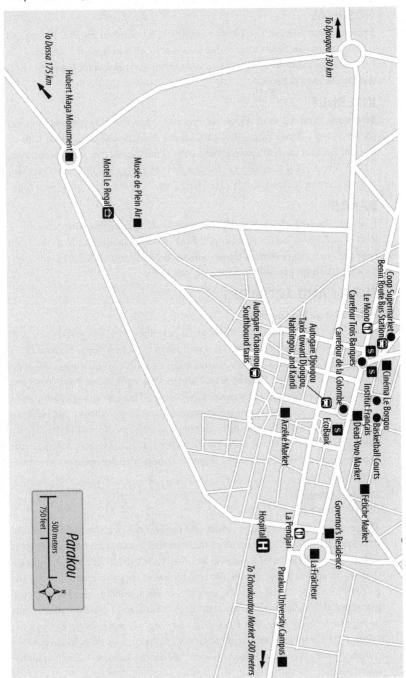

To Djougou 130 km

To Dossa 175 km

Hubert Maga Monument

Motel Le Regal

Musée de Plein Air

Coop Supermarket
Benin Route Bus Station
Le Mono
Carrefour Trois Banques
Carrefour de la Colombe
Autogare Tchaourou
Southbound taxis
Autogare Djougou
Taxis toward Djougou,
Natitingou, and Kandi
Cinéma Le Borgou
Institut Français
Basketball Courts
Dead Yovo Market
EcoBank
Arzéke Market
Fétiche Market
Governor's Residence
Hospital
La Pendjari
La Fraîcheur
Parakou University Campus

To Tchoukoutou Market 500 meters

Parakou
500 meters
750 feet
N

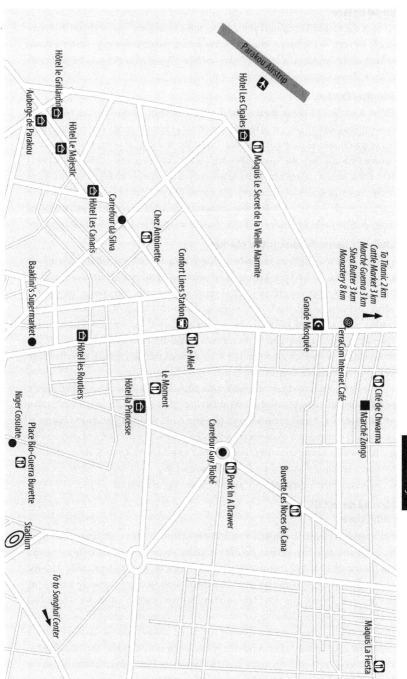

Parakou Airstrip

Hôtel le Grillardin

Auberge de Parakou

Hôtel Les Cigales

Maquis Le Secret de la Vieille Marmite

Hôtel Le Majestic

Hôtel Les Canaris

Carrefour da Silva

Chez Antoinette

Confort Lines Station

Baaklini's Supermarket

Hôtel les Routiers

Hôtel la Princesse

Le Miel

Le Moment

Grande Mosquée

To Titanic 2 km
Cattle Market 3 km
Marché Guema 3 km
Shea Butter 3 km
Monastery 8 km

TerraCom Internet Café

Cité de Chwarma

Marché Zongo

Niger Cosulate

Place Bio-Guerra Buvette

Carrefour Guy Riobé

Pork In A Drawer

Buvette Les Noces de Cana

Stadium

To to Songhai Center

Maquis La Fiesta

Alibori & Borgou

Royal Palace

Go visit the king of Parakou! If you drop in at the right time, you might catch a ceremony. Be sure to ask for permission before taking pictures. See page 34 for a guide to king-related etiquette. *Location: Near the Hubert Maga Monument on the south side of town. Zemidjans should know where it is.*

Songhaï Center

This is a satellite of the original Songhaï Center in Porto-Novo. You can visit to see some of Songhaï's innovative activities, which range from experimental agriculture to honey production to livestock breeding. While the center itself is about 15 kilometers outside Parakou, they also have a shop within the city where you can buy their products. *Location: Zemidjans usually know where the shop within Parakou is located. To go to the center outside Parakou, arrange for a zemidjan or a taxi driver to take you there and wait to take you back to Parakou—you won't be able to find another zemidjan for the return trip. To pay a zemidjan to wait for you, the standard price is FCFA 1,000 per hour.*

Chak-i-ti-boum Tchoukoutou Market

This is a collection of grass huts where people hang around on Saturday afternoons and drink local millet beer, known as *tchoukoutou* (pronounced choo-koo-too) or *tchouk* (chook). Get your fill of it while you're in the north: *tchouk* originates in the north, and even today, you'll be hard-pressed to find it south of Dassa. At a *tchouk* market, you enter a hut and sit down on a log bench, and the vendor—who is almost always a woman—ladles a bit of *tchouk* into a calabash bowl for you to taste. If you like it, tell her how much you want: FCFA 50 of *tchouk* fills the calabash about halfway, while FCFA 100 fills it nearly to the brim.

Since *tchouk* is so cheap, the market is a popular place to hang out, especially for people who can't afford bottled drinks at *buvettes*. It's a good place for visitors to chat with the locals, not least because they'll give you credit for trying their local beverage. However, the market is a common place for singles to meet a partner, and women who go there without male company should expect to get hit on. *Open Saturday, mid-afternoon until dusk. Location: on the paved road leading east from the Carrefour de la Colombe, after the hospital and just past the University of Parakou.*

Marché de Bétail
Cattle Market

This market is run by the Fulani, a nomadic herding tribe that originally comes from the Sahel and now ranges throughout West Africa. If you don't want to buy a cow, you can browse other Fulani merchandise: broad straw hats, swords, handmade daggers, and the colorful woven scarves that the herders wear to shield themselves from the sun and dust. Even if you don't buy anything, it's worth going just to see. The Fulani retain their traditional lifestyle, customs, and dress more than almost any other ethnicity in Benin. The men wear flowing robes and headscarves, and always carry a sword and a concealed dagger, while the women wear ornate jewelry and headdresses. Their complex, musical language is spoken throughout West Africa. Location: On the far north end of town, along the highway to Malanville.

Grand Marché Arzéké
Arzéké Main Market

You can find anything from produce to suitcases to traditional fabric in this vast, covered market. Just tell someone what you're looking for, and they'll either point you in the right direction or take you there themselves. Visitors might take interest in the beautifully carved Fulani and Bariba calabash bowls, as well as in the large selection of colorful fabric, which you can take to a tailor or seamstress and get made into a traditional outfit (*Culture,* p31). Hold on to your bag, and get permission from vendors before taking pictures of them or their merchandise. *Hours: Opens around 9am and gets going around 10–11am, and stays open until evening. Open daily, but most active on Saturday. Location: South side of the town center, straddling the main north-south road. Very hard to miss.*

Dead Yovo Market

Located near the Arzéké Market, this is where to find Western clothing and footwear. Most of it is secondhand—hence the morbid nickname—but prices and selection are good. The market lines the street leading north from the Carrefour de la Colombe; if you follow this street to the end, you'll see more stalls selling jeans along the dirt road to your right. Further down that dirt road, there's a market for Vodoun talismans and an area where livestock are butchered. *Hours: same as the Arzéké Market. Open daily, though some vendors may be closed on Sundays. Location: north of Carrefour de la Colombe.*

Marché Zongo and Marché Guéma

These are two of Parakou's smaller markets. You can get the feel of a thriving open-air market without the Arzéké Market's sometimes overwhelming atmosphere. They only sell food and basic supplies like soap. *Open daily. Location: zemidjans know them both by name.*

Institut Français
The French Institute

Like its sister-center in Cotonou, the French Institute in Parakou has a library and a gallery space with rotating exhibits. It's a good source for tourism information on the Borgou and Alibori regions. Newspapers, magazines, and other media are available to the public with proper identification. There are occasional concerts, lectures, films, and plays depicting West African history and culture. Animated tennis and basketball courts are attached to the cultural center and are open to anyone wanting to watch or get in on a game. (In both Cotonou and Parakou, the Institut Français has replaced the earlier Centre Culturel Français.) *Location: town center (see map).*

Grande Mosquée
Great Mosque

Most of Parakou's population is Muslim. This imposing structure is the largest mosque in the city and is worth a visit, though non-Muslims aren't allowed inside. *Location: town center; hard to miss, and zemidjans all know it by name.*

L'Université de Parakou
The University of Parakou

This campus is part of Benin's small public university system and is the primary university for northern Benin. It focuses on training professionals in several fields, including economics, political science, law, technology, medicine, agronomy, and languages. As in other Beninese universities and professional schools, the vast majority of professors and students are men. While the recently-built campus includes lecture halls, residence halls, a cafeteria, and a library, it's poorly maintained: locals use the neglected grounds to grow crops and graze sheep, and discard their trash in the broken fountains. *Location: On the paved road leading east from the Arzéké Market, past the hospital. Zemidjans know it as "l'Université."*

Monastery

Surrounded by charming gardens, tree-lined paths and flower bushes, this monastery is a great place for a quiet stroll. The main attraction is the monastery boutique, where you'll find an array of fresh juices, handmade soaps, balms, candles, fruit wines, syrups, and natural remedies, all made by the religious community. The kiosks and supermarkets in Parakou also sell the monastery juices and syrups, whose contact information is found on the product labels. It is best to call and make sure the boutique is open before making the trip. *Location: a few kilometers outside of the city, along the highway to Malanville. It's best to either go in a hired car, or take a zemidjan and pay him to wait for you—it would be nearly impossible to find another zem for your return trip. Pay him FCFA 1,000 for each hour he waits.*

ARTISANS

Hôtel les Routiers Local artisans sell a variety of jewelry and woodwork at a stand just outside the hotel.

Leatherwork A stand where artisans sell various leather products: bags, wallets, keychains, and so on. *Location: Across the street from the customs office, which zemidjans know as "Chez les Douanes." Please note that the location is not on the map.*

Hand woven cloths A local woman named Charlotte makes traditionally-woven cloths that you can use as placemats, blankets, or table runners. You have to order in advance. The order will take a few days to fill, but you can stop by her house to see how she works and choose the thread colors for a personalized piece. *Tel: 96.35.64.10*

Paintings This is a local artist who paints the people and scenery of the area. He's very friendly and always has plenty of paintings on hand. *Tel: 97.08.61.37*

Shea butter Butter derived from the shea plant is renowned for its effect on skin. You can find shea butter products sold at high prices by brand-name cosmetics companies in Europe and America, or you can buy them for cheap from the Africans who produce them. A union of 16 shea-producing women's groups is headquartered in Parakou. Their products, sold under the cosmetics line SOMBOU, include lotions, soaps, and skin creams. Their friendly and dynamic president is always happy to answer questions about the shea process, and if you come by on the right day you'll get to see the women at work. *Tel: 97.11.11.51 / 95.86.80.54. Location: Approximately two kilometers north of the Grande Mosquée, take a right at Titanic (p168) and travel one more kilometer.*

SUPERMARKETS AND BAKERIES

While the range of Western groceries available in Parakou is relatively limited, it's the best selection you'll find in northern Benin.

Baaklini's Overall, this is the best supermarket in Parakou. It's not comparable to larger supermarkets in Cotonou, but they stock basic Western groceries and have a decent wine and cheese selection. The owner is a Beninese-born Lebanese man who enjoys dressing like Tarzan. *Hours: 8am–12pm, 3–7pm. Closed Sundays. Location: A small building on the road leading northwest from Carrefour Trois Banques (known to zemidjans as Route de l'Aviation or Route de l'Aéroport). If you're coming from Carrefour Trois Banques, it's on your left, and if you reach Hôtel des Routiers you've gone too far. A big sign on top of the building says BAAKLINI.*

Co-op Pronounced as one syllable, "coop," this is another decent supermarket. It stocks most of the basics. *Hours: 8am–12pm, 3–7pm. Closed Sundays. Location: The large red building on the northwestern side of Carrefour Trois Banques.*

La Franchise It has the best wine selection in Parakou, and sells shea butter products as well. *Hours: 8am–12pm, 3–7pm. Closed Sundays. Location: A small building near Carrefour da Silva. Not on map.*

Pâtisserie Run by the owner of Baaklini's supermarket, this bakery sells pastries, cakes, and desserts. You can also dine in and have a hamburger with fries, a mini pizza, or schwarma. *Hours: 8am–12pm, 3–7pm. Closed Sundays. Location: Next to Baaklini's supermarket (see above).*

EATING AND DRINKING

Parakou offers a full range of dining options, though the selection of non-African cuisine is far more limited than in Cotonou.

High-end

Hôtel les Routiers The hotel restaurant, which serves excellent three-course French meals, offers Parakou's most European—and most expensive—dining experience. The menu includes a variety of meats and pasta dishes. *Meals: FCFA 4,000–8,500. Drinks: FCFA 1,000–3,000. Hours: the hotel gates close at 10pm. Open daily. Location: Route de l'Aviation, northwest of the Carrefour Trois Banques. Zemidjans know it by name.*

Le Moment Aside from the restaurant at Hôtel les Routiers, this is the most Western restaurant in Parakou. They serve pizza, steak, hamburgers, salads, and sandwiches in a setting that, after you step off Parakou's dusty streets, feels rather swanky. However, portions can run a bit small, and drinks are expensive. Prices go up slightly if you sit in the air-conditioned interior, rather than in the partially-enclosed patio. *Meals: FCFA 2,500–5,500. Drinks: FCFA 700–2,000. Air-conditioned indoor and covered* *patio seating. Hours: about 12pm–9pm. Closed Sundays. Location: Near Hôtel la Princesse. Zemidjans often don't know Le Moment by name, since it was renamed a few years ago, but they'll know the hotel.*

Midrange

⊗ **Chez Antoinette** You may not expect to find Italian cuisine in northern Benin, but here it is. A friendly Italian couple runs this restaurant, which offers salads and a variety of Italian pasta dishes, as well as some Beninese cuisine. Get there before 8pm—they often run out of food. If you say something nice in Italian, you might get a free drink. *Meals: FCFA 1,000–2,500. Drinks: FCFA 250–900. Patio seating, covered or open-air. Hours: about 11am–10pm, with food served before 2pm and after 6pm. Closed Sundays. Location: west of Confort Lines, off the Route de l'Aviation, and near Carrefour da Silva. Some zemidjans know it by name, while others know it only as the restaurant run by the white lady.*

⊗ **Cité de Chwarma** Home of delicious schwarma. You can get lamb or chicken, or the vegetarian option. The owner and chef, Nestor, provides excellent service and enjoys chatting with foreigners. When you walk in, he may put on a DVD of American music videos for you. *Meals: FCFA 1,000–2,000. Drinks: FCFA 250–700. Indoor or curbside seating. Hours: about 12pm–8pm. Closed Mondays. Location: Near Marché Zongo. It's a bright green building on the cobblestone road leading away from the main paved road. If you're coming from Marché Zongo, it will be on your right.*

Les Noces de Cana A large, clean restaurant and *buvette* serving pricey Beninese cuisine and some Western dishes, including chicken and fries. They also serve omelettes and instant coffee in the morning. Service can be slow, but the ambience is pleasant (unless they have music blaring) and the open walls allow the breeze to cool you off. Be aware that while they list a variety of European dishes on their menu—including steak and *bananes flambées*—most of them are prepared off-site, and you'll probably be waiting an hour or two if you order them. *Meals: FCFA 1,000–3,000. Drinks: FCFA 250–1,200. Covered patio seating. Hours: about 8am–11pm. Location: Nouveau Quartier, on the cobblestone road leading northwest from Carrefour Guy Riobé, and just around the corner from another buvette called Axe Beni Chic. Almost all zemidjans know either Les Noces de Cana or Axe Beni Chic by name.*

La Fraîcheur This restaurant and *buvette* sits next to a large traffic circle. You can sit on the covered patio or in the surprisingly tranquil park-like area in the middle of the traffic circle. They serve huge plates of couscous, fried chicken, and French fries. While it's a good place to chill out, avoid it if you're in a hurry: preparing your meal may take longer than the siege of Troy. Also, do not attempt to order chicken or fries separately. The fries come with the chicken. *Meals: FCFA 1,500–2,000. Drinks: FCFA 250–1,200. Seating: covered patio or open-air. Hours: about 12pm–10pm. Closed Sundays. Location: at the Carrefour Bio Guerra, just north of the hospital. Most zemidjans know it by name.*

Titanic A bar that serves great grilled fish with fries in the evening. *Meals: FCFA 800–1,200. Drinks: FCFA 250–1,200. Hours: about 12pm–10pm, with food served around dinnertime. Location: Approximately 2 kilometers north of the Grande Mosquée, near Marché Guéma, which most zemidjans know.*

Budget

⊗ **Maquis la Fiesta** Here you can try a range of northern Beninese cuisine—pounded yam, *wagasi* cheese, guinea fowl, peanut sauce, and red, white, and black *pâte*—in a clean, comfortable setting. You'll often see Parakou's wealthier citizens eating and drinking here, both to get a good meal and to rub shoulders: the proprietress' husband is the mayor of Parakou. *Meals: FCFA 500–1,000. Drinks: FCFA 250–1,200. Indoor and covered patio seating. Hours: about 12pm–2pm. Closed Sundays. Location: Nouveau Quartier. Most zemidjans know it by name.*

Pork In A Drawer The nickname says it all. The women here slow-cook chunks of pork in a drawer-type oven. When you arrive, they'll open the drawer to let you pick out your pork, which they serve with *piron* and ground hot peppers. They cook all parts of the pig, so look carefully and don't pick an ear or chunk of liver (unless that's what you want). *Meals: FCFA 550–1,100. Drinks: FCFA 250–900. Covered patio seating. Hours: lunch only, about 12pm–3pm. Closed Sundays. Location: The east side of Carrefour Guy Riobé.*

Carrefour Guy Riobé There are a few low-cost food options around this large, quiet traffic circle. At lunch or dinnertime, you can find good *igname pilée* at a shack on the traffic circle's western side. On the southern side, a couple of women sell sandwiches in the evening. You can get avocado, beans, rice, egg, tomato, onion, *wagasi*, meat, fish, or salad in your sandwich. They start running out of food around 7pm. Pork In A Drawer is also located here (see above). *Meals: Igname pilée with meat or cheese FCFA 200–400, sandwiches FCFA 150–500. Location: most zemidjans know it by name.*

Maquis Le Secret de la Vieille Marmite This clean, friendly lunch spot, whose name means "The secret of the old cooking pot," serves local cuisine that's a step above what you'd buy at a roadside shack. You can get *pâte*, rice, beans, or *igname pilée* with a wide selection of sauces, meats, fish, and *wagasi* cheese. *Meals: FCFA 500–1,000. Drinks: FCFA 250–1,200. Indoor or covered patio seating. Hours: about 12pm–2pm. Closed Sundays. Location: Near the airport and next to Hôtel les Cigales. Most zemidjans know it by name.*

Le Mono Serves a wide variety of local cuisine, including some items—such as fish and fried plantains—that are more typical of southern Beninese cooking and harder to find in the north. *Meals: FCFA 400–1,000. Drinks: FCFA 250–1,200. Hours: about 12pm–10pm, with food served for both lunch and dinner. Location: Near the Carrefour Trois Banques and the ATT bus line office.*

La Pendjari Another lunch spot serving good Beninese cuisine: *igname pilée* or rice with meat or *wagasi* cheese and a variety of sauces. *Meals: FCFA 400–800. Drinks: FCFA 250–1,200. Hours: about 12pm–10pm, with food served around lunchtime only. Location: Near the Governor's Residence ("La Maison du Préfet"), which most zemidjans know.*

Alibori & Borgou

ACCOMMODATIONS

⊗ **Hôtel les Routiers** This is Parakou's most luxurious hotel. It offers clean and comfortable rooms, all air-conditioned and with hot running water. The hotel is set among beautifully-kept gardens and has the best swimming pool in Parakou, which non-guests can use for FCFA 2,000. It's also home to Parakou's most European restaurant, serving a variety of excellent (and expensive) French dishes. It is located near the center of town, a few minutes walk away from the main Arzéké Market, the major taxi station, and several *buvettes* and supermarkets. Not coincidentally, it houses the French Vice-Consulate for northern Benin. *FCFA 20,000–45,000. A/C, satellite TV, and private bathroom with hot water. Meals: FCFA 3,800 for breakfast, FCFA 4,000 for a dish à la carte, FCFA 8,500 for a full multi-course meal. Tel: 23.61.04.01. Location: a few blocks north of the Carrefour Trois Banques. It's a major landmark and most zemidjans know it by name.*

Hôtel le Grillardin This relatively high-end hotel offers comfortable lodging, pleasant landscaped grounds, and a pool. The restaurant serves a range of European cuisine and pizza. The bar has wine and liqueur, as well as the typical beer and soda, which cost about double what you'd pay in a *buvette*. *FCFA 21,500–29,500. A/C and private bathroom. Meals: breakfast 1,500–3,200, lunch and dinner 4,000–7,000. Tel: 23.61.27.81. Location: on the west end of town. Zemidjans usually know it by name.*

Hôtel de la Colombe This hotel offers decent rooms in a quiet location. The restaurant serves a mix of Beninese and European cuisine. It's about a 20-minute walk, or a short zem ride, from the center of town. *FCFA 8,500 with fan, FCFA 15,500 with A/C. Meals: breakfast FCFA 800–1,500, lunch and dinner FCFA 5,500. Tel: 23.61.11.65. Location: near Rond Point Papini, a few meters off the cobblestone road. Zemidjans usually know it by name.*

Hôtel Les Cigales This midrange hotel offers clean rooms and a pleasant bar and dining area that's decorated with colorful African fabric and wooden sculptures. It's a great place to while away the hot afternoon hours, listening to music with a cold drink and a stack of cards. The restaurant serves delicious European cuisine, including pizza. Order your food well in advance. *FCFA 6,500–10,500 with fan, FCFA 17,000 with A/C. The lower-priced rooms share a common bathroom. Meals: breakfast FCFA 2,500, lunch and dinner FCFA 2,500–3,000, pizza FCFA 3,500–4,500. Tel: 97.89.11.98. Location: on the west end of town, by the airport.*

⊗ **Hotel Les Canaris** This hotel offers clean rooms, with pastel green doors set around a central cement courtyard. The staff is friendly, albeit a bit sleepy. Just up the road, a corner eatery is a convenient spot for a cheap breakfast. *FCFA 6,500 with fan, FCFA 15,000 with A/C. Private bathroom. Tel: 23.61.11.69. Location: off the road between the airport and Bank of Africa, well indicated by signs.*

Motel Le Regal This is one of the first places visitors will see when arriving from Cotonou, and it is also a good spot for a snack and a cold drink. The rooms are basic and clean, and a particular attraction is the large and seemingly frustrated caged baboon in the courtyard. *FCFA 6,000–8,500 with fan, FCFA 10,500–15,500 with A/C. Private bathroom. Meals: FCFA 2,500 and up. Tel: 23.61.26.82. Location: near the southern entrance of town, between the Carrefour Hubert Maga and the Musée de Plein Air.*

N'Dali

N'Dali lies 60 kilometers north of Parakou, on the north-south highway. There is a major customs checkpoint here that regulates all north-south commercial traffic. It's also a crossroads between the highway and the dirt road leading to Nikki and nearby Nigeria.

Nikki

Nikki is the historical Bariba capital of the northeast. It is the seat of an ancient royal palace that still presides over a vast territory, including a large part of northeastern Nigeria. At the height of the dry season, you'll notice the effects of the encroaching desert in this quaint town of dusty paved streets. For travelers sticking to Benin's paved roads, a side trip to Nikki may be the best opportunity to visit a culturally charged locale that, with the exception of the period of the Gaani Festival, is relatively untouched by tourists. Nikki also provides a glimpse into some of Benin's authentic, rural agricultural town life. Despite being off the main roads, Nikki has a bustling daily market and town center, and offers all of the basic amenities an adventurous traveler would need for a day trip or overnight stay.

GETTING THERE

The easiest way to reach Nikki is by getting a bush taxi in Parakou, where Nikki-bound taxis leave throughout the day. You can also take a taxi to N'Dali and change to another taxi to complete the trip. For the return trip, taxis leave Nikki for Parakou several times a day. If you're making a day trip from Parakou, you can arrange (possibly for a small fee) for your taxi driver or a local zemidjan to notify you before the last taxi of the day leaves Nikki.

SIGHTS AND ACTIVITIES

Palais Royal
Royal Palace

Before colonization, the King of Nikki reigned over a vast territory comprising parts of present-day northeastern Benin and northwestern Nigeria. Today, he remains a guardian of the culture of the Bariba people, who still inhabit this region. Visits to the palace are conducted through the Mayor's office, whose *Chef de Culture* can provide directions and a guide. If he's home, the king may receive you in his throne room. The best day to visit is Friday, when noblemen from all corners of the Borgou region come in traditional dress to greet the king or bring issues to his attention. Remember to ask before taking pictures, and to offer a donation of about FCFA 1,000 to the king and to anyone who helps you. See *Etiquette* (p34) for more information about visiting local kings. *Open daily. Location: on the east side of town.*

Alibori & Borgou

Horsemen of Nikki

If you're visiting Nikki outside of the period of the Gaani Festival, you might wonder where all the horses and riders are located. There are no obvious stables to be seen, and most of the horseback riding takes place out in the fields or on the hunting grounds. The horses are actually stabled in familial compounds throughout the town, and are kept behind closed doors when not being ridden. Any teenage school student with adequate language skills will be able to guide visitors to a home with a stabled horse. With a little negotiation, the rider may be willing to show his horse and conduct a bareback tour of the town, or down a peaceful dirt road to the town's large water reservoir. The horses are high-strung and accustomed to dancing parades, so it is best that the owners stay nearby. While there's no official price, you should pay about FCFA 3,000 per person for a horseback ride, depending on the length of the ride. Keep in mind that the horsemen usually leave early in the morning to work in the fields and come back at nightfall, so a visit should be arranged a day in advance.

EATING AND DRINKING

Roadside stands offer local fried snacks, or rice dishes. In the morning and at lunchtime you can find *igname pilé*, the signature dish of the north, served with a tomato sauce and fresh local cheese or meat. Ask around for a stall serving *igname pilé*, or just follow your ears to where you hear the rhythmic pounding of the yams. Despite its small size and Muslim majority, Nikki houses a good number of bars. Some of the best watering holes include **La Refuge** (on the way to the *barrage*, or reservoir), **Le Campement** (across from the Mayor's office), and **Le Secret** (a bit hidden, past the customs checkpoint, right off the road going to Tchikandou/Nigeria), where from the roof you can enjoy a drink while watching the sunset.

> The most Western dining options in Nikki are Chez John's Hotel and La Belle Princesse, where one can get a choice of meat with fries, rice, or couscous for FCFA1,500-3,000

Cafeteria Okpé Oluwa A polite and friendly gentleman cooks up spicy omelet sandwiches, spaghetti, and coffee or tea from his modest roadside cafeteria. *At the southwest entrance of town, by the road to N'Dali; Meals FCFA200-600; Open daily, early mornings (7am) and evenings.*

La Fête de la Gaani

Nikki's main cultural attraction is the Gaani Festival, a spectacular celebration featuring Bariba horsemen. Visitors flood the town to watch the riders and their decorated horses provide elaborate displays of traditional horsemanship. The king and his dignitaries parade around town as the ceremonial grounds vibrate with the sound of drums and trumpets, and the clamor of the crowd. Other events include craft shows, dances, musical events, and even a 5k run.

The Festival's dates vary each year. It usually takes place around Maoloud (the birth of the Prophet Mohammed) and lasts about a week. Contact the Hôtel Kpe Lafia (see Accommodations, below) to ask about specific dates. If you're planning to stay in Nikki at this time, you'll need to get hotel reservations well in advance.

Chez Ezaco Ezaco and his lovely family will prepare all the classic cafeteria dishes. At times, homemade yogurt is also available. *Near the royal palace; Meals FCFA200-600; Open Mon-Sat, 7am-10pm.*

Chez Tata This hole-in-the-wall restaurant is run by a Fon lady and is a favorite of locals. She serves up delicious garbanzo beans (pois chiche) in palm oil—usually they're freshest at lunch—as well as other traditional plates. *The eastern edge of the meat market, just behind the old radio tower; Meals FCFA200-600; Open Mon-Sat, 7am-10pm.*

ACCOMMODATION

Hôtel Kpe Lafia This place offers basic rooms, and the price is right. The restaurant serves basic fare, such as rice and chicken, to order. *FCFA 2,500 with fan, FCFA 5,000 with A/C. Private bathroom. Meals: breakfast FCFA 1,500, lunch and dinner FCFA 3,000. Tel: 95.02.92.42, 96.63.39.02 (manager's cell). Website: hotelkpelafianikki.com. Location: outside of town, on the road leading to Parakou.*

Hotel Chez John This hotel was built to accommodate the flood of visitors who come once a year for the Fête de la Gani. Apart from that week long festival in the spring, the hotel remains open but quite empty.

This two story building houses clean and basic rooms at great prices. A deluxe room with a/c is being built and should be ready to house guests for a higher fee in 2010.

Attached to the hotel there is a restaurant and *buvette* serving tasty Beninese meals including hearty breakfast omelets, rice or couscous dishes, and chicken and fries from FCFA1,000 per dish. It is all made to order, so guests should place requests in advance. A hopping underground night club at the hotel is popular with the locals on weekend nights. *From the west entrance of town, the first dirt path to the left before the marketplace. Indicated by signs; FCFA5,000 and up; fan, private shower and toilets.*

Campement de Nikki A series of comfortable bungalows dot the dusty hotel courtyard. An open air restaurant offers basic Beninese cuisine, and is the favorite watering hole of local functionaries and visiting NGO workers. *West side of town, across the intersection from the mayor's office; FCFA5,000 and up; fan, private shower and toilets.*

Kandi

Kandi, on the north-south highway 200 kilometers north of Parakou and 110 kilometers south of Malanville, developed as a rest stop along the ancient caravan routes. The settlement became an important chiefdom under the rule of the Bariba King of Nikki. The main entrance to the W National Park is at Alpha Koara, 40 kilometers north of Kandi. You can also enter the park at Kofonou, 15 kilometers from Karimama, or at Sampeto via Founougo.

Alibori & Borgou

GETTING THERE

A bush taxi should cost FCFA 3,000–3,500 to or from Parakou and FCFA 1,500 to or from Malanville.

EATING AND DRINKING

There is a wide choice of bars and *buvettes* around Kandi, most of which are concentrated around the marketplace. Here are a couple recommended spots.

Maquis Aefi offers a range of Beninese cuisine: rice, *pâte*, couscous, *wagasi*, turkey wings, and chicken and fries. *Location: at the southern roundabout near the cotton factory.*

Chez Maman Sans Prix is a good choice for local cuisine. They serve *igname pilée* with either *wagasi* or a variety of bush meat. *Location: behind the cotton factory.*

ACCOMMODATIONS

Auberge de Kandi Set in a vast courtyard of multiple buildings, this inn offers pleasant and simple rooms. There are a total of seven rooms: five with A/C and two with a fan. Some rooms have satellite television. The open-air restaurant and bar are always open and serve African and French dishes. It's the only place in Kandi that serves beer on tap. The hotel staff can arrange a tour of the Chutes de Koudou. *Single occupancy: FCFA 10,500 with fan, FCFA 15,500 with A/C. Double occupancy: FCFA 12,000 with fan, FCFA 17,000 with A/C. Private bathroom. Meals: FCFA 4,000. Tel: 23.63.02.43 / 93.05.21.90. Location: almost two kilometers north of town, on the road toward Malanville.*

Motel de Kandi This small hotel offers clean, simple rooms. They have an in-house restaurant and bar. *FCFA 8,500 with fan and shared bathroom, FCFA 15,500–18,500 with A/C and shared bathroom, FCFA 25,000 for suite with A/C and private bathroom. Meals: breakfast FCFA 1,500, lunch and dinner FCFA 2,500–3,000. Tel: 23.63.03.03. Location: north of town, on the road toward Malanville.*

Auberge La Rencontre This hotel has a friendly atmosphere and ten clean rooms with double beds. There are satellite TVs in each room. There's a nice rooftop bar and restaurant, but be sure to order food in advance. *FCFA 7,500–14,500. Fan or A/C, shared or private bathroom. Location: near the taxi station, on a side street off the paved road. Turn right two streets after the Pharmacie Na Siara, or one street after La Maison Blanche nightclub if coming from the south.*

Auberge la Pension de l'Alibori This centrally-located hotel has eight rooms with double beds. Two of them have A/C, but they don't always work. If the A/C's working, the price is FCFA 12,000. There's a good restaurant on-site, but be sure to order meals in advance. *FCFA 6,500–12,000. Fan or A/C, private bathroom. Location: in the center of town on the old road to Banikoara and near the Banikoara taxi gare.*

Parc National du W

The W National Park is one of Benin's two safari parks, the other being Pendjari National Park in the northwest. The "W," pronounced "doole-vay" in French, refers to the shape of the section of the Niger River that forms the border between Benin and Niger within the park. The park was created in 1954 and has since been named a UNESCO World Heritage Site and a UNESCO Biosphere Reserve. While its one million hectares include land in Benin, Burkina Faso, and Niger, most of the reserve is in Benin.

The park belongs to the multinational W-Arli-Pendjari park complex, a 50,000-square-kilometer reserve that stretches across the borders of Benin, Burkina Faso, and Niger. Twelve thousand square kilometers of the park complex, comprising parts of the Pendjari and W National Parks, are located within Benin.

The Niger River, which flows through the reserve, is the third-largest river in Africa (after the Nile and Congo Rivers) and an important flyover landmark for migratory birds. Over 350 species of birds have been identified within the park.

Park W has significant populations of hoofed mammals, such as buffalo and warthogs, as well as baboons, aardvarks, elephants, and hippopotami. There are smaller populations of cheetahs, leopards, lions, caracals, servals, and the rare West African manatees. The park's wetlands, important to many forms of life, perform a critical role in water quality and availability in the region by trapping and filtering the ground water. The rainy season displays a lush version of the landscape, with more watering holes and diverse flora.

Humans have lived along the Niger River since Neolithic times. Today, the Fulani people inhabit parts of the park and herd their cattle throughout, while Bariba and Dendi farmers cultivate fields around the perimeter. The conflict between the local populations' reliance on the park's resources for their livelihoods and the efforts of park authorities to conserve the natural habitat is a constant source of friction.

VISITING THE PARK

As with Pendjari National Park, the best time to spot animals is February though April. This is the latter half of the dry season, when water is scarce and animals concentrate around the few remaining watering holes. Much of the brush has dried out or been burned, making it easier to spot animals. However, this is also the hottest part of the year; afternoon temperatures can reach 50° Celsius, or 120° Fahrenheit. The landscape is also less scenic than during the rainy season, when lush green vegetation covers the park.

PARK ENTRY FEES

Tickets are available at the park's entrance.

FCFA 10,000 / person (foreigner)

FCFA 6,000 / person (Beninese citizen)

FCFA 3,000 / fishing license

Alibori & Borgou

PARK GUIDES

You must have a guide to enter the park. One recommended guide is **Aziz**. Reach him at 64.06.31.84.

The CENAGREF office in Kandi can also put you in contact with a guide, as well as help you make hotel and camping reservations within the park. Reach them at 23.63.00.80.

SIGHTS IN THE PARK

Les Chutes de Koudou
The Koudou Falls

The remote area around these waterfalls has been developed to allow for comfortable tent-camping and wildlife-viewing. Lions, elephants, and hippopotami frequent the area. However, the falls disappear during the dry season.

Point Triple

Located on the west side of the park, the *Point Triple* is where the countries of Benin, Niger, and Burkina Faso meet. There's a rough track here that runs between Park Pendjari and Park W, but it's passable only with an all-terrain vehicle and a driver familiar with the area.

EATING AND DRINKING

There are no restaurants within the park. Eat at the campsite where you're staying, or buy non-perishable food in Kandi or Parakou and bring it in.

PARK ACCOMMODATIONS

Campement de Chutes de Koudou This remote camp is run by the French Auberge chain. To reach this point, a 4x4 vehicle is recommended in the dry season, and necessary in the rainy season. The camp is comprised of 11 tents, permanently installed on teak structures with roofs. Reservations can be made from the Auberge de Kandi or the CENAGREF office in Kandi. Though there is no electricity, radio communication is possible between the camp and Kandi over the park guide network. The camp also has kayaks to tour the Mekrou River. *FCFA 20,000. Extra bed FCFA 3,000. Mosquito net, private shower and toilet. Meals: FCFA 4,000. Tel. (Kandi office): 23.63.02.43. Location: 120 kilometers northwest of Kandi, via Banikoara and just past the Sampéto entrance.*

Staying across the border

There are other campsites on the Burkina Faso and Niger side of the park. These include Point Triple, Tapoa, Karey Kopto, Boumba, and Mare. Arrangements can be made through CENAGREF in Kandi. Before staying in Niger, see page page 71 for information on *Safety and Security*.

Malanville

Malanville sits on the banks of the Niger River, which forms the border between Benin and Niger. A bridge connects Malanville with the Nigerien town of Gaya. The border with Nigeria is also nearby, to the southeast. Malanville is an international town, with heavy Arabic influence and a largely Muslim population that peacefully shares the town with a Christian minority. Its weekend market is renowned throughout the Sahel, though it's been recently relocated, and the steep cost of stalls at the new market has driven many vendors away. You'll also find a night market on weekends. Because it's so close to Niger and to Park W, Malanville attracts some tourists, though security concerns have caused tourism in Niger to drop off in recent years (see Security, p71).

GETTING THERE AND AROUND

If you're coming from Cotonou, take a bus or bush taxi to Parakou, then switch to another bush taxi for the rest of the trip. You can take a direct Malanville taxi for FCFA 4,500, or take a taxi to Kandi for FCFA 3,500 and then another taxi from Kandi to Malanville for FCFA 1,500. The Parakou–Kandi road has recently been repaired, making this leg of the trip relatively quick and comfortable.

EATING AND DRINKING

Omega 2000 Overall, this is the best food in Malanville. They serve chicken and fries, and sometimes rabbit. They also have the best beer selection in town. *Meals: FCFA 2,000. Drinks: FCFA 350–1,200. Location: down the street from the TV and radio building.*

Nigerian Pub In this makeshift structure of reeds, you can eat pork and drink Nigerian beer. *Meals: FCFA 500–1,500. Drinks: FCFA 350–1,200. Location: near the stadium.*

Buvettes For street food or a cold drink, you can find *buvettes* all along the main road through town.

Grocery store Malanville has a small shop that sells some Western goods. *Location: next to Pharmacie Sahel.*

ACCOMMODATION

Relais du Soleil This recently-renovated hotel offers pleasant and comfortable rooms, as well as newly-constructed bungalows. Some rooms have satellite TV. The restaurant serves hearty meals, including fresh grilled fish from the river, for about FCFA 3,000. The staff can arrange tours into Park W, camel or horse rides, and boat trips up the Niger River. They have a swimming pool, which non-guests can use for FCFA 1,500. *FCFA 12,500–22,000. Fan or A/C, private bathroom. Tel: 23.67.01.25. Location: on the southern edge of town, near the taxi station.*

Hôtel Sota In association with Parakou's Hôtel Le Majestic, the Hôtel Sota offers classy accommodations. It offers a swimming pool, a bocce ball court, and a small playground. Niger River tours by pirogue can also be arranged. The attached restaurant, Le Calao, offers African and European meals for FCFA 2,500–4,500, while the bar, Le Baobab, serves mixed drinks in the evenings. *Tel: 97.64.97.48; FCFA 18,000–22,000; fan or A/C, private bathroom.*

Motel Issifou This is the best budget option in town, with clean, basic rooms and large bathrooms. The restaurant serves local meals starting at FCFA 1,500. *FCFA 5,500. Fan, private bathroom; Location: off the paved road at the southern end of town.*

Guéné

Guéné is located at a fork in the road 26 kilometers south of Malanville. The paved road to the east leads to Malanville and the border with Niger, while the dirt road leading northwest goes to Karimama. The main attraction in Guéné is the market every Thursday, which is known for its livestock. Fulani and other traders come from afar to trade cattle, sheep, and goats. This is a great place to find Fulani clothing and accessories, as well as the beautifully carved calabash bowls that the Fulani use to carry milk.

Atakora & Donga

Like the northeastern Alibori–Borgou region, the Atakora–Donga presents a sharp contrast to regions further south: a slower pace of life, calmer towns, and friendlier people. Heading north, you move from the flat, scrubby landscape of the Donga to the

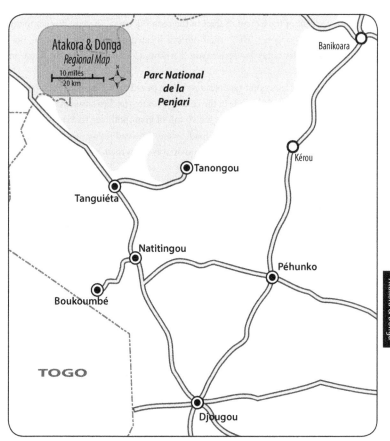

low, rocky mountains of the Atakora Range—some of the most beautiful country in Benin, especially during the rainy season.

Djougou, the main town of the Donga, acts as a major center of trade between Benin and other countries in the region, especially Togo. Natitingou, main town of the Atakora, is arguably Benin's most scenic city. Numerous ethnicities and languages call Natitingou home, including peoples hailing from nearby Togo and Burkina Faso. From Natitingou, you can go on safari at the Pendjari National Park, visit the waterfalls at Kota and Tanongou, and take a day trip to Boukoumbé to see traditional fortified houses called *Tata Sombas*.

Djougou

Djougou is an important market town and one of the largest towns in northern Benin. Buses and taxis stop here en route between Parakou and Natitingou. The majority of the community here is Muslim.

GETTING THERE AND AWAY

Buses stop in front of the Cinema Sabari in the center of town. The best bus company operating out of Djougou is ATT. Their office is located in the Cinema Sabari. Taxis leave several times a day for Natitingou, Parakou, Cotonou, and nearby Kara, in northern Togo.

The road from Djougou to Parakou was once paved but hasn't been maintained, and is now among the worst roads in the country. Some stretches have entirely reverted to dirt road, while other stretches are so full of giant potholes that drivers prefer to drive through the grass next to the road. Avoid this road if you can—go south to Dassa, then back up north to Parakou. If you do travel this road, be aware that the trip can take up to 5 hours.

Destination // Taxi price // Bus price

Cotonou // FCFA 7,000 // FCFA 7,000

Parakou // FCFA 2,500 // –

Natitingou // FCFA 1,500 // FCFA 1,500

Savalou // FCFA 4,500 // –

HOSPITAL

Djougou's main hospital is located west of the town center, on the road to N'Dali.

BANKS

Djougou has two banks, **Ecobank** and **Bank of Africa**. Ecobank is near the Cinema Sabari in the center of town, while Bank of Africa is located on the road to Parakou.

SIGHTS AND ACTIVITIES

Djougou has a well-reputed handicraft trade. You can find woven fabrics, jewelry, and sculptures in the little boutiques around town. Northwest of the market, the Zembougou-Beri neighborhood houses silver jewelers and blacksmiths who weld recycled metal into large ladles, royal canes, and ornaments. On the west end of town, near the hospital, traditional weavers sell beautiful shawls and wraps from their workshop. Another craftsman nearby fabricates unique leather flasks and small boxes. Just west of the market, an artist displays his abstract paintings in his little studio. At the **Espace Tissage** (Weaving Area) in the neighborhood called Quartier Yalwa, you can watch apprentices learning to weave traditional West African fabric.

The **regional market** takes place in the center of Djougou, behind Bank of Africa, every four days. The **Djougou Royal Palace** is located off the road to Togo, where the king welcomes visitors in exchange for a small gift—a suggested donation is FCFA 1,000.

North of Djougou, the hillside **Tanéka** villages off the highway near Copargo are worth a visit. These semi-nomadic communities have established settlements of stone-walled huts with shale covered courtyards. Only the witch doctors, elders, and children remain in the village while all able bodied persons travel as seasonal workers. The village chief carries a long, curved pipe made of copper, which is constantly lit. Though the community is friendly, visitors should enter with particular caution and respect, and of course ask permission before taking photographs. Inquire at one of the hotels in Djougou or Natitingou for a local guide to take you into the villages.

EATING AND DRINKING

Foreigners generally like much of the regional cuisine here, which is good, because that's all you'll find in Djougou. There are food stands and local eateries all over the place serving rice, couscous, *waché* (a somewhat spicy brown rice with a smattering of beans), *wagasi* cheese, meat, and fish. Some good local eateries include **Le Rencontre des Amis** (Meeting Place for Friends), **Le Sans-Rancune** (Without a Grudge), and **Le Flamboyant**. If you're not feeling adventurous, the most Western-style restaurants (though not necessarily serving Western-style food) are located at the Motel du Lac, Hôtel de la Donga, and Hôtel Sabou. For a refreshing drink along the road, try **L'Escale des Routiers** (Trucker Stop), located on the road toward Parakou.

ACCOMMODATION

Motel du Lac Set in a well-kept and tranquil garden, this hotel offers clean and spacious rooms with elaborate African décor and satellite TV. The owner, Madeline, is quite helpful and can provide information on visiting the region, such as the best way to go to the Tanéka villages and when to visit the king. She promotes local craftsmen by keeping a collection of their work on display. The restaurant, located in the courtyard, serves excellent meals. *FCFA 12,000–15,000 with fan, FCFA 15,000–18,000 with A/C. Tel: 97.54.06.56. Email: thamazighrol@yahoo.fr. Location: on the road south toward Cotonou.*

Atakora & Donga

Hôtel de la Donga This centrally-located hotel offers basic but spacious rooms. Suites are available for double the price, but the only difference is that you have a separate living room. You can't get a room with two beds, so if you're traveling with a friend, be ready to snuggle. *FCFA 15,500 with fan, FCFA 20,500 with A/C, FCFA 40,500 for a suite. Tel: 97.19.10.35 / 97.11.75.54. Location: on the road toward Parakou.*

Hôtel Sabou Located in a quiet neighborhood away from the main street, this hotel has a pleasant courtyard and a restaurant offering good local cuisine. However, rooms are quite small. *FCFA 5,500–8,000 with fan, FCFA 13,000–14,000 with A/C. Tel: 96.00.30.90 / 94.44.40.99. Location: Quartier Sassirou.*

The Monkeys of Kikélé

The village of Kikélé, six kilometers from Bassila, houses a small family of monkeys known locally as the *singes magistraux*, the masterful monkeys. They reportedly belong to a near-extinct species and are a spectacular sight, with an unusual howl. To visit, first go to Bassila: take a bush taxi from Dassa or Djougou, or take a Djougou- or Natitingou-bound bus from Cotonou and tell the driver you want to get off in Bassila. At the taxi station in Bassila, look for the Kikélé zemidjans in their green shirts. The zem ride to Kikélé should cost FCFA 500. There is no set organization or official guides, but if you ask around the village, you can find someone to guide you for about FCFA 1,000. You may be asked to visit the home of a local traditional leader first.

Péhunco

Escape the regular tourist track by stopping in Péhunco. Also known as Ouassa-Péhunco, this is a major crossroads and market town on a dirt road between Parakou and Natitingou. In the markets you'll find *tchoukoutou*, northern millet beer, as well as jewelry sold by the significant Fulani population. The dominant ethnic group here is the Bariba, and their culture is on full display. On national holidays and other important occasions, the village hosts ceremonies and parades featuring the king on horseback. Although there isn't much in particular for tourists to do, it's a good example of the daily life and culture of a large and vibrant northern village.

> In the north, the rainy season is the worst time to travel to towns that are only accessible by dirt roads, as the roads sometimes wash out and fill with potholes.

GETTING THERE

Since Péhunco is a rural town, it's accessible only by a rough dirt road, and taxis don't arrive or depart as regularly as in larger towns. The following table shows approximate taxi departure times and prices. The departure times are the same whether you're going to or departing from Péhunco. Remember that, due to occasional bandit attacks, it's unwise to travel on rural dirt roads after sunset.

Route // Approximate departure time // Price (can vary)

Péhunco–Natitingou // Noon and evening // FCFA 2,500

Péhunco–Djougou // Noon and evening // FCFA 2,500

Péhunco–Parakou // Throughout the day // FCFA 4,000

Péhunco–Kérou // Noon // FCFA 3,000

As with elsewhere, taxis only leave once the car is full of passengers, which can take a while. To avoid a long wait at the taxi station, give your phone number (if you have a Beninese phone) to the driver and ask him to call you when he's ready to go. If you don't have a phone, you can tell a zemidjan where you'll be waiting and offer to tip him a couple hundred francs if he comes to let you know when the taxi's ready.

EATING AND DRINKING

Le Triomphe This *buvette* has recently expanded to serve food. They now offer good-quality Beninese cuisine after 7pm. However, they're sometimes blasting music. *Meals: FCFA 200–600. Location: On the road to Djougou.*

Other easy-to-find and well-managed *buvettes* include **Petit à Petit**, located on the road to Parakou, and **Le Chateau**, located across from the taxi station.

ACCOMMODATION

Hôtel Prestige If you opt to spend the night in Péhunco, Hôtel Prestige is your only real choice. The rooms are clean and basic, and the staff is friendly. Friday and Saturday are dance nights and can get noisy. They recently renovated several rooms and built a second building. You can stay in the older rooms for a cheaper rate, or go for the more expensive newer rooms, which have television and A/C. *Older rooms, single or double, with fan: FCFA 5,500. Newer rooms, single or double, with A/C: FCFA 10,000–12,000.*

Natitingou

Built along the sides of two mountain ridges in the rocky Atakora Range and in the narrow valley the runs between them, Natitingou is the most scenic major town in Benin. It balances the laid-back tempo of village life with a selection of good hotels, restaurants, and other amenities.

Natitingou is a natural stopover for travelers to the Atakora. From here you can take a day trip to Boukoumbé, Tanguiéta, or the waterfalls at Kota or Tanongou. If you're going on safari at Pendjari National Park, your guide will probably pick you up here and take you to your lodging in or near the park.

You'll also want to take some time to explore the town itself. Natitingou is increasingly cosmopolitan, with significant populations of the Bariba, Dendi, Ditammari, Fon, Fulani, Waama, Yoruba, and many other ethnicities, but it hasn't lost the hospitality and charm of a village, from the quiet dirt streets to the people's striking eagerness to help out lost visitors. The town is scenic at any time of the year: in the rainy season, flowering trees and shrubs cover the mountainsides, while a fine red dust coats the town during the dry season.

Atakora & Donga

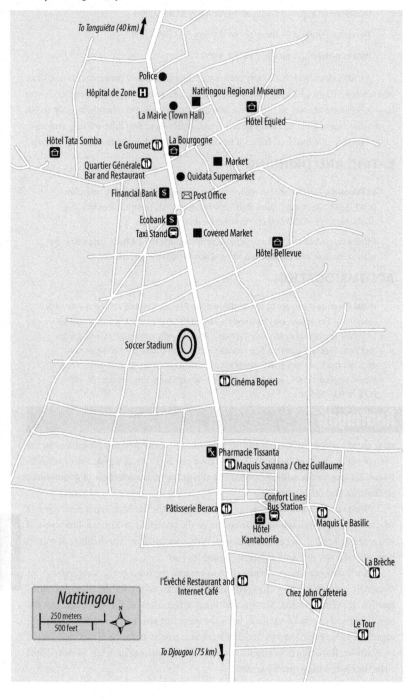

To Tanguiéta (40 km)

Police

Hôpital de Zone

Natitingou Regional Museum

La Mairie (Town Hall)

Hôtel Equied

Hôtel Tata Somba

Le Groumet
La Bourgogne

Quartier Générale
Bar and Restaurant

Market

Quidata Supermarket

Financial Bank

Post Office

Ecobank

Taxi Stand
Covered Market

Hôtel Bellevue

Soccer Stadium

Cinéma Bopeci

Pharmacie Tissanta

Maquis Savanna / Chez Guillaume

Confort Lines
Bus Station

Pâtisserie Beraca

Hôtel
Kantaborifa

Maquis Le Basilic

La Brèche

l'Évêché Restaurant and
Internet Café

Chez John Cafeteria

Le Tour

Natitingou

250 meters
500 feet

To Djougou (75 km)

HOSPITAL

Natitingou's main hospital is the **Regional Hospital (Hôpital de Zone)**, located on the main road north of the town center. For contact information for recommended doctors based at the hospital, see *Emergency Call Numbers* (p73).

INTERNET

Natitingou's best internet café is located at the Évêché restaurant, located near the Diocese of Natitingou (*"évêché"* meaning "diocese"). Zemidjans all know it by name; just say "l'Évêché," pronounced "lay-veh-shay."

BANKS

Natitingou has three banks: Ecobank, Bank of Africa, and Orabank. Ecobank and Bank of Africa have ATMs that are open 24 hours and accept Visa cards. Ecobank and Bank of Africa can also change Euros and U.S. dollars during business hours. Ecobank is open through the lunch hour and on Saturday mornings. All three banks are located on the main paved road through town, near the main traffic circle.

GETTING THERE

Bus

The bus companies ATT, La Poste, Tunde, Confort Lines, Benin Routes, and Intercity Lines operate routes between Natitingou and Cotonou. A seat on one of the newer air-conditioned buses (operated by ATT, La Poste, and Tunde) should cost around FCFA 7,500. The other companies, which operate older buses, charge slightly lower rates.

Buses leave and arrive from the large traffic circle on the north side of town. It may cost FCFA 200 for a zemidjan ride to get out there.

It's best to buy bus tickets the day before your departure. If you show up in the morning without a ticket, it may be hard to find a seat. You can buy tickets at the bus company offices (tell a zemidjan which bus company you're looking for), or from the ticket vendors who are usually hanging around the post office, in the center of town.

Bush Taxi

Taxis going to Tanguiéta pick up passengers on the highway just north of Quidata Supermarket. Taxis going to Djougou are on the highway just south of the Évêché restaurant. Both of these leave several times every day. Most taxis for other destinations depart from the taxi station and leave once a day.

Zemidjan

It's easy to find zemidjans in the market area and along the main road through town. It should cost FCFA 100–150 to go almost anywhere in town.

Unlike in towns further south, you shouldn't negotiate the price before getting on the motorcycle in Natitingou. Just pay the driver FCFA 100 or 150, depending on how long the ride seemed, when you arrive at your destination. If you try to negotiate the price beforehand, it tells him that you don't know what the price should be—and that's when he tries to rip you off.

SIGHTS AND ACTIVITIES

Musée Regional de Natitingou
Natitingou Regional Museum

This excellent museum is housed in a former French colonial mansion. It focuses on the history of the region, with displays of traditional hunting tools and weapons, as well as miniature reconstructions of Tata Sombas. On the museum grounds, you'll find several good artisans' shops selling high-quality beads, masks, batique prints, dolls, and other items. If you bargain a bit, you should be able to get a good price. *Hours: Mon–Fri 8am–12:30pm and 3pm–6:30pm, Sat–Sun 9am–12pm and 4pm–6:30pm. Entry fee: FCFA 1,000. Location: between the Hôtel Bourgogne and the police station.*

Artisans' Market

There's a small artisans' market in the center of town. The vendors sell a variety of souvenirs, from jewelry to wood and bronze statues to ceremonial swords. While you will need to negotiate the price, they won't try to rip you off as much as vendors further south will. *On the main paved road through town, next to a gas station and across the street from the post office ("La Poste"). Usually closed Sundays.*

Local Paintings

Joseph Njie is an artist who lives and works in Natitingou. He paints gorgeous original pieces and makes all of his own paint pigments from stones that he mines from the Atakora mountains surrounding Natitingou. He enjoys visiting with foreigners and has been a good friend to many Peace Corps Volunteers over the years. If you're in Natitingou, you can go to his home, which doubles as his studio, to look at (and maybe purchase) his work, as well as to chat about art, African politics, and food—he speaks impeccable English. He can also give you advice on traveling in the region. Call 98.62.40.42 or 96.08.46.90 and say that Jonny sent you.

Other Handicrafts

Several smaller boutiques, including **Le Carrefour des Artisans**, **Tresors d'Afrique**, and **Nouvelle Galerie**, sell typical West African crafts. Location: lining the brick road between the Hôtel Tata Somba and the main paved road.

Les Chutes de Kota
The Kota Falls

Tucked away in the hills about 15 kilometers southeast of Natitingou, the *Chutes de Kota* aren't as tall as the Tanongou Falls (p194), but make for an equally pleasant adventure. To arrive, pedal a bike, ride in a car, or hire a zemidjan (FCFA 2,500 one-way). The road gets curvy and rocky, so if traveling by car, go in a 4x4 vehicle, because a bush taxi might not make it. The easiest way to get there is to follow the highway ten kilometers toward Djougou, then turn left on the dirt road to Kouandé. After three kilometers, a sign on the right indicates a narrower dirt road to the falls. There is a small visitor's center set up at the entrance, though the guard is not always present. If he is, an entry fee of FCFA 200 is usually required. From here, a hiking path goes down the steep slope to the bottom of the falls, where a shaded pool is open for swimming. Depending on the season, the path can get overgrown and is difficult to see, so take care not to get lost.

Kouandé

Located 50 kilometers east of Natitingou, Kouandé is the historical capital of the Bariba peoples in the Atakora. The Kouandé Kingdom was founded in the 18th century by Worou Wari, the son of a prince who had fled the Kingdom of Nikki in the east. You can get there by bush taxi for FCFA 1,500, or by zemidjan for FCFA 2,500. The trip from Natitingou takes about an hour. The royal palace of Kouandé is an interesting place to visit. A tour includes a visit with King Bagana Sorou III and recountings of the region's legends.

EATING AND DRINKING

⊗ **Maquis Savanna / Chez Guillaume** In the opinion of many, this is the best place to eat in Natitingou. Guillaume is a French- and Moroccan-trained chef who turns out a wide variety of appetizers and entrées: salad, soup, or hummus, followed by antelope, Guinea fowl, Nile perch, or brochettes de gésier, and accompanied by French fries, couscous, or green beans. He also serves pizza cooked in a wood-fired oven; homemade pastries and ice cream; and Moroccan lamb, chicken, pigeon, or vegetarian tagine. For drinks, choose between fresh fruit juices or reasonably-priced beer or soda. Guillaume provides excellent service and is one of the friendliest people you'll meet in Benin. Free delivery, and live jazz on Saturday nights. *Meals: FCFA 1,500–4,000. Drinks: FCFA 350–1,200. Location: On the main road, across from Pharmacie Tissanta.*

Bar-Restaurant Chez Daniel This is another excellent restaurant that boasts a remarkable chef. Daniel's specialties include antelope, salad, and sautéed potatoes. He can prepare excellent multi-course meals with advance notice. *Meals: FCFA 1,000–3,000. Drinks: FCFA 250–800. Location: across from the Mairie (town hall). Tell a zemidjan "Chez Daniel, en face de la Mairie" or "Chez le Waama, en face de la Mairie." (Daniel is of the Waama ethnicity; while not everybody in town knows his name, they all know he's the Waama with the successful restaurant.)*

Fulani and Lokpa Whipping Ceremonies

The nomadic Fulani (Peul or Peuhl in French) herders of the Sahel hold an annual flagellation ceremony as a rite of passage into manhood. These rituals are typically held during the dry season in the marketplaces of towns in northern Benin, such as Boukoumbé and Ouaké, near the Togo border. To prove their manhood, young Fulani men must stand motionless as their elders slash them across the torso with tamarind whips, creating welts and drawing blood. Fulani women gather around, clapping and singing to the rhythm of drums, while each young man defies bodily pain and sings songs of praise.

The Lokpa people also hold whipping ceremonies. Instead of being passively whipped, their young men fight each other with whips. Just after sunrise the morning before the ceremony, there's a dance-filled procession through the village. The most notable Lokpa whipping ceremonies take place in Ouaké and Badjoudé.

Atakora & Donga

QG This is among the coolest bars in Nati. Drinks are always cold—not something to be taken for granted in Benin—and they often have live music. A variety of street food vendors set up shop around the bar, and you can bring their food in. The owner, Justin Tagili, has long been a friend of local Peace Corps Volunteers. He's well-connected and can find you good taxi drivers, zemidjans, and anything else you need in Natitingou. *Meals: FCFA 300–1,500. Drinks: FCFA 250–800. Hours: about 11am–11pm. Open daily. Location: in the center of town, on the cobblestone road leading west from the paved highway toward the Hôtel Tata Somba. While the bar's full name is Quartier Général, everyone knows it as QG.*

La Brèche Located on a mountainside, La Brèche probably has the best view of any *buvette* in Natitingou—bring your camera. It's also built next to a *Tata Somba*, a traditional fortified house. However, service ranges from slow to rude. They offer basic dinners of Guinea fowl or chicken with French fries, but the quality is sub-par and you may be waiting two hours or more for your food to arrive. Have a drink here at sunset, then go eat at one of Natitingou's better restaurants. *Meals: FCFA 1,500-2,000. Drinks: FCFA 250-1,200. Location: on the southeast side of town. Tell a zemidjan "la Brèche de Natitingou."*

L'Évêché The chef here was trained at Chez Guillaume, and consequently the food is good. Their specialties include pizza, spaghetti carbonara, and grilled fish. If you come for breakfast, you'll get an omelette, fruit and yogurt, and real coffee—a rarity in Benin. However, it has an over-lit and unromantic ambiance, and service takes a while. The best internet café in town is located here. *Meals: FCFA 1,500 for breakfast and FCFA 2,000-3,000 for lunch or dinner. Drinks: FCFA 250–800. Location: near the Diocese of Natitingou ("évêché" meaning "diocese"). Zemidjans all know it by name; just say "l'Évêché," pronounced "lay-veh-shay."*

Le Tour Le Tour offers a fantastic view of Natitingou, cold drinks and hearty dishes of meat or cheese with couscous, fries, rice, or spaghetti. Food may not be available at all hours of the day, so either check in advance or just come for a drink. *Meals: FCFA 1,000–3,000. Drinks: FCFA 300–800. Hours: 12pm–11pm. Open daily. Location: up the road from the Hôtel Kantaborifa, indicated by a sign.*

Chez John Cafeteria This basic eatery offers some Western-style food, such as chicken and fries, sandwiches, and a variety of omelettes. *Meals: FCFA 700–1,500. Drinks: FCFA 250–800. Hours: 8am–11pm. Location: on the southeast side of town, along the dirt road leading to Le Tour and La Brèche.*

NIGHT LIFE

One recommended nightclub in Natitingou is **Le Village**, located behind Ecobank. Your zemidjan should know how to find it. Say "Discothèque le Village, derrière Ecobank."

ACCOMMODATIONS

La Bourgogne Run by Thérèse, a Frenchwoman who's lived in Natitingou for 20 years, this hotel caters mainly to the tourist crowd—you'll seldom see any Africans staying or eating here. Rooms are small but pleasant. The upscale restaurant serves a variety of French dishes for lunch and dinner, and a breakfast of croissants, yogurt, fresh fruit, and real *café au lait*. It's also the headquarters for Benin Adventure Tourism, which can arrange tours of Pendjari National Park. *FCFA 25,000. Meals: FCFA 3,000–6,000; breakfast FCFA 3,000. Private bathroom, hot water, fan or A/C. Tel: 23.82.22.40. Website: hotelbourgognebenin.com. Location: on the main road, just north of the market, indicated by a sign.*

Hôtel Bellevue Set in grounds full of trees and flowers, this pleasant hotel offers both thatched bungalows and traditional rooms. The main building, which houses the restaurant, is built in the colonial style and was once the police headquarters. The restaurant offers pricey local cuisine, but certain dishes are often not available. *Bungalow FCFA 7,000–9,000; bungalow with A/C and hot water FCFA 14,000–16,000; hotel room FCFA 17,000–18,000. Meals: FCFA 1,500–3,000. Location: up the dirt track from the Cinema Bopeci, indicated by a sign.*

Hôtel Tata Somba Once one of Natitingou's premier hotels, the Tata Somba is now government-run. Rooms are small and dreary, bathrooms clean but tiny. It does have spacious grounds and a large swimming pool, though the tennis court has fallen into disrepair. The restaurant offers good local cuisine at astronomical prices: a meal for two with drinks will easily cost FCFA 20,000. In this price range, there are better hotels in Natitingou. *FCFA 30,000. Location: at the northwest end of town, at the end of the brick road off the main paved road, indicated by a sign.*

Hotel Kantaborifa This hotel has comfortable rooms and a breezy courtyard restaurant. A full meal usually consists of salad, a main dish, and some fruit. *Single occupancy: FCFA 6,500 with fan, FCFA 12,500 with A/C. Double occupancy: FCFA 8,500 with fan, FCFA 15,500 with A/C. Private bathroom. Meals: FCFA 2,500–3,500. Tel: 23.82.11.66. Location: on a dirt road at the south end of town.*

Boukoumbé

Boukoumbé, a village located west of Natitingou and near the Togo border, is famous for its **tata sombas**, the two-story fortified houses traditionally built by the Ditammari people as protection against enemy tribes and dangerous animals. It's also home to one of the regional Fulani whipping ceremonies. You'll also want to check out the *tchoukoutou* market, which takes place every four days, and the gorgeous natural scenery of the area. **Mount Koussou-Kovangou**, the highest point in Benin, is located nearby.

GETTING THERE

Visitors generally go to Boukoumbé as a day trip from Natitingou. Taxis to Boukoumbé leave the Natitingou taxi station a couple times a day and cost FCFA 1,500. They're most frequent on Boukoumbé market days, which take place every four days.

A zemidjan from Natitingou to Boukoumbé costs FCFA 2,000. The zemidjan ride is more comfortable and much more convenient than a taxi—it's worth the extra 500 francs if you don't have much luggage.

When you get a zemidjan in Boukoumbé for the return trip to Natitingou, the driver may try to tell you that you have to pay double because he won't be able to find another passenger in Natitingou to take back to Boukoumbé. Do not believe him. You may have to wait around for a while, but eventually somebody will take you for the right price.

SIGHTS AND ACTIVITIES

Tata Touristique

If you want to visit a tata somba without walking uninvited into someone's home, go to the model tata somba. It's located just outside of Boukoumbé and is run solely for tourists. Inquire at the Maison des Jeunes or at the restaurant Chez Koubetti for a guide. Ask for Josephine Koubetti and say that Josh Kora Kora sent you.

You can take a two- to three-hour hike to the tata somba for FCFA 5,000, or go by motorcycle for FCFA 2,000. You can also spend the night on the roof of the tata somba for FCFA 3,000. Sleeping mats, mosquito nets, and a private bathroom with a shower and flushing toilet are provided. Bring bottled water for drinking. You can eat breakfast, lunch, or dinner at the tata somba for FCFA 1,000–2,000. To arrange an overnight stay, call the Tata Touristique at 96.00.66.36.

Tchoukoutou Market

If you've read a few other sections of this guide, you're probably familiar with *tchoukoutou*, the locally-brewed millet beer that's popular throughout northern Benin. Boukoumbé holds its market every four days because of *tchouk*: it takes three days to ferment, and on the fourth day you sell it. As elsewhere, you sit in a stall and the vendor serves you a 50- or 100–franc portion in a calabash bowl. It'll still be fermenting as you drink it. When you get down to the white yeast at the bottom of the bowl, dump it on the ground.

In Boukoumbé you'll find two varieties of *tchouk*, a stout variety and a lighter variety. Try asking for a mixture of the two, called *Kora Kora*. Say "*N'pah spessidia Kora Kora.*"

Tata Sombas

Boukoumbé's traditional fortified houses were designed to protect the inhabitants and their livestock from enemy tribes and wild animals. The first level of the tata somba houses the family's livestock—cows, goats, sheep, and chickens—while the family lives on the upper level. Grains are stored in silos made of palm leaves on the upper level, safe from the livestock.

According to tradition, when a son is ready to build his own home, he climbs to the top of his parents' tata somba and shoots an arrow as far as he can. Where the arrow lands is where he will build his own tata somba. The entrance to a tata somba always faces west, which is believed to be the direction of life, and is surrounded by talismans and altars to traditional deities.

Tanguiéta

As you can tell from the colonial architecture around town, Tanguiéta was the seat of French colonial administration for the Atakora-Donga region. This small town of 20,000 includes populations of the Dendi, Waama, Nateni, and Biali ethnicities. It also houses the office of the Pendjari National Park, the ultimate destination of most tourists who pass through here. The park entrance is a short drive to the north.

GETTING THERE

From Natitingou, a bush taxi to Tanguiéta costs FCFA 1,500. From Cotonou, the bus company ATT operates a direct route to Tanguiéta. The bus leaves from the ATT office at the Place de l'Étoile Rouge at 6:30 in the morning and gets to Tanguiéta around 6:30 in the evening. Buy your ticket the day before from the ATT office. It should cost FCFA 8,000.

To go directly to Cotonou from Tanguiéta, take the ATT bus that leaves Tanguiéta at 6:30am. It leaves from the Quidata supermarket, which is the tallest building in town.

EATING AND DRINKING

Hôtel Baobab and **Hôtel Atakora** have in-house restaurants. Some good *buvettes* include **Chez Julie**, which is affiliated with APP Hotel, and **Bon Coin**, located on the southwest side of town. The **Maison des Jeunes**, located on the far north side of town, is a good lunch spot.

Tanguiéta's specialty market product is watermelon, though they're only seasonally available. If they're in season, you'll see them for sale in mounds in the town center.

> If you're headed to Pendjari National Park, Tanguiéta is the last place you'll be able to stock up on inexpensive food—the few eateries in and around the park are pricey, and the surrounding villages have little or no street food available.

ACCOMMODATIONS

Hôtel Baobab This hotel has a large, pleasant courtyard with places to sit in the shade, have a cold drink, and recover from a long day of traveling in the north. The rooms are set in bungalows around a flowery courtyard. The hotel restaurant serves higher-end African meals that include a salad; a main course of rice, couscous, or fries with chicken, fish, or guinea fowl; and fruit. While this was once undoubtedly the best hotel in Tanguiéta, it has recently lowered its standards under new management. *Single-occupancy: FCFA 6,000 with fan; double-occupancy: FCFA 13,000 with A/C or FCFA 8,000 with fan; camping: FCFA 3,000 with tent and mattress provided; FCFA 1,500 if you bring your own equipment. Private bathroom. Meals: breakfast FCFA 1,500, lunch or dinner FCFA 5,000, vegetarian meal FCFA 4,000. Drinks: FCFA 500 and up. Tel: 90.66.56.95. Location: on the north end of town, near the official Pendjari Park office and along the highway to the Burkina Faso border.*

Hôtel Atakora This place offers a range of accommodations at prices similar to the Hôtel Baobab. Two suites even have a balcony and a fridge. *Single-occupancy: FCFA*

Atakora & Donga

6,000 with fan, FCFA 12,000 with A/C; double-occupancy: FCFA 8,000 with fan, FCFA 15,000 with A/C; suites with fridge: FCFA 15,000 with fan, FCFA 20,000 with A/C. Meals: breakfast FCFA 1,500, lunch and dinner FCFA 5,000. Location: in the town center.

APP Hotel / Chez Basile If you're looking for a budget backpacker-style room for the night, this is it. Rooms are very basic, and you'll be using a common pit latrine in the courtyard. There is a popular nightclub attached, so it can be quite loud on weekends. The rooftop dining area is a pleasant place to spend evenings or to enjoy bread and coffee at sunrise, before the grueling daytime heat. *FCFA 5,000. Some rooms have a fan; shared shower and pit latrine. Location: in the center of town, off the dirt road to Tanongou.*

SIGHTS

Tanguiéta is the nearest town to the **Tanongou Falls** and **Pendjari National Park**. The Hôtel Tata Somba in Natitingou can provide much of the information necessary for visiting Pendjari and the Tanongou Falls. You can also explore Tanguiéta's market, held every Monday.

Pendjari National Park

Le Parc National de la Pendjari, or **Pendjari National Park**, is Benin's premier safari park and a highlight of any visit to Benin. While it's not as extensive as the safari parks of East Africa, you'll likely see elephants, lions, water buffalo, hippopotami, crocodiles, baboons, warthogs, and several species of antelope, monkeys, and exotic birds. Over 300 species of birds have been identified within the park. You may also see hyenas and cheetahs, though their populations within the park are relatively small.

Pendjari owes its wide range of animals to its diverse ecosystems, which provide the animals' habitats. The park is a UNESCO Biosphere Reserve and contains the most important forest and wetland ecosystems in the area. An impressive gallery forest lines the base of the Atakora mountains, while savannah and swampy meadows stretch throughout the park.

The park belongs to the multinational W-Arli-Pendjari park complex, a 50,000-square-kilometer reserve that stretches across the borders of Benin, Burkina Faso, and Niger. Twelve thousand square kilometers of the park complex, comprising parts of the Pendjari and W National Parks, are located within Benin.

Three ethnicities inhabit the zones bordering the park and retain the use of the resources found within. Their main activities are agriculture, animal husbandry, fishing, and hunting. Use and management of natural resources remains a significant source of contention between park authorities and local villagers.

VISITING THE PARK

The best time to spot animals is February through April. This is the latter half of the dry season, when water is scarce and animals concentrate around the few remaining watering holes. Much of the brush has dried out or been burned, making it easier to spot animals. However, this is also the hottest part of the year; afternoon temperatures can reach 50° Celsius, or 120° Fahrenheit. The dried- and burned-out landscape is also less scenic than during the rainy season, when lush green vegetation covers the park.

You must have a guide to enter the park. (See below for a list of recommended guides.) Your guide can pick you up in Natitingou or Tanguiéta and will drive you around the park in a Land Rover or similar vehicle. Many guides have seats on top of their vehicles, allowing you to spot animals from a higher vantage point. Since there are dangerous wild animals around, you aren't allowed to leave the vehicle and walk around the park, except at watering holes with designated observation platforms.

Hunting is permitted within a dedicated section of the park. You must be accompanied by local guides and respect the park's game rules, which keep the number of each species hunted each year at sustainable levels. You must also pay a significant fee to the park for each animal killed. For more information, contact the park directly.

PARK ENTRY FEES

You can buy tickets at the park entrance.

FCFA 10,000 / person (foreigner)

FCFA 3,000 / person (Beninese citizen)

FCFA 3,000 / vehicle

PARK GUIDES

You must have a guide to enter the park. You can find guides in Natitingou or Tanguiéta. While you can hire a driver and guide separately, it's best to hire a guide who also drives his own vehicle (he'll have a 4x4 vehicle that's better able to handle the terrain, and he'll take care of any car issues along the way). Guides with vehicles generally charge FCFA 50,000–60,000 per day, plus gas.

The Hôtel Tata Somba in Natitingou and Hôtel Baobab in Tanguiéta both organize trips to the park and can link you up with their recommended guides. You can also contact a guide yourself.

For guides, we highly recommend **Bernard** (tel: 97.39.64.65) and **Adamou** (tel: 97.35.45.58 / 94.78.43.40). They can both pick you up in Natitingou or in Tanguiéta.

EATING AND DRINKING

The only place to eat and drink in the park is at the Hôtel Campement de la Pendjari. Because it is so remote, it can be expensive. To save money, stock up on food in Natitingou and have a picnic at the observation tower at one of the watering holes.

PARK ACCOMMODATION

Hôtel Campement de la Pendjari This hotel offers the only accommodations within the park. Electricity comes from gas generators, and there are no landlines or cell phone reception. However, the hotel includes a plush restaurant and lounge, with a full bar at its center. Drinks are expensive because they have to be brought from far away. There is a swimming pool where you can refresh after a long trip across the parched landscape. *Double room with A/C FCFA 28,000; single room with*

Atakora & Donga

fan FCFA 20,000; bungalow with fan and exterior shower and toilet FCFA 16,000; extra bed FCFA 3,000. Meals: breakfast FCFA 2,500, lunch or dinner FCFA 6,000. Open Dec. 15–May 31. Tel: 23.82.11.24 / 23.82.20.99 / 97.04.02.83 / 90.04.24.78 through the Hôtel Tata Somba in Natitingou (a list of reservations is sent daily by car).

Hôtel Campement de Porga This is surprisingly luxurious for a hunter's lodge, though it does not have the same amenities as the Hôtel Campement de la Pendjari. There is no pool and the restaurant is not as high-end, but the food is good. *Double room with fan FCFA 19,000; bungalow FCFA 15,000; extra bed FCFA 2,000. Meals: breakfast FCFA 2,500, lunch or dinner FCFA 6,000. Open Dec. 15–May 31. Tel: 23.82.20.39 / 23.82.11.24 / 23.82.20.99 / 23.82.22.00. Reservations made through the Hôtel Tata Somba in Natitingou.*

Le Relais de Tanongou Though it's not located in the park, you can stay here during your visit to the park. See *Tanongou* below.

Camping in the Park

You can camp within the park with advance permission from the park office in Tanguiéta. Your party must be entirely self-sufficient, and the park strongly recommends that you hire a local guide to accompany you. Camping costs FCFA 3,000 per person per night, payable at the park entrance. You can rent camping equipment in Tanguiéta; none is available at the park.

Tanongou

Tanongou is a tiny village at the foot of the Atakora range, 30 kilometers northeast of Tanguiéta along the dirt road to Batia in Pendjari National Park. It sits beside the best-known waterfalls in the country, *les Chutes de Tanongou*.

GETTING THERE

If you hire a Pendjari guide, you can usually have him pick you up in Natitingou or Tanguiéta and bring you to Tanongou, whether you're spending the night there or just want to visit the waterfalls. Otherwise, you'll have to hire your own bush taxi or take a zemidjan—Tanongou is so small that bush taxis don't regularly go there. If going by zemidjan, keep in mind that the road gets very dusty during the dry season. The road to Tanongou skirts the park, and you may see wildlife such as monkeys and birds. Eucalyptus, mango, and acacia trees border the cultivated fields, a sign of local agroforestry practices.

SIGHTS AND ACTIVITES

Chutes de Tanongou
Tanongou Falls

The **Tanongou Falls** are a great place to swim, and those daring enough can leap from a cliff some meters above the pool. Visitors must pay a FCFA 1,000 entry fee to visit the falls. Boys and men from the village come to offer their assistance along the slippery rocks to reach the upper part of the falls. If you accept their services, which may not be entirely optional, they'll expect a tip of a couple hundred francs per guide.

Hiking

The staff at Le Relais de Tanongou (see the following *Accommodation* section) can arrange a guided hike to the source of the Tanongou Falls. The hike takes about four hours. You can opt to stay overnight in straw huts at the source. The guides will prepare a traditional dinner on site. The hike costs FCFA 2,000 per person, and the overnight camping costs FCFA 3,000 per person plus food costs.

ACCOMMODATION

Le Relais de Tanongou Set at the foot of the Tanongou Falls, this camp is remote but comfortable. There are six bungalow rooms, a low-key restaurant, and a pleasant outdoor *buvette* serving beer and soda. Motor-generated electricity runs for only a few hours each night, so bring a flashlight. Rooms are spacious and tidy. In the bungalows with private toilets and showers, the running water may or may not be working. *Bungalow with private shower and toilet FCFA 9,000; bungalow with external shower and toilet FCFA 7,000; fan, powered by generator that runs for a few hours at night. Meals: breakfast FCFA 2,500, lunch or dinner FCFA 5,500. Drinks FCFA 500–1,000. Reservations made through the Hôtel Tata Somba in Natitingou.*

EATING AND DRINKING

Beyond the Relais de Tanongou, there are no dining options in Tanongou. To save money, stock up on breakfast items in Natitingou. You can kindly ask the kitchen staff at the Relais for hot water in the morning.

Across the stream from the Relais lies a more rustic hunters' camp of straw huts and a makeshift kitchen. You might glimpse a vehicle of hunters as they return from a successful trip with an antelope or a water buffalo. A portion of this meat will be divided and shared among the villagers of Tanongou.

Language Reference

Signs in French

Here are translations of terms in French that you're likely to see on signs in Benin. For everyday French phrases, see *Useful Translations* at the beginning of this book.

Accès interdit // Entry forbidden

Accueil // Reception, front desk

Aéroport // Airport

Ambassade // Embassy

Arrêtez // Halt

Atelier // Workshop

Attention! // Watch out!

Auberge // Inn

Autogare // Taxi and/or bus station

Banque // Bank

Boutique // Small shop

Buvette // Casual bar offering soda and beer, and sometimes local food

Caisse // Register (in a store), teller (in a bank)

Carrefour // Intersection

Centre artisanal // Artisans' market

Commissariat // Police station

Contrôle de police // Police checkpoint

Crédit // Phone credit

Cyber // Internet café

Défense / Défendu // Forbidden

Direction // Management, headquarters

Entrée // Entrance

Fermé // Closed

Gare Station // Used either as shorthand for *autogare* or *gare routière*, or to refer to a former station of Benin's defunct railroad system

Gare routière // See *autogare*

Gendarmerie // Gendarme (military police) station

Gérant // Manager

Guichet // Teller (in a bank)

Guichet automatique // ATM

Interdit // See *défense*

Maison des jeunes // Community center

Maquis // Informal eatery offering local cuisine

Marché // Market

Marché artisanal // See *centre artisanal*

Marché de bétail // Livestock market

ONG // NGO (non-governmental organization)

Ouvert // Open

Péage // Toll station

Privé // Private

Ralentir / Ralentissez // Slow down

Réception // See *accueil*

Rond-point // Traffic circle

Siège (régional) // (Regional) headquarters

Sortie // Exit

Sortie de secours // Emergency exit

Supermarché // Supermarket

Travaux // Construction, road work

Toilettes // Restroom or latrine, depending on circumstances

WC // See *toilettes*

Local Language Phrase Guide

This section includes phonetically-written phrases from some of Benin's most wide-ly-spoken languages. French is spoken throughout the country, though not by every-one. The other languages are spoken only in the regions indicated.

AJAGBE (ADJA)

Spoken in parts of the Mono-Couffo region.

Good day // Okodo gnidonmé

Good evening // Okodo fiéssi

How are you? // Lémidédo?

Fine, thanks // Nle nyoende

Thank you // Akpé

Goodbye // Mayiagbo

How much is it? // Nenido?

That's too much. // Evohodi

Give me the change. // Naheji

I'm looking for a taxi. // Ji hun deka nam

I'm looking for a zemidjan. // Ji kéké deka nam

BARIBA

Spoken primarily in the Alibori-Borgou region, and in parts of the Atakora-Donga region.

Good morning // Akpounando

Good afternoon // Ka sonson

Good evening // Ka yoka

How are you? // Akpounando

Fine, thanks // Alafia

Thank you // Nasiara

Goodbye // N'kwa sosi / N'kwa sia

How much is it? // Y eh was?

That's too much. // Yakpé ato.

Give me the change. // Ané ko sí ta ma.

Okay // Ya wa

I'm looking for a taxi. // Na kéké ka su.

I'm looking for a zemidjan. // Na zemidjan ka su.

I'm going to _____. // Na _____ do.

BIALI

Spoken in the area surrounding Tanguiéta, in the Atakora département.

Good morning // La saam

Good afternoon // La yémtoune

Good evening // La péém

How are you? // Lafié bo? / Narou bo?

Fine, thanks // Lafié bo maghli

Thank you // A diahin (singular) / I diahin (plural)

Goodbye // L't sade

OK // Too / L'soui

How much is it? // I touéri?

That's too much. // L'péi bams maghle

Give me the change. // M'moinane tchahanlme

I'm looking for a taxi. // M'yémse sahou

I'm looking for a zemidjan. // M'yémse zémidjan

I'm going to _____. // M'pa _____.

DENDI

Spoken throughout northern Benin.

Good morning // Nasuba

Welcome // Nakayo

How are you? // Mete gah? / A fono kokari?

Fine, thanks // Baani

Thank you // Nagbei

See you later // Achi densu

See you tomorrow // Achi suba

I would like _____. // A bar _____.

DITAMMARI

Spoken in parts of the Atakora-Donga region.

Good morning // A hentaa

Good afternoon // A tuunaa

Good evening // Ne kuyuoku

Goodnight // Ne keyenke

Welcome // Ne mucemmu

How are you? // A douhaa? / A kpenna?

Fine, thanks (and you?) // Iyo, (a duo meta?)

Thank you // Ne mutommu

See you later // Dek paa de bo yi eme

Goodbye // De kpa de boyeme

How much is it? // De bo yi dendi?

That's too much. // De donku deu fa.

Give me the change. // Nduonni feyoonfe.

What? // Ba?

I'm looking for a taxi. // N wanti tesante.

I'm looking for a zemidjan. // N wanti zemidjan.

I'm going to _____. // N kori _____.

FONGBE (FON)

Mahi-speakers will also understand these phrases. Fon is spoken throughout southern Benin, while Mahi is spoken in some areas of the Zou-Collines region.

Good morning // A fon ganji a?

Good afternoon // Kudo hwemé

Good evening // Kú dó gbadà

Welcome // Kwabo / Mi kwabo

How are you? // Né a de gbon?

Fine, thanks // Un do ganjí / Un fon ganjí

Thank you // Awanou / Ooh

Goodbye // Edabo

How much is it? // Nabí wé?

That's too much. // Axivéxívé

Give me the change. // Cé akwé

OK // Yoh

I'm looking for a taxi. // Bà nyé taxi

I'm looking for a zemidjan. // Un jlo kéké

I'm going to _____. // Olo _____ yiwé.

FRENCH

Spoken, to some extent, by much of the population throughout the country. Some of these phrases differ from French as spoken in Europe. Translations followed by phonetic spellings.

Good morning // Bonjour *(bohn-jure)*

Good afternoon / evening // Bonsoir *(bohn-swa)*

How are you? // Comment ça va? *(como sa va?)*

Fine, thanks // Ça va bien, merci *(ca va bee-in, mair-see)*

Thank you // Merci *(mair-see)*

See you later // À tout à l'heure *(ah toot ah leur)*

Goodbye // Au revoir *(oh reh-vwar)*

What? // Quoi? *(qwa?)*

How much is it? // C'est combien? *(say com-bee-in?)*

That's too much. // C'est trop. *(say tro.)*

Give me the change. // Donne-moi la monnaie. *(dohne-mwa la moh-nay.)*

I'm looking for a taxi. // Je cherche un taxi. *(jhe shersh uhn taxi.)*

I'm looking for a zemidjan. // Je cherche un zemidjan. *(jhe shersh uhn zem-idjan.)*

I'm going to _____. // Je vais à _____. *(jhe vay a _____.)*

FULFULDÉ (FULANI / PEUL / PEUHL)

Spoken throughout central and northern Benin, but only by members of the Fulani ethnic group.

Good morning // Djaam waali / Waali djaam

Good afternoon // Djaam gnali / Gnali djaam

Good evening // Djaam hiiri / Hiiri Djaam

How are you? // Fôfô / Non bannu

Fine, thanks // Séi djaam / Djaam taam

Please // Atchanaam Haakè

Thank you // Mi yééti

Goodbye // Waadi dégoom / Waddi minm djiitoyii

OK // Éddum woddi / Woddi

How much is it? // Nonyiinum?

That's too much. // Éddum tchaadi / Éddum wodi tchèdè

Give me the change. // Hôkaam tchèouddè / Tchéouddè aam

I'm looking for a taxi. // Mii darta lorrè / Mii filor laanan

I'm looking for a zemidjan. // Mii darta mon zémidjan / Mii filor mon zém-idjan

I'm going to _____. // Mii yaaha _____.

Gengbe (Mina)

Spoken in parts of the Mono-Couffo region.

Good morning // Mi fon yónéndéa

Good evening // Mi kudo wetro

How are you? // Mi le yónendea?

Thank you // Akpe

Goodbye // Mayi ma va

That's too much. // Eveci

Give me the change. // Namcéhji

I'm looking for a taxi. // Nleji ehunde kanam

I'm looking for a zemidjan. // Nle jikéké deka

GÚN

Spoken in and around Porto-Novo.

Good morning // Mi kaaro

Good afternoon // Mi kaasan

Good evening // Mi kualé

Welcome // Mi kwaabo

How are you? // Mi to ganji a?

Fine, thanks // Ehh, uhn to ganji.

Welcome // Mi kaabo

Thank you // Abayi

Goodbye // Edabo

Have a good day // Egbe an nyon

How much is it? // Nebi wé

That's too much. // É vé kwé.

Lower the price a little. // Depo kpede.

Give me the change. // Nami changee.

I'm going to _____. // Uhn dje yi _____.

IDAATCHA

Spoken in and around Dassa, in the Collines département.

Good morning // Ékoni

Good afternoon // Ékòsón

Good evening // Ékáàlè

How are you? // Owaré?

Fine, thanks // N'waré

Please // Éjàré

Sorry // Éjáré

Thank you // Okoutchè

Goodbye // Odabo

How much is it? // Égbéloo

That's too much. // O han din

Give me the change. // É funm li shenji

I'm looking for a taxi / zem. // N'wa wo kèkè

I'm going to _____. // N'lèko lí _____.

NAGOT

Tchabé- and Yoruba-speakers will also understand these phrases. Dialects of Nagot, Tchabé, and Yoruba are spoken in parts of the Ouémé-Plateau region, throughout the Zou-Collines region, and in parts of northern Benin.

Good morning // Ékáàro

Good afternoon // Ékasan

Good evening // Ékalé

Welcome // Ékáàbo

How are you? // É dji dáàda?

Fine, thanks // Adukpé

Thank you // Okuchébé

Goodbye // Odáàbo

See you tomorrow // Odola / Odáào

OK // O da

How much is it? // É lo?

That's too much. // O mo kupo.

Give me the change. // Ba mi changi.

I'm looking for a taxi. // M'bo taxi.

I'm looking for a zemidjan. // M'bo zé.

I'm going to _____. // M'lo _____.

Index

Contact us at

www.otherplacespublishing.com
info@otherplacespublishing.com